FootprintItalia

Umbria & Marche

Introducing
the region

About the region

Central Umbria

Valle Umbria &
southeast Umbria

Southwest
Umbria

Northern Umbria

Northern Marche

Central & southern Marche

Practicalities

Contents

About the author

Julius lived in a flat in the centre of Perugia for four months to write this guide, during which time he wrote off his car on a mountain road, got trapped in some Roman ruins, picnicked on Mussolini's nose and spent long evenings on the roof terrace gazing at the stunning views. Julius has written for Footprint and various other travel publishers on Bolivia, Morocco, England and many different Italian regions; Umbria is his favourite.

Acknowledgements

Thanks to Cristina for renting us her great flat, and to Martin and Tessa for finding her. Thanks to Adriana Vacca and everyone at Umbria Tourism for their help. Thanks to Carolyn for looking after us so well and to Ann and Michael in Canalicchio for their warm hospitality and cool swims. Thanks to Matt, Phil, Kerry, Claire and Richard for visiting. Thanks to Giampiero Bea at Paolo Bea, Elisa Mori at Palazzo Ricci, Letizia at Madonna del Piatto, Michela at Pietrarubbia, Patrick Nicholas in Orvieto, Roberto at Narni Sotterranea, Alessandro Graziani, Tamsin Langrishe, Rose Thompson, Linda Lyne, everyone at The Hill that Breathes and so many others for all their help and friendly advice. Thanks to Zachary Nowak for his invaluable insights. Thanks to Nick and Shona for reminding me that I wasn't alone. Thanks to Beverley for her patient and meticulous editing, and to Alan, Kassia and everyone at Footprint for their help and hard work. And thanks to Clair for all her assistance, support, marking up maps and, especially, for salads and Sagrantino on the roof terrace.

About the book

The guide is divided into four sections: Introducing the region; About the region; Around the region and Practicalities.

Introducing the region comprises: At a glance, which explains how the region fits together by giving the reader a snapshot of what to look out for and what makes this region distinct from other parts of the country; **Best of Umbria & Marche** (top 20 highlights); **A year in Umbria & Marche**, which is a month-by-month guide to pros and cons of visiting at certain times of year; and **Umbria & Marche on screen & page**, which is a list of suggested books and films. **About the region** comprises: History; Art & architecture; Umbria & Marche today, which presents different aspects of life in the region today; **Festivals & events**; Sleeping (an overview of accommodation options); **Eating & drinking** (an overview of the region's cuisine, as well as advice on eating out); **Entertainment** (an overview of the region's cultural credentials, explaining what entertainment is on offer); **Shopping** (the region's specialities and recommendations for the best buys); and **Activities & tours. Around the region** is then broken down into six areas, each with its own chapter. Here you'll find all the main sights and at the end of each chapter is a listings section with all the best sleeping, eating & drinking, entertainment, shopping and activities & tours options plus a brief overview of public transport.

Map symbols

i	Informazioni Information	**Ⅱ**	Monumento Monument
○	Luogo d'interesse Place of Interest		Stazione Ferroviaria Railway Station
🏛	Museo/Galleria Museum/Gallery		Escursioni a piedi Hiking
	Teatro Theatre	**M**	Metropolitana Metro Station
○	Negozi Shopping		Mercato Market
✉	Ufficio postale Post Office		Funicolare Funicular Railway
†	Chiesa Storica Historic Church		Aeroporto Airport
	Giardini Gardens		Universita University
......	Percorsi raccomandati Recommended walk		

Picture credits

Contents

Farmhouse near Deruta.

Introducing the region

Introduction

Umbria is Italy's only landlocked region, and though a long Adriatic coastal strip forms part of the Marche, it feels like an anomaly, for this part of the country is dominated by its hills. The high Apennines are less a barrier between the two regions than a glue that holds them together – a commonality of landscape and lifestyle.

Equidistant from Rome and Florence, Umbria and Marche have long been marked by the comings and goings to the north and south, but never swamped by them. Essentially rural, their hill towns are often exceptionally beautiful but are usually beacons of stone in a green, hilly, wooded world. And though the Etruscans and Romans dominate the museums, it is the medieval period that has left the deepest impression on the contemporary urban psyche, with many streets having changed little in 500 years.

Religion has made its mark here, but even at its holiest it is a pastoral spirituality – not for nothing did St Francis go to live in the woods, preach to the birds and befriend the wolf.

The food and wine may not generally be complex but they are no less delicious for that. And the art and architecture is astounding but also approachable, largely because few of Tuscany's tour groups make it this far south or east.

But to characterize Umbria and Marche as 'Tuscany without the tourists', as many do, is to do them a disservice, for this is an area proud of its own nature. It is rustic but also creative and individual, seldom brash or ostentatious, and all the more wonderful for that.

At a glance
A whistle-stop tour of Umbria & Marche

The green heart of Italy has hills aplenty – many topped with medieval towns – as well as mountains, lakes and a Mediterranean coast.

From ancient Rome to the Renaissance, from Raphael to Ravanelli, the wealth of historical and artistic treasures in places such as Assisi and Orvieto is extraordinary, while towns such as Perugia and Urbino have lively universities to add youthful spice to the cultural mix.

The landscape is stunning, with enormous panoramic vistas around every corner. The spine of the region, the Apennine range – snow-capped in winter and then enrobed in spring flowers – makes ideal walking country. Or you could fling yourself off the top with help from a paraglider, or rush down white water rapids in a raft. Alternatively, laze on a sandy Adriatic beach with great local wine and delicious pasta, flavoured with the mysterious truffles that grow under the roots of the region's trees.

Central Umbria

Perugia, the region's biggest city, and **Assisi**, its biggest tourist attraction, sit facing each other across the northern neck of the **Valle Umbra**, a large plain that was once under water. Still living a watery existence – just – is **Lago Trasimeno** to the west. Perugia and Assisi are very different places: the former a lively university town famed for its summer jazz festival and its chocolate; the

Via Fagiano, Perugia.

latter one of the holiest places in Christendom, home of Sts Francis and Clare, and the site of frescoes that changed the face of art.

Stray from the souvenir-laden main streets of Assisi, or the wide, paved thoroughfare of Perugia, and you will find yourself lost among a maze of narrow medieval lanes, with cats lying in the shade of ancient arches and women hanging washing from high windows. And Perugia's cultural life goes much deeper than its summer festivals: late into the night, when the rest of Umbria has long since gone to bed, music issues from chic wine bars and gritty student pubs.

Shallow Lake Trasimeno is a cool antidote to the two towns, with regular boats to its indolent islands and a beach life of sorts around its edges. And there are other escapes too – behind Assisi, **Monte Subasio** rises steeply, with good summer walking and cross-country skiing in winter.

Valle Umbra & southeast Umbria

South of Assisi, a series of steep hill towns presides over the flat plains below, each prettier than the last. **Spello**, **Trevi** and **Spoleto** all retain their strong medieval identities, while **Montefalco** adds the bonus of a successful wine industry. **Bevagna** is flatter, but no less lovely.

The striking town of **Norcia** was the birthplace of the twin saints Benedict and Scholastica, the first Western monk and nun. Beyond, further south and east, the landscape changes: the Apennines rise to some of their most spectacular heights in the **Parco Nazionale dei Monti Sibillini**, straddling Umbria and Marche, a mountainous land of wild boar, wolves and morning mists. Beech woods cling to folds in the hills while the enormous high plains are home to wild flowers and fields of lentils.

Southwest Umbria

The town of **Orvieto**, built on, and into, a huge layer cake of volcanic rock, is another of Umbria's centres, dominated by a gargantuan cathedral visible from afar. Decorated both inside and out with fascinating, if occasionally nightmarish,

The lowdown

Money matters
Staying in a cheap *agriturismo* and eating picnics, you could just about get by on €75 a day per person. Double that for a more comfortable holiday, with swimming pool, truffles and Sagrantino.

Opening times
Most shops and tourist attractions close at lunchtime. Almost no shops open on Sundays and museums are often closed on Mondays.

You can often buy combined tickets that let you into several sights, though the savings aren't always great. Students and children usually go half price.

Tourist information
Even small towns have tourist information offices, where you can get a map and advice on the best sights. Most also have lists of accommodation. *Agriturismi* (see page 50) are worth booking before you arrive (agriturismumbria.com/eng).

In the university towns, look out for student-produced information. Perugia's *The Little Blue What To Do* (in English) is especially useful; livingitaly.com offers a wealth of historical and cultural information, plus tours.

Prosecco is a traditional aperitivo, usually accompanied by bar snacks.

bas-relief and frescoes, it is one of the region's must-see buildings. Orvieto is a wine centre too – its crisp white is a good accompaniment to a meal in one of its excellent restaurants.

Nearby **Todi** is yet another hill town, with an excellent September arts festival and some huge Roman cisterns underneath its striking piazza. **Narni**, from which CS Lewis probably took the name for his fantasy land Narnia, is a little-visited town with a fascinating underground network. The geographic centre of Italy, it has remarkable Roman remains, which residents of pretty nearby **Amelia** see as rather modern – their town having been founded before Rome itself. To the north there is more of ancient Rome, in the shape of the abandoned town of **Carsulae**, whose romantic ruins occupy a bucolic spot among thickly wooded hills.

Pick of the picnic spots

Central Umbria If you've climbed Mount Subasio from Assisi a picnic at the top will taste all the better, though you can also drive up. Anywhere overlooking Lago Trasimeno would also be good, especially one of the many peacefully scenic spots on Isola Polvese.

Valle Umbra & southeast Umbria There are some good short walks from the abbey of San Pietro in Valle (see page 142) which could culminate in a picnic in the woods or down by the River Nera. For more expansive views, the hills around the Piano Grande near Castelluccio are hard to beat.

Northern Umbria The summit of Monte Cucco (see page 206) has enormous views in all directions, or you could find a more sheltered spot among the beech trees near Ranco at the end of the road up into the Apennines.

Northern Marche For both the views and the bragging rights, a picnic on Mussolini's broken nose (see page 226) is not to be missed. For a less political lunch, follow the road round to the left from the top of Urbino until you get to the grassy slope looking back over the town.

Central & southern Marche The beaches at Portonovo and Sirolo make good picnic spots; both have less frequented ends that are easily reached by a stroll along the seafront.

Northern Umbria

Less visited than the regions further south, northern Umbria has some excellent walking, not to mention world-class hang-gliding, on its eastern fringes. On the edge of the **Parco del Monte Cucco**, **Gubbio** has a Roman theatre, an extraordinary medieval town hall and a very special cable car, which whisks passengers two at a time up Monte Ingino in fragile-looking baskets. To the west, in the Upper Tiber Valley, **Città di Castello** sits at the heart of a tobacco-growing area where you can find much of the region's *agriturismo* (rural farm) accommodation. Home to one of Italy's foremost 20th-century artists, it also houses significant art collections. Nearby, little **Montone** hosts Umbria's film festival each July.

Northern Marche

Urbino is one of the most picture-perfect Renaissance towns and has been a great centre of learning and the arts for hundreds of years. The huge Palazzo Ducale dominates the surrounding landscape and the town retains much of its 15th- and 16th-century structure, as well as being home to 21st-century contemporary university life. To the north, the **Montefeltro** is an isolated area, with craggy outcrops topped with

Above: Fountain in piazza Arringo, Ascoli Piceno. Opposite page: View across Umbria towards Assisi and Monte Cucco.

castles rising precipitously out of the landscape. **San Leo** has a spectacularly sited fortress at the top of a cliff, and there are lots of other villages to explore. Out on the coast, **Pesaro** and **Fano** are old-fashioned resorts, but both have good beaches and handsome antique centres to compensate for their garish seafronts. North of Pesaro, where the hills reach right to the sea, **Gradara** is another castellated town with a tragically romantic past.

Central and southern Marche

The busy Adriatic port of **Ancona** has a quiet old centre with some good museums and some exceptional seafood restaurants. Just to the south, the **Parco del Conero** is one of Italy's most attractive stretches of coast, with rare wild beaches and green hills that reach right down to the sea. **Portonovo** is a pleasant little beachside village

Spello, Trevi and Spoleto all retain their strong medieval identities, while Montefalco adds the bonus of a successful wine industry. Bevagna is flatter, but no less lovely.

with some good restaurants and hotels and, just around the coast, cliff-top **Sirolo** has pastel-painted houses and a great beach at the foot of a steep path. **Macerata** is a little-visited university town with an outdoor summer opera festival, and nearby **Loreto** is the site of Mary and Joseph's house – flown here by angels or reconstructed by crusaders, depending on who you believe. **Ascoli Piceno**, a buzzing town with a stunning stage-set piazza, is the centre of the Marche's south, from where the high and often snowy peaks of the **Monti Sibillini** are not far away.

Best of Umbria & Marche

Top 20 things to see & do

❶ Corso Vannucci
Perugia's main street is one of the most beautiful in Italy. With the cathedral and the exquisite storyboard of the 13th-century Fontana Maggiore at one end, and the Renaissance treasures of the Palazzo dei Priori en route, it makes the perfect setting for posh shopping or an evening *passeggiata*. Page 71.

❷ A night out in Perugia
In general, night-time in Umbria is for sleeping. Unless cheesy beach discos are your idea of fun, it's little better in Marche. Perugia, however, is a different story: its cosmopolitan mix of international students ensures that the bars are lively, and whether beer and indie rock or wine and contemporary jazz is your thing, you'll find plenty going on after midnight. Page 111.

❸ Cookery lesson at Alter Ego, Perugia
A cookery lesson at this excellent and friendly restaurant costs little more than a good meal, and the wine is thrown in too. There's none of the preciousness you find in some places, and you get to eat the fruits of your labours at the end of the day. Page 113.

2 Bottega del Vino, Perugia.

5 Basilica San Francesco, Assisi.

4 Umbria Jazz, Corso Vannucci, Perugia.

④ Umbria Jazz

Europe's most important jazz festival overwhelms Perugia with an atmosphere of indolent enjoyment. Street bands and free piazza concerts fill the medieval centre, and people come as much for the stunning setting as the music. Page 48.

⑤ Basilica di San Francesco, Assisi

Few galleries in the world have either the quantity or the beauty of the art found in the two churches, one atop the other, of Umbria's holiest town. Perched on the edge of Assisi, the basilica has been expertly restored to its former glory since the 1997 earthquake. Page 87.

⑥ A boat trip on Lago Trasimeno

There are regular ferries from Castiglione del Lago out to the two peaceful islands. But for a real treat, charter a private boat, complete with prosecco and fruit, for a VIP cruise on Italy's fourth biggest lake. Page 96.

⑦ Paragliding off Monte Subasio

Strong updrafts all along the western side of the Apennines make it a prime spot for hang-gliding or paragliding. Monte Cucco often stages hang-gliding world championships, but for the chance to sail down on the breeze over Assisi, Monte Subasio takes some beating. Page 124.

⑧ Eating alfresco at a summer festa

Many of the region's old towns have an extraordinary attachment to traditions that go back hundreds of years. Festivals usually involve dressing up in medieval costumes and waving flags, playing music or running up mountains carrying heavy objects. The best of them, in the ancient quarters of towns such as Città di Castello, Montefalco and Gubbio, also involve *taverne*, or outdoor restaurants, serving traditional fare such as truffle-laden pasta and wild boar at bargain prices, sometimes on benches in the streets, sometimes in settings such as old cloisters. Page 46.

9 Trevi

It often seems that the southern part of Umbria has a medieval hill town around every corner. Little changed for hundreds of years, they sit like intricate sandcastles above the plains, seductive invitations to leisurely wandering. Quiet Trevi has fewer obvious sights than most, but it is one of the most intact and perfectly formed. Page 132.

10 Spring flowers on the Piano Grande

From Castelluccio, a romantically isolated town deep in the Sibillini Mountains, a high plain stretches out across the bottom of an enormous basin. Views of it in spring, carpeted with flowers against a backdrop of snow-covered peaks, feature on many a postcard. Page 149.

11 Rafting in the Sibillini

Other places in the world may have more adrenaline-inducing rapids, but the region's highest and wildest mountains, where wolves and even a bear or two roam, are a stunning place for going downstream. Page 153.

12 Duomo di Orvieto

Fear was clearly a prominent driving force behind the design of the 52-m tall façade of Orvieto's extraordinary Gothic cathedral. In exquisite and often painful detail, bas-reliefs from the 14th century illustrate a particularly hellish version of what might happen to you if you're bad. Inside, Signorelli's frescoes are similarly memorable and equally nightmarish. After all the suffering and anguish, you'll need one of Orvieto's exceptionally good ice creams. Page 173.

13 Monte Cucco

At the top of the Parco Regionale di Monte Cucco, on the Apennine ridge separating Umbria from Marche, beautiful beech woods blanket the mountains, and paths climb to the summit – from which there are extraordinary views. Page 206.

14 A ride in one of Gubbio's cable cars

Standing in a small and slightly rickety basket to be whisked up a steep mountainside might not be everybody's idea of fun, but Gubbio's cable car has just the right mix of exhilaration and huge views to be vertiginously memorable. Page 205.

15 Mussolini's broken nose

High above the Gola del Furlo, one of the steep gorges slicing through the Apennines, *Il Duce* had a large stone profile of his face built into the mountain. It was later blown up by partisans, but

9 A shrine in the hilltop town of Trevi.

not completely destroyed, and it's possible to walk up through the forest to stand on his broken nose, from where there is an awesome view down into the gorge below. Page 226.

⑯ Palazzo Ducale, Urbino
One of the Renaissance's most fêted buildings, the Ducal Palace dominates the university town of Urbino. It's now a museum, and visitors can walk through its arcaded squares and elaborately decorated bedrooms and imagine 15th-century life in the court of Federico da Montefeltro. Page 223.

⑰ Gradara
In the far north of Marche, the tiny medieval walled town and castle of Gradara are almost completely intact. The setting for the tragic love story of Francesca and Paolo, immortalized by Dante and later by Rodin, it meets all the requirements for a proper fairy-tale castle. Page 234.

⑱ A sunset over Monte Carpegna
In a region over-endowed with jaw-droppingly beautiful views, the sight of the sun dropping behind the Parco Naturale Sasso Simone e Simoncello from the restored castle at Pietrarubbia is especially memorable. Page 229.

⑲ Lazing on the beach after walking in the Parco del Conero
The Adriatic coast of Marche is at its most beautiful just to the south of Ancona, where the rolling rural landscape of the hinterland reaches right down to the sea. Free of the blight of development, small beaches have space to breathe. Page 252.

⑳ Grotte di Frasassi
Deep inside the Apennines, the Grotta Grande del Vento cavern in the Frassasi caves is the largest in Europe, big enough to hold Milan's cathedral. Nor is it the only attraction here: spectacular stalagmites and stalactites, both large and small, make the 1.5-km route through the caves an awesome experience. Page 254.

Five of the best

Frescoes

❶ **Perugino** Collegio del Cambio, Perugia (page 77).
❷ **Raphael** San Severo, Perugia (page 79).
❸ **Giotto** and **Cimabue** Basilica di San Francesco, Assisi (page 87).
❹ **Pinturicchio** Cappella Baglioni, Spello (page 121).
❺ **Signorelli** Cappella di San Brizio, Orvieto (page 173).

17 Gradara's steeply sloping streets lead to the castle at the top of the hill.

19 The beach at Sirolo, in the Conero Park.

Month by month

A year in Umbria & Marche

The last night of the Spoleto Festival sees a classical concert played in the town's piazza.

January

Capodanno (New Year) is welcomed with fireworks, feasting and lentil soup. Umbria Jazz Winter (see page 46) brings gospel singing to Orvieto's Duomo and jazz concerts to start the year. Snowfalls are fairly common across the region and the temperature drops close to or below freezing at night. At higher levels, cross-country skiing is popular. The weather is often crisp and sunny – January is the second driest month of the year.

February

Another cold month, with some snow likely, especially in the hills. Carnival is an especially big deal in Ascoli Piceno (see page 47) where there's a week of feasting and processions.

March

Spring can be slow in arriving, especially at higher altitudes, where the snow lingers. Even at lower levels the temperature rarely hits 15°C.

April

Easter is celebrated with plenty of pomp and ceremony, especially in the religious heartland of Assisi. At night the temperature drops and there can still be frosts, but the days are warmer, with an average maximum of 17°C.

May

As the mountain snows melt, the carpets of wild flowers bloom on the Piano Grande, near Castelluccio. Timing depends on the weather, but crocuses, blue squill, orchids and narcissi usually flower first, followed by geraniums, buttercups, peonies and tulips in June and then cornflowers,

Top: The Basilica of St Francis. Above: Wild horses on the Piano Grande.

Concert-goers sit on the steps of the Palazzo dei Priori for free jazz in Perugia

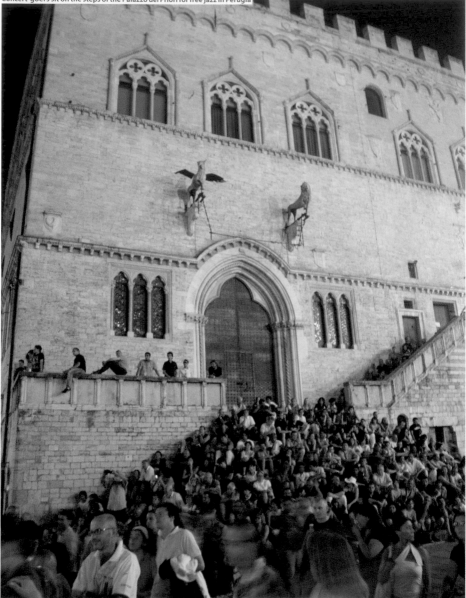

daisies and poppies. Butterflies also enjoy the show. On 15 May the age-old *Corso dei Ceri* in Gubbio pulls in the crowds, as teams race up the mountain carrying huge wooden 'candles'. At lower levels May is usually pleasantly warm, with maximum temperatures averaging 22°C.

June

The last remnants of snow on the high mountains melt away as the weather heats up. The average maximum temperature is 26°C. The first of the region's many summer festivals get under way.

July

The average maximum temperature is 29°C: in hot weather it can reach the mid-30s, though nights are seldom oppressively warm. The hills offer a cool respite and the beaches become busy with Italians and northern Europeans on their summer holidays. Umbria Jazz turns Perugia into a huge festival site, and many other towns host age-old celebrations, often with a medieval theme. Ice creams become an almost obligatory part of the evening *passeggiata*.

August

Inland, the towns empty of people as Italians head to the sea. On the coast you may have to fight to get a beach umbrella. Hot, sunny weather predominates, punctured by occasional heavy thunderstorms. Many of the locals who stay behind are involved in traditional festivals, and improvised outdoor eateries spring up in the medieval hill towns. On 15 August Italy comes to a complete standstill for *Ferragosto*. Figs ripen and the shops fill with delicious local tomatoes.

September

The greatest heat of summer tails off, and there are occasional mists in the mornings over the valleys, as Italians troop back to work. Grapes ripen on the vines.

October

Eurochocolate in Perugia turns the town brown, along with the leaves on the many millions of trees in the region. Nights are often cold, and mists linger. Grapes are harvested and the first snows may fall on the peaks of the Sibillini. Porcini mushrooms, gathered from the woods, become increasingly popular on restaurant menus.

November

Usually the wettest month, the average temperature drops below 10°C for the first time, but there can still be some pleasantly warm days. The first new olive oil pressings become available from the year's crop and are best consumed fresh.

December

What is claimed to be the world's biggest 'Christmas tree' is illuminated on the mountain above Gubbio. Snow is possible, though white Christmases are more likely at higher levels. On average the temperature falls to only 9°C, but December is usually drier than November, and sometimes seasonally crisp, frosty weather creates a festive mood.

Screen & page

Umbria & Marche in film & literature

Umbria and Marche are largely undiscovered territories in books and on film, though the landscape has starred in several movies.

Films

Brother Sun, Sister Moon
Franco Zeffirelli, 1972
Zeffirelli used the wide open spaces of the Piano Grande, as well as other settings around the region, for his Oscar-nominated biopic of St Francis, in which the saint is depicted as the great forerunner of the hippy movement.

La Vita è Bella (Life is Beautiful)
Roberto Benigni, 1997
Though the Italian part of this Oscar-winning film is set in and around nearby Arezzo, over the border in Tuscany, the concentration camp scenes were filmed in Terni in southern Umbria.

My House in Umbria
Richard Loncraine, 2003
Dame Maggie Smith and Timothy Spall, plus a straight Ronnie Barker, star in this slow and thoughtful adaptation of William Trevor's 1991 novel about terrorism and community.

Books

Fiction & poetry
Divine Comedy
Dante Alighieri, 1308-1321
Though hardly light holiday reading, nothing else can explain Italy and the Italians quite like the *Divine Comedy*. References to it can be seen all over Umbria and Marche: in Perugia, which he wrote

about, in the depictions of Hell on the façade of Orvieto's Duomo, and in the story of Francesca and Paolo from Gradara. And if you're learning the language it might help too: speak to an Italian about Italian and they'll probably tell you that Dante invented it.

Selected Poems
Giacomo Leopardi, 1818-1837, translated by Eamon Grennan, 1997
One of Italy's favourite poets, Leopardi was born in Recanati in Marche in 1798.

Ratking
Michael Dibdin, 1988
A detective story featuring Aurelio Zen, an archetypal, lonely, middle-aged detective, who is sent to Perugia to investigate a kidnapping and gets sucked into a complicated world of relationships and lies.

After Hannibal
Barry Unsworth, 1996
Keen, cutting observations on ex-pats in Umbria, their relationships and follies. Lots of precisely drafted characters out-of-water.

Non-fiction
The Dark Heart of Italy
Tobias Jones, 2003
An incisive and unsentimental look at contemporary Italy, which attempts to explain football, the media and Silvio Berlusconi.

An Appetite for Umbria
Christine Smallwood, 2005
A cookbook, coffee-table book and restaurant guide rolled into one. Interviews with the people behind Umbria's best restaurants are followed by some of their trademark recipes, and Eddie Jacob's wonderful photos of the people, places and food turn the book into a thing of great beauty (available from appetiteforumbria.com).

Umbria and the Marches
Georg Henke, 2005
The best guide to walking in Umbria and Marche, with careful instructions and generally excellent maps, Georg Henke's book would make an excellent companion to this guide.

I Segni del Paesaggio
George Tatge, 2007
A rare photography book on Umbria, this captures the rural spirit of the place without sentimentality or sunsets. The black-and-white photos come from an exhibition in Todi in 2007 and feature mud and dead trees, decrepit fences and mist, fig trees growing through the windows of ruined houses, as well as some beautiful landscapes.

Sculture nella città: Spoleto 1962
Giovanni Carandente, 2007
A beautiful and occasionally humorous coffee-table book looking back at the Spoleto sculpture festival of 1962 in black-and-white photographs. It's a great study of the Italians' easy interaction with art, and a sumptuous portrait of a gorgeous town, which, of course, has barely changed at all in the interim.

Contents

About the region

Waiting for the sun to fade on the Duomo in Orvieto.

History

Disproving the common belief that Italian culture started with the Romans, Umbria and Marche are rich sources of some sophisticated pre-Roman remains. The first populations probably migrated to central Italy from eastern and central Europe around 1500 BC, initially to the fertile plains around Perugia, then increasingly into the hills.

Earliest inhabitants

Little is known about the Umbri, the first sophisticated, organized civilization in the region. Pliny the Elder, writing in the first century AD, called them the oldest people in Italy, and their lands probably stretched to cover much of modern-day Tuscany and Marche as well as Umbria. There was a distinct and strict Umbrian social structure, probably based on military rank. The Iguvine or Eugubian Tablets (see page 201), bronze plates discovered by a farmer near Gubbio in the 15th century, are engraved with Umbrian inscriptions that tell of religious rituals including sacrifices.

Etruscan culture

As the Etruscans spread from the northwest, the Umbri were pushed east, so that by around 700 BC the River Tiber was the dividing line between the

Hypogeum of the Velimna Family, Perugia.

Museo Archeologico, Perugia.

two cultures, and the Etruscans controlled previously Umbrian towns such as Perugia and Orvieto. They traded extensively with the ancient Greeks, to the extent that around three-quarters of all Ancient Greek pottery discovered to date has been found in Italy.

Etruscan civilization was highly developed, of unknown origins, and with a mysterious non-Indo-European language. Modern genetic experiments on people living in the region suggest their Etruscan ancestors may have come from the Eastern Mediterranean. They seem to have been a loosely affiliated society, without a centralized power base. No history written by the Etruscans exists, though there are plenty of funerary inscriptions. The Etruscan tombs outside the walls of Orvieto (see page 177) are a rich source of information. There are also Etruscan tombs outside Perugia, and many sarcophagi in its archaeological museum. These carved stone coffins often portray the deceased reclining on the lid.

In comparison with ancient Greece, women seem to have been given more prominence in Etruscan society, with tombs possibly suggesting a matriarchal line of descent. Etruscan women, unlike Greek women, attended banquets, and some Etruscan carvings show affection between couples, which is usually absent from Greek depictions.

There is debate about the extent to which the Etruscans influenced the Romans – certainly much of Etruscan architectural style was adapted by the Romans, and some go as far as to suggest that the name Rome itself may be Etruscan. Ancient Etruscan walls and city gates can be seen in Orvieto and Perugia, where Emperor Augustus later added his stamp to one of the Etruscan gates.

The Picenes are the most obscure of the region's ancient peoples. A warlike bunch, they inhabitated a small strip of present-day Marche, giving their name to the town of Ascoli Piceno. Many were buried in full battle garb, with swords (imported from the Balkans) and spears.

In 309 BC Perugia was defeated in battle against the Roman army and gradually, over the next 150 years, the entire Etruscan, Umbrian and Picene region fell under the control of Rome.

The Roman Empire

A power struggle followed the murder of Julius Caesar in 44 BC. Caesar's great-nephew Octavian forced Mark Antony's brother Lucius Antonius out of Rome; when he took refuge in Perugia, Octavian (now Emperor Augustus) destroyed the city, and with it the last remnants of Umbrian independence. The *Arco Etrusco* (Etruscan Arch) still bears the inscription that the emperor had placed on it – 'Augusta Perusia' – renaming the city after himself and stamping his authority on the region.

By this time Rome was already the dominant force in the whole region. Historians disagree about the exact level of the Etruscans' influence on the early Roman Empire: some believe that they may have had an important part to play in the founding of Rome itself. Once the two powers were competing for control of the region, however, the loose structure of Etruscan government was no match for the centralized power of Rome.

Roman settlements

The important via Flaminia, which connected Rome with the Adriatic at Fano, had a major influence on the region for many centuries. A part of the road, paved with stones on which Roman cartwheel grooves are still visible, can be seen at Carsulae (see page 186), where it passes through the *Arco di Traiano* (Trajan's Arch), and much of the original Roman route is still used, including, at the Gola del Furlo, a tunnel through the rock constructed by Vespasian in AD 77.

As trade flowed through the region, Roman towns grew up, and earlier Umbrian towns expanded. Umbria became increasingly prosperous and strategically important. Romans took their holidays in Umbria, and emperors partied at the Fonti del Clitunno (see page 135). Roman towns such as Interamna Nahars (Terni), Spoletium (Spoleto), Fulginium (Foligno) and Perusia (Perugia) thrived; historians described Narnia (Narni) in such glowing terms that CS Lewis later borrowed its name for his heavenly fictional world.

Roman Carsulae (see page 186), in the hills north of Narni, grew up almost entirely because of its position on the road, and became a staging

In search of the Romans

The newly reopened archaeological museum in Assisi is one of the best for Roman remains, and gives access to the Roman forum itself, underneath the piazza del Comune. In Todi (see page 179) there are enormous Roman cisterns under the central piazza, and in Perugia (see page 78) a narrow pedestrian street follows the route of the Roman aqueduct.

Piazza del Comune, Assisi.

post complete with a theatre and amphitheatre complex, temples and a large triumphal arch. The via Flaminia was subsequently re-routed around the town, however, and an earthquake may have hastened its demise. Abandoned for centuries, it is now an important and idyllic archaeological site.

Life was not always simple for the Romans – they suffered one of their worst military defeats here in 217 BC, when the Carthaginian general Hannibal, having led his army, complete with elephants, over the Alps, lured a Roman army under Flaminius into an ambush and killed at least 15,000 soldiers.

Though the region's urban buildings are often of medieval origin, the layouts of many towns still follow the original Roman city plan, with a central piazza where the Roman forum once stood, and a main street that follows the route of the original east-west *decumanus maximus*. Towns such as Assisi were built over Roman foundations, and the front section of the original Roman temple still stands, now adapted into a church.

Almost everywhere you can find Roman carvings and columns reused by subsequent generations – the Tempietto sul Clitunno (see page 135) was thought to be a Roman temple, until it was realized that early Christians had reused parts of earlier Roman ruins to build their church. Many other churches in the region feature recycled Roman capitals and stones.

Eventually, the road that had given the region so much prominence also brought problems. As trade had travelled along the via Flaminia in the years of the Roman Empire, so Vandal and Visigoth invaders used it in subsequent centuries, and with the fall of the Western Empire the region was subjected to many major battles that ushered in a new, less ordered era.

The Dark Ages – early Christian & Gothic

As the Roman Empire declined and fell, into the post-Roman (Byzantine) era stormed the eastern Germanic Goths. Umbrian towns were destroyed as they found themselves caught in a strategically significant position between the two battling forces. With the disintegration of central government the region fragmented; the hills of Umbria, and the monastic traditions and practices they gave birth to, were to be essential to the survival of western Christianity.

The Lombards & the Duchy of Spoleto

The Goths ruled central Italy until the western Germanic Lombards, under King Alboin, successfully invaded in AD 568. The Lombards' Duchy of Spoleto covered most of modern-day Umbria, though the Byzantines retained a strip of central Italy from Rome to the Adriatic, including Narni and Perugia, cutting off the Duchy from the Lombard centre of power to the north but also giving it a degree of independence.

The Lombards had arrived with a fearsome reputation, but as they settled in the region they became less warlike, gave up their Arianism to embrace Catholicism, and contributed to the construction of abbeys. It was, eventually, a time of renewed stability and an era of importance for Spoleto, though little remains from the Lombard era – the Chiesa di San Pietro in Valle (see page 142) is an exception.

To the north, the Lombards overstretched themselves when they invaded Ravenna, upsetting the pope. In AD 754, Pope Stephen III consolidated the papacy's earthly power when he asked the Franks, under Pepin the Short and subsequently his son Charlemagne, to take up arms against the Lombards. Though the Duchy of Spoleto continued to exist as an entity until 1250, the balance of power had swung away from the Lombards, and the eighth century marked the beginning of a long and often uneasy relationship between the Franks and the pope; nominally partners in the Holy Roman Empire they were often bitterly opposed as they fought for economic control, not just of Italy but of the whole of Western Europe.

CHARLEMAGNE.

('peace, prayer and work'), was designed to set the foundations for religious communities living together. Widely adopted by monks and nuns ever since, it has been so successful that St Benedict is generally regarded as the founder of Western monasticism, his sister as the first nun.

The pope & the Holy Roman Empire

Struggles between the pope and the state have a long history in Italy, and Umbria and Marche have always been either involved in or affected by them.

In AD 776 the Duchy of Spoleto fell to Charlemagne and his Frankish army. Twenty years earlier, Charlemagne's father Pepin the Short, having captured Ravenna from the Lombards, had given it to the papacy in return for influence and titles. The Duchy of Spoleto was now also given to the pope, though Charlemagne retained the right to name its dukes. In AD 800, Pope Leo III crowned Charlemagne Holy Roman Emperor. It was a hugely significant moment for Western Europe, and central Italy was largely shaped by it for the next 1,000 years.

In creating the notion of a Holy Roman Empire, Charlemagne built an entity to rival the power of the Byzantine Church to the east, merging Germanic power with historical memories of the Roman Empire and the spiritual authority of the papacy. At the same time the Papal States were born and the pope became involved in temporal power to an unprecedented extent, becoming a political and economic power as well as a spiritual one.

Guelphs & Ghibellines

The tensions created by this relationship between pope and emperor, and the vexed question of whether the Church gave authority to the emperor or vice versa, were played out at local levels, with powerful families and towns taking (and often switching) sides to suit their own ends.

By the 12th century, the faction on the side of the papacy had become known as the Guelphs; those in favour of the emperor were the Ghibellines. ('Guelf' was probably derived from the Bavarian

Birth of monasticism

While these power struggles were being played out, in the Umbrian hills, Benedict and Scholastica were born in Norcia in AD 480; they initiated a long spiritual tradition in the region that looked not to the grandiose papal style of Rome but to a more humble, meditative religion, which centuries later would culminate in the philosophy of St Francis (see page 90).

At the same time the Benedictine influence gave to Western Europe a quiet – and at the time unheralded – tradition of learning, in the process preserving history and literature. Benedict founded 12 communities of monks and his 'Rule', the code by which the monks lived, was highly influential, though he never set out to found anything as far-reaching as a monastic order and was not canonized by the Roman Catholic Church until 1220. The Rule, actually a book of precepts summed up in the words *pax, ora et labora*

dukes of the Welf, and 'Ghibelline' from the rival Hohenstaufens of Swabia, who used Waiblingen, the name of their castle, as a battle cry.) Associations were loose, however, and more often local than national. Guelphs often came from rich mercantile backgrounds and Ghibellines from agricultural estates. Born in Assisi in 1181, St Francis himself fought in this strife, taking part in battles against Perugia, where he was captured and imprisoned.

This background of centuries of local squabbles and bitter rivalries helped to create the Umbria and Marche landscape that still exists today, with fiercely protected castles and walled hill towns guarding local *comuni* (communes/municipalities), and strongly held local identities. Castles such as Gradara (see page 234) date from this period, and even important farms had their own watchtowers and defences, some of which still survive.

At times, larger forces washed over these local battles. When Frederick Hohenstaufen, known in

Italy as Barbarossa, became emperor in 1152, he marched south, brutally overpowering and often destroying Umbrian cities that stood up to him, such as Spoleto. This imperial violence did not mean, however, that papal governors were received any more favourably – the rich, noble families of Perugia were particularly unhappy to be governed from Rome.

Pope Innocent III came to Umbria in 1216 to try to firm up his authority, but he died, probably poisoned, in Perugia. The regional antipathy towards the pope was political rather than religious, but a new-found religious enthusiasm was inspired by St Francis and had a profound influence on the region. And while it was often an anarchic and bloody period, in some ways the local competition and one-upmanship also paved the way for the architectural and artistic flowering of the Renaissance, as well as fostering the area's independent spirit.

Five of the best

Castles

❶ **Rocca del Leone,** Castiglione del Lago (page 97).

❷ **Rocca Albornoziana,** Spoleto (page 137).

❸ **Rocca di Albonoz,** Narni (page 185).

❹ **Castello di Pietrrubbia,** San Leo (page 229).

❺ **Castello di Gradara,** Gradara (page 234).

Rocca del Leone, Castiglione del Lago.

The Renaissance & the end of self-government

The first green shoots of the Renaissance began to appear early in the region, when the papacy was split between Avignon and Rome in the 14th century – the so-called Western Schism. With Europe's attention focused elsewhere, Umbria and Marche were left largely to their own devices, and the *comuni*, which already enjoyed a degree of independence, flourished. Many of the structures of 21st-century Umbria and Marche date from the 14th and 15th centuries, years when the *comuni* had enough power and economic strength to define their own destinies.

Papal domination

It would, however, be wrong to characterize the medieval period as a golden era for the region. Bitter infighting continued, and it was a time notable as much for its bloodiness as for its cultural blossoming. Foreign *condottieri*, or mercenaries, were hired to fight on behalf of local towns and cities, increasing the violence. The streets of Perugia are said to have flowed with the blood of the murdered. Then there was the Black Death, which killed more than half the population in 1348. There was no understanding that bubonic plague was passed on by fleas on rats, and the disease recurred many times after the main outbreak was over. And there were earthquakes too. Eventually, weakened by fighting between themselves, the towns and cities of the region all fell to the papacy, and long centuries of neglect followed.

La Guerra del Sale – the Salt War – is a good example of the different military and economic influences of the times. In 1540, Pope Paul III told the citizens of Perugia that thenceforth they would be forced to purchase only papal salt, at a price that was more than double what they were currently paying. The justification given was that the income was needed to support the papal troops. The people of Perugia were not impressed and, after the failure of negotiations, war broke out between the city and the papacy. The pope won, took away all Perugia's independence and built a huge castle, the Rocca Paolina (see page 80), on top of the city quarter where the rich Baglioni family had previously lived. It is said, perhaps apocryphally, that the absence of salt in the region's traditional bread dates from this point.

Artistic & intellectual growth

Given the misery and violence of everyday life in late medieval times, the flourishing of the arts seems incongruous, but it was around this time that the Renaissance court of Federico da Montefeltro became a famous centre of artistic patronage. Pietro Vannucci, better known as Perugino, was born in Città della Pieve in 1446; 37 years later his most famous student, Raphael, was born – the son of an artist at the Urbino court.

It was also a period of wider intellectual flowering. The first copy of Dante's *Divine Comedy* was printed in Foligno, in southern Umbria, in 1472, by which time universities were already thriving in Perugia and Macerata. It may have felt like an era of change and hopefulness, but it wasn't to last.

Palazzo dei Consoli, Gubbio.

The new religion

Trade, money and civic pride meant that secular building, such as the construction of the Palazzo dei Consoli in Gubbio (see page 201), built in 1332, began to rival and often overtake religious architecture.

Under the firm but distant thumb of papal rule the region largely stagnated – isolated, rural and forgotten – until unification.

The Risorgimento to the present day

The Salt War was the final struggle of years of discord between the *comuni* and the papacy. Nearly 200 years earlier Pope Innocent VI had employed Cardinal Albornoz to subdue the region, and many of the papal fortresses he had built still lord it over towns such as Assisi and Spoleto today.

After Perugia finally caved in to the power of the papacy, the region entered a slow decline, though some towns, such as Urbino and Città di Castello, did manage to retain some independence for a while. In many ways this mirrored the fate of Italy in general – after the Renaissance, the European cultural and political status of the whole peninsula began to ebb away to the north.

Between the 16th and 18th centuries Umbria and Marche became something of a backwater. Depopulated and riven by banditry – in the late 16th century the papacy executed over 1,000 bandits a year – the area languished as a largely unloved and isolated source of papal taxation. At the end of the 18th century Napoleon came and took control, then left again after a brief period of economic growth, having plundered the region's art and other treasures.

Unification & war

When, in 1859, Perugia rose up in favour of the Risorgimento (the movement to unify Italy), it can have come as no great surprise. When unification finally arrived, the inhabitants of the city celebrated by immediately demolishing the huge Rocca Paolina, the castle that had represented so many years of papal rule.

Despite the revival of the name 'Umbria' in 1870, life under the new Italian Republic was not much easier than before. Opened up to national competition after centuries of torpor, the Umbrian and Marche economies struggled to cope.

Local politics

The region's continued left leanings (in 2006, 56% in the Marche and 57% in Umbria voted for Romano Prodi) may not tally with national politics, but at a local level government is largely getting things done, eventually, such as Perugia's expensive but impressive Minimetrò system, which opened in 2008.

And when, in the early 20th century, opportunities to escape presented themselves, thousands did so, emigrating to America in huge numbers. Those left behind turned increasingly to socialism and communism in search of economic solutions, though their hopes of change were dashed under the regime of Mussolini, who left his profile built into the Marche rocks at the Gola del Furlo (see page 226). In the Second World War Foligno was badly bombed by Allied forces, as was Terni, whose armaments factories made it a strategic target. Many towns were also left scarred when the German forces retreated, destroying infrastructure as they went.

Reinvention

In the second half of the 20th century, despite continued emigration, civic pride returned as power filtered down to the regions, and Umbria and Marche began to benefit from tourism and small-scale business. Transport links were improved, and cultural events – from revived medieval festivals to new seasons of jazz and opera – brought some zest to the area. Also important has been the renaissance of Umbrian food, which is increasingly exported to the rest of Italy and beyond.

The 1997 earthquake (see box, page 91) was a setback for a region increasingly reliant on tourism. For some years people stayed away, and there was also some disquiet over the way money was channelled into big projects and not into re-housing the homeless. Now, however, most Umbrians look to the future with some optimism: theirs is a region finally on the up.

Art & architecture

Amalassunta Blu, Osvaldo Licini, Ascoli Piceno.

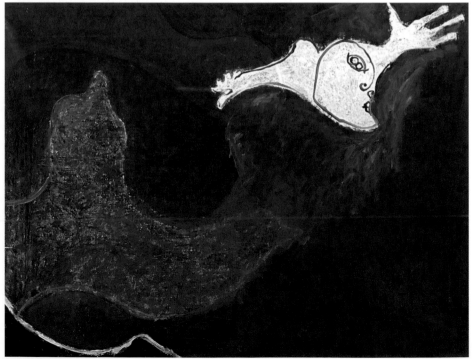

Though it is a region often defined by its verdant landscape, what makes Umbria and Marche so special is the way that humans have interacted with this landscape for the last 2,500 years, leaving their mark in the forms of buildings, roads and farms. The continuity is remarkable – town walls built before the Roman era have been patched up now and again but still survive, and even where the original structures no longer stand, designs for (and often stones from) buildings erected by the Romans have been reused.

Art, too, has made its mark on the region: Raphael was born here, and some of the most important art ever painted adorns the Basilica of di San Francesco in Assisi. It is a land of religious art, of Perugino, Pinturricchio and the Crivelli brothers, but also of the beginnings of something else: the region's landscape makes some significant appearances, and some of its portraits, such as those of Federico da Montefeltro and his wife Battista Sforza, are instantly recognizable. It's also a region with – somewhat unusually for Italy – some excellent 20th-century art, especially the Burri Collection in Città di Castello and the sculpture and paintings of Spoleto, Marcerata and Ascoli Piceno.

Etruscan & Roman art

Despite the wide spread of the Umbri across the region, they left little of their building and art. The Etruscans, however, seemingly obsessed with death and rituals, left a large body of artefacts in tombs around Umbria, and Romans built upon their legacy.

Richly decorated pottery and carved stone sarcophagi tell us most of what we know of Etruscan civilization. The Museo Archeologico Nazionale in Orvieto (see page 175) has frescoes from two Etruscan tombs, with figures attending a funeral banquet, which show an elegance in Etruscan art that is often overlooked. The tombs themselves, just outside Orvieto, are solid, square, stone structures.

Where to see Etruscan tombs

The sculpture on Etruscan tombs is elaborate, with the deceased usually depicted reclining on the lid of the sarcophagus and bas-reliefs around the sides. The best examples can be seen at the Ipogeo dei Volumni (see page 82) outside Perugia, and in the archaeological museums of Perugia and Orvieto.

Five of the best

Paintings to see

❶ Piero della Francesca's *Polyptych of St Anthony*, Galleria Nazionale dell'Umbria, Perugia (see page 75).

❷ Ghirlandaio's *Coronation of the Virgin*, Museo della Città di Narni, Narni (see page 184).

❸ Luca Signorelli's *Martyrdom of San Sebastian*, Pinoteca Communale, Città di Castello (see page 209).

❹ Raphael's *La Muta*, Galleria Nazionale delle Marche, Urbino (see page 223).

❺ Carlo Crivelli's *Madonna and Child*, Pinoteca, Ascoli Piceno (see page 263).

Etruscan pottery
Much of the pottery found in Etruscan tombs comes from Greece. In fact, so keen were the Etruscans on Greek pottery that a lot of it was made with this export market in mind, and more Ancient Greek pottery has been found in Italy than in Greece. In time, the Etruscans copied and developed the Greek styles. Gradually, figures and animals appeared, almost always in profile. Oriental patterns appeared around 700 BC, and the characteristic 'black-figure' pottery, with human figures against a red ground, followed in the same century. This style was subsequently reversed, so that red figures appear against a black background.

Bucchero ware is the black, usually polished, pottery most often associated with the Etruscans, and there are plenty of examples in museums around the region, especially in Orvieto and

Where to see Roman architecture

Many towns have Roman walls and theatres; some of the latter, such as those in Spoleto and Gubbio, are still used for performances. Urbs Salvia (see page 259), near Macerata, has a wonderful oval amphitheatre overgrown with trees. The region's best Roman remains are at Carsulae (see page 186), where an intact triumphal arch crosses the via Flaminia and there is a ruined theatre and amphitheatre.

Perugia. The colour was achieved by firing the pots in an atmosphere of carbon monoxide instead of oxygen. The best pieces are from the seventh and sixth centuries BC, influenced at first by Phoenician and Cypriot designs and later by Greek pottery.

Roman advances

Etruscan towns were designed, rather than growing organically, and had two main axes: the north-south *cardo* and the east-west *decumanus*, dividing each town into four quarters. The form was later adopted by the Romans, who also developed other Etruscan features, such as barrelled arches, good roads and excellent drainage systems and sewers. Rome had the military might, however, and came to dominate the region, building towns around the important via Flaminia, the road that connected Rome with the Adriatic. The Romans' invention of concrete in the first century BC meant that, while they took up Etruscan forms, their buildings could be bigger and stronger; their use of marble also meant that their decorations and statues were finer, and lasted longer.

Though there are few, if any, intact Roman buildings in the region, there are plenty of ruins, and also many Roman elements that were reused in later buildings. The Tempietto sul Clitunno (see page 135) contains so many Roman elements that it was long considered to be a Roman structure; the entire front section of the Temple of Minerva in Assisi (see page 93) was retained when it became a church; and the Basilica di San Salvatore in Spoleto (see page 141) uses Roman columns, capitals and carvings in a comically haphazard fashion.

Medieval art & architecture

After the Romans, art and architecture suffered for centuries – medieval works were either forgotten, or were destroyed in the many battles, and little of that period survives today. From around AD 1000 to the start of the Renaissance the conflict continued, but despite the Guelph-Ghibelline chaos (see page 30), or in some cases because of it, towns began to grow and prosper.

Competition between rival towns, and between Church and State, led to unprecedented architectural and artistic one-upmanship. While the wealthier and more powerful Church built bigger churches and cathedrals, towns such as Gubbio tried to exert their independence by building bigger and more impressive town halls and public buildings. Increased private wealth amongst merchants also meant that grand homes were constructed.

Byzantine art

The Church employed artists to decorate its new buildings, initially in a largely Byzantine style, with front-on portraits of the Madonna and Child on patterned backgrounds of gold leaf. As the period wore on, these became more sophisticated, culminating in the extraordinary storytelling frescoes of Giotto and Cimabue in the Basilica di San Francesco in Assisi (see page 87), a crucial stepping-stone in the path towards the Renaissance and a modern concept of art.

Five of the best

Beautiful churches

❶ **San Pietro** Perugia (see page 81).

❷ **Santa Maria Sopra Minerva** Assisi (see page 93).

❸ **San Silvestro** Bevagna (see page 127).

❹ **Sant'Eufemia** Spoleto (see page 141).

❺ **San Pietro in Valle** Valnerina (see page 142).

The church of San Silvestro in Bevagna.

From Romanesque to Gothic

This was also a time of changing styles in architecture. The Romanesque style, so-called because it used many of the round forms of ancient Roman architecture, can be seen in some of the region's oldest churches, such as at San Pietro in Valle (see page 142) and Sant'Eufemia in Spoleto (see page 141), both largely constructed in the 12th century. Buildings of this type combine sturdy walls with round arches, barrel vaults and large towers. Their symmetrical layouts are generally simple and their windows small.

Gothic style, which originated in France, was long regarded as inferior in central Italy – indeed the Italians coined the description 'Gothic' as an insult, because they equated the style with something barbaric. Nevertheless, it became increasingly influential, with its more complex ribbed vaulting, flying buttresses, pointed arches and high, light, stained-glass windows. The upper church in the Basilica di San Francesco is a good example of Umbrian Gothic at its best.

As Umbria and Marche came under papal control, political influence and power drained away; many towns in the region stagnated after the 15th century, retaining their medieval buildings and traditions. Wander around the centres of Umbrian hill towns such as Gubbio, Perugia or Assisi, and you might feel that in 500 years nothing much has changed.

The Renaissance

After the often flat, decorative, Byzantine-influenced religious art of the medieval period, the artistic flowering of the Renaissance in the 15th century was a dramatic change. Influenced by the work of Giotto and a rediscovery of the forms and shapes understood in ancient Roman times, artists started painting three-dimensional space, light and shadow, rendering architectural perspective and including landscape and domestic detail. Though most art remained nominally religious, contemporary faces and emotions appeared in

Where to find Umbria's great artists

Perugino's best work in the region is in the Galleria Nazionale dell'Umbria in Perugia (see page 75).

Pinturicchio's masterpiece is the Cappella Baglioni in Santa Maria Maggiore in Spello (see page 121).

Despite **Raphael**'s birth in Urbino, few of his paintings can be seen in the region. A glorious exception is his delicate *La Muta*, or *Portrait of a Gentlewoman*, in the Galleria Nazionale delle Marche in Urbino (see page 223).

The Umbrian landscape, notably around the shores of Lake Trasimeno, features strongly in Perugino's art, and he clearly took his studies of perspective seriously. It is easy to see links between his painting and that of his pupil Raphael, but it is also possible to see how Raphael improved on what he had learnt.

Pinturicchio was a contemporary (and assistant) of Perugino, and is often overshadowed by him, sometimes rather unfairly. Though he was not an innovator like Perugino, Pinturicchio's decorative paintings exhibit a detached, careful draughtsmanship that has aged well and often appears quite contemporary next to Perugino's sentimentality. Born Bernardino di Betto in Perugia in 1454, Pinturicchio worked with Perugino on frescoes in the Sistine Chapel and later decorated rooms in the Vatican Library. His finely observed plants and landscapes mark him out as an artist with a very keen eye, and many of his paintings are embellished with fascinating minutiae.

Raffaello Sanzio (known in English as Raphael) was born in Urbino in 1483. His father Giovanni Santi was also an accomplished painter and poet, and was court artist to Federico da Montefeltro. Raphael was orphaned at the age of 11, but by then he had already worked with his father, and as a teenager he showed precocious talent. There is debate about when he worked as an assistant, and perhaps as an apprentice, to Perugino in Perugia, but by 1501 he was already described as a fully trained master. The depiction of Daniel in one of Perugino's sumptuous paintings in the Collegio del Cambio (see page 77) is probably a portrait of Raphael, and his own first documented fresco is also in Perugia, in the Cappella di San Severo (see page 79).

works that were often paid for by rich families. This patronage in turn created a cult of personality, and painters – who had previously been largely anonymous – became the celebrities of the age.

Umbria's great artists

Pietro Vannucci, known as Perugino, was born in Città della Pieve in 1446. His work marks the beginning, and arguably the apotheosis, of the so-called Umbrian school of Renaissance art. Perugino worked in the studio of Andrea del Verrocchio, alongside Leonardo da Vinci, and he may have also studied under Piero della Francesca. His greatest achievement was probably his tutoring of Raphael, though at his peak he also produced some great Renaissance art, before falling back into saccharine cliché later in his career. He was one of the most famous and successful painters of the time, and was called to Rome by the pope to paint the Sistine Chapel.

Renaissance architecture

Though the region's great architecture is mainly medieval, there are some notable Renaissance buildings too, such as La Forteza in San Leo (see page 228) and the Palazzo Ducale in Urbino (see page 222). Many medieval buildings, such as the Cattedrale di Santa Maria Assunta in Spoleto (see page 137) were given Renaissance additions.

Under papal rule, the region's art and architecture largely stagnated for centuries. This lack of development has left many artistic treasures unspoilt, but it has also stunted artistic life. A 20th-century rebirth of sorts centred around Alberto Burri in Città di Castello (see page 211). His abstract sculptures, full of pain and suffering, were a response to the violence of the period. His legacy has left sculpture as one of the region's foremost artistic outlets – Arnaldo Pomodoro's sculpture park and museum at Castello di Pietrarubbia in Marche (see page 229) is a fine example.

Burri's use of post-industrial space in the tobacco-drying sheds of Città di Castello is also one of the region's best examples of contemporary architecture. A drive through the ugly suburbs of Perugia or Ancona provides graphic evidence that interesting architecture of modern times is concentrated on reusing existing structures rather than on building beautiful new ones.

Five of the best

Places to see contemporary art

❶ **Galleria Civica d'Arte Moderna**, Spoleto With colour and movement, an uplifting international collection (see page 140).

❷ **Collezione Burri**, Città di Castello Two museums dedicated to Alberto Burri, the region's most important contemporary artist (see page 211).

❸ **Pietrarubbia**, Montefeltro Fine sculpture, in a museum and scattered around a medieval village (see page 229).

❹ **Museo Palazzo Ricci**, Macerata A fabulous collection of works by just about everyone who mattered in 20th century Italian art (see page 258).

❺ **Galleria d'Arte Contemporanea**, Great temporary exhibitions (see page 263).

Above: Galleria Civica d'Arte Moderna, Spoleto. Opposite page: *Madonna in Gloria* by Perugino.

Umbria & Marche today

Tourism on a small scale

Bypassed by Italian development for much of the 20th century, Umbria and Marche can still feel like regions in a time warp, much further from the politics of Rome or the money of the Italian north than they actually are. Sundays are still soporifically slow, shops and businesses close for long siestas, and in August inland towns empty of residents as everyone heads for the beach. Assisi aside, tourism often feels like a novel concept in Umbria, and a completely alien idea in Marche. There are few of the crowds encountered in Tuscany, and out of season – which in some places means for most of the year – you can travel a long way without seeing another foreigner.

But the region is slowly changing, with small enterprises cottoning on to the idea that there is money to be made from virgin landscapes and traditional Italian culture. The wine industry and food producers are beginning to open their doors to visitors, and the many *agriturismi* in the region are widening their horizons to attract foreign visitors, not just the Italians who have traditionally made up most of their clientele.

Above: Taking life easy in Bevagna.
Opposite page: The traditional art of flag waving, Gubbio.

Traditionally unconventional

It would be misleading to exaggerate the extent to which Umbria and Marche are traditional Italian regions. Each has a strong identity of its own, often in antipathy to big brother Tuscany, and a somewhat surprising anti-establishment streak, born of centuries of papal misrule and central government neglect. Indeed, both regions have rather left-leaning political instincts, and a forward-looking creative streak, in contrast with the rest of Italy's sometimes moribund fascination with the past.

As power has seeped down to a regional level, so local government has been able to do some good, investing in local projects, especially in festivals (see page 46), of which there seem to be several every week, and which are held in even the smallest towns. And while many take place without attracting a single tourist, others, such as Umbria Jazz, are now major international events, with plenty of accompanying inward investment.

Tradition is still upheld enthusiastically in events such as Gubbio's centuries-old *Corso dei Ceri* (see page 47) but there are new revivals of the past too, including Bevagna's *Mercato delle Gaite* (see page 47). Such things help not only to encourage tourism but also to inculcate a sense of pride in the region.

The shock of the new

Found under her duvet with her throat cut in November 2007, Meredith Kercher was a 21-year-old British student studying at the Università per Stranieri in Perugia. The international media circus that has accompanied the murder case has shaken a region unaccustomed to being in the news at all, except when local television reports the latest truffle finds. Famous for its murders in medieval times, Perugia had seemed such a peaceful place in the 20th century. Whether the Kercher case will have any long-lasting effect on the city remains to be seen. For the time being it has brought an unwanted notoriety and a loss of innocence.

Nature & environment

Below: Morning mist over the valley below Perugia. Opposite page: Chianina cattle have lived in the region for centuries.

Dominated by hills, Umbria and Marche are predominantly rural regions. Apart from a narrow strip along the Marche coast, and the flat, central Valle Umbra in Umbria, most parts have few people and lots of wildlife. The Apennines, the mountains running down the spine of Italy, are especially spectacular here, and there are lakes too, notably Lago Trasimeno, Italy's fourth largest.

The striking natural landscape has done much to define the region, with characteristic small walled towns and villages overlooking valleys that were once strategically important as the only routes through difficult terrain. The isolated valleys were perfect places for hermits and monks, enhancing the region's religious importance and its preponderance of saints. And the existence of animals such as wild boar, which still roam the uplands, has influenced the cuisine here for millennia.

Mountains & marshes

The discovery of the 'Gubbio Layer' (see page 205) near Gubbio in the 1970s changed the world's thinking about the extermination of the dinosaurs 65 million years ago. One of the reasons that this geological fingerprint was so well preserved is that until relatively recently this area was under the sea, the most recent uplift of hills having occurred between 24 million and a mere 1.6 million years ago, in the Miocene and Pliocene eras.

The Apennine Mountains are mainly limestone, and stone quarried from them has been used since before Etruscan times for building in the region, giving the local towns their characteristic pale appearance. (The slightly pink tinge of the stone from Monte Subasio gives Assisi its warm glow.)

The high mountains of the Sibillini, on the Umbria-Marche border, are characterized by large, distinctive karstic plains. Formed originally by glaciers, natural ditches drain rain and melted snow from the surface into an underground drainage system. On occasion these can get blocked, resulting in temporary lakes.

In Roman times the Valle Umbra, the flat, fertile plain spreading south from Perugia, was an area of marshy lakes: Lacus Umber and Lacus Clitorius. It was first drained by the Romans and is now relatively highly populated. Over the centuries there have been various plans to drain the shallow Lago Trasimeno to the west, but these days the main threat to it is global warming.

Wolves, boar & porcupines

Wild boar have been roaming the central Italian hills for millennia – Etruscan pottery shows that it was already a favourite dish 2,500 years ago, and the tradition of hunting boar is deeply ingrained in Umbrian tradition. These days the boar are mostly of Eastern European stock, the original species having at one point nearly died out. The incomers have bigger litters and have bred successfully, especially in regional and national parks, where they are protected from hunters, to the point that in some areas they are considered pests. If you are lucky you may come across a family of them in the mountains.

The Apennine wolf, also known as the Italian wolf, is a subspecies of the grey wolf. Growing up to 1.5 m long and weighing 25-40 kg, it hunts smaller mammals such as deer and boar. The mountains of Umbria and Marche were traditionally a part of the wolf's stronghold, and the animal features strongly in the folklore of the region, including the story of St Francis and the wolf.

Above: Sun shines through the beech trees in the Sibillini mountains. Opposite page: Olive harvest above Spello.

Between 1801 and 1825, wolves in Italy were thought to have killed more than 70 people, but there have not been any attacks on humans since the Second World War. By the 1970s human activity had nearly wiped out the wolf population, with numbers believed to be down to around 100. Since then, however, public and political opinion about the wolf has changed, and it is thought that there are now around 500 in the country, many of them in the central Italian Apennines.

Other, less vaunted mammals, such as wildcats and porcupines, also live in the Umbrian and Marche uplands, and you may find porcupine spines on paths, though the animals themselves are elusive. Rabbits and hares are more common, if they can avoid being turned into pasta sauce, and a lone bear has made his home in the region's mountains (see box, page 150) having travelled north from the Abruzzo.

In the central Italian skies, you may spot golden eagles and other birds of prey circling over the high hills, and at lower levels there are many migratory birds, though the surfeit of hunters eager to shoot anything with feathers means that there is considerably less birdlife than you might expect.

Look out for *Vipera aspis* – untreated bites from the venomous viper, or asp, can be fatal.

Beech trees, truffles & poppies

The much-vaunted greenness of Umbria comes mainly from its thick blanket of trees – in Marche the eastern slopes of the Apennines tend to be steeper and rockier. At lower altitudes the woods are often predominantly holm oak, with beech and deciduous oak woods higher up, before the larger vegetation peters out leaving the highest areas to thick grasses and wildflowers. Chestnut and cypress trees are also common.

It is in the wooded hills that the region's most sought-after delicacy, the truffle (see page 54), is hunted using special dogs. Three varieties of the fungus are found here: the black truffle, the prized white truffle and the *scorzone*, or summer truffle. Porcini mushrooms also grow wild in the woods and are much used in cooking, especially in the autumn.

The Piano Grande (see page 149), a karstic plain at an altitude of 1400 m in the Sibillini Mountains, is the largest and most famous of the region's wildflower pastures. The plain is a vast flat area of grassland surrounded by mountains, which bursts into a sumptuous display of colour from late spring onwards. Wild geraniums, orchids, daisies, buttercups and poppies are among the flowers you'll see.

Olives, grapes & lentils

The best-known agricultural product from Umbria and Marche is olive oil, with wine not far behind. Lentils are also grown in the area, and all these crops have influenced the landscape. Almost all the region's flat areas, which were once marshes or lakes, are now fertile agricultural land.

The region's olive oil is highly regarded, especially that of Umbria, which has been sought after since Roman times. Most olive trees do not react well to the lower temperatures that prevail away from the lowlands, but those trees that will grow on the slopes yield especially tasty olives. On higher ground, olive growers cultivate at the edge of what is possible in order to achieve this high quality, but crops can sometimes fail. Some olive trees in Umbria are thought to be over 1,000 years old. Olives are usually harvested in October and November, often by hand rather than with the machines that are generally favoured further south.

Grapes are grown for wine, especially around Montefalco and Orvieto in Umbria, and Cònero and Macerata in Marche, where lines of vines stripe the landscape, their leaves turning to golden shades in the autumn after the grapes are harvested. Lentils are the traditional crop on the Piano Grande near Casteluccio, and a small, multicoloured bean, once thought extinct, has been rediscovered and is now cultivated near Lago Trasimeno.

Festivals & events

It can seem at times as if Umbria and the Marche have more festivals than inhabitants. From major international music festivals to a couple of loosely linked local events in a remote village hall, there is always something going on somewhere. Add to these a rich history of local traditions, often going back many hundreds of years, and you have a busy calendar.

January

Umbria Jazz Winter
Associazione Umbria Jazz, piazza Danti 28, Perugia, T075-573 2432, umbriajazz.com.
In Orvieto, an offshoot of the main Umbria Jazz festival includes a special Mass on New Year's Day, with gospel singers performing in the magnificent cathedral.

Sant'Emiliano (27th)
Trevi.
The feast day of Trevi's patron saint is marked by a torchlit procession carrying his statue through the streets.

The Corpus Christi procession in Orvieto.

February

Carnevale
Carnival is celebrated everywhere, but nowhere with quite as much gusto as Ascoli Piceno, where masked parades and accompanying parties go on for a week.

San Valentino (14th)
Terni.
Valentine's Day is marked in the saint's birthplace with a fair and fireworks.

April

Easter
Easter in Assisi is a holy affair, with solemn processions by torchlight on Good Friday.

Coloriamo i cieli
Castiglione del Lago, coloriamoicieli.com.
The town holds a kite festival over several days in late April or early May.

May

Calendimaggio
Assisi, calendimaggiodiassisi.it.
A medieval festival revolving around competition between the two halves of the city, the *Parte di Sopra* (upper part) and the *Parte di Sotto* (lower part), which plays itself out in dance, theatre, archery and flag-waving over two or three days in the first half of the month.

Corsa all'Anello
Narni, corsallanello.it.
Narni's biggest festival climaxes on the second Sunday in May and involves medieval dressing up, baroque music, wine drinking and a joust where riders try to drive their lances through a ring. The event commemorates the writing of the medieval town's first laws in 1371.

Five of the best

Romantic spots

❶ **Perugina chocolate factory** Industrial and corporate, but over a million kisses a day (see page 82).

❷ Watching the sunset from the eastern shores of **Lago Trasimeno** (see page 96).

❸ **Camera delle Dame**, Castello di Monterone, Perugia (see page 100).

❹ **Piano Grande** in spring (see page 149).

❺ **Gradara** Relive the Francesca and Paolo story (see page 234).

Corso dei Ceri (15th)
Gubbio.
There are several medieval celebrations here throughout the year, but the *Corso dei Ceri* is the biggest, with dressing up and a race up the mountain carrying the *ceri* – huge wooden 'candlesticks' topped with statues of saints. Later in the month, the *Palio della Ballestra* is a crossbow competition between Gubbio and rival Sansepolcro, across the border in Tuscany.

June

Mercato delle Gaite
Bevagna, ilmercatodellegaite.it.
This new week-long festival around the middle of the month celebrates old customs: traditional work practices such as paper- and candle-making are recreated, in the obligatory medieval costumes.

L'Infiorata
Spello.
On the Sunday nearest 21 June, Spello is given over to flower power when it hosts a festival in which the streets are decorated with works of art made entirely from thousands of petals.

Festival dei Due Mondi
Spoleto, festivaldispoleto.com.
This classical music festival in June and July celebrates American and European music (hence the two worlds of the title). Outdoor concerts have a stunning setting in the piazza in front of the cathedral.

July

Umbria Film Festival
Montone, umbriafilmfestival.com.
The second week of the month sees a screen erected in the piazza for the town's bijou film festival, subtitled 'Alternative Voices in European Cinema'. It's no Cannes, but there can be few more idyllic spots to watch films alfresco.

Sferisterio Opera Festival
Macerata, sferisterio.it.
The strangely wide Sferisterio (see page 259) was built for a now obscure sport, but makes a great open-air setting for Marche's top opera festival, which runs into August.

Umbria Jazz
Piazza Danti 28, Perugia, T075-573 2432, umbriajazz.com.
One of the world's biggest jazz festivals, Perugia's annual musicfest is a joyous jamboree, and a festival that many other places in the region have tried to copy. The whole town is completely taken over, and accommodation and decent restaurant tables can be hard to come by. New Orleans bands march through the streets, Italian groups cover Frank Sinatra classics outside the cathedral and American songstresses wail in the piazzas, while bigger names play ticketed gigs in the stadium. It's a great experience if you can find somewhere to stay: the city buzzes and the atmosphere is genial. The jazz theme is often stretched a little – in 2008, for example, Editors and REM headlined.

Ancona Jazz
anconajazz.com.
At more or less the same time as Umbria Jazz, this festival takes place on the Adriatic coast.

August

Palio dei Quartieri (14th)
Gubbio.
In enthusiastically medieval Gubbio, they dust down their flags, crossbows and costumes again for a day of competition between the four ancient quarters of the town. As well as the flag-throwing and archery in the piazza, the *quartieri* lay on feasts on benches around the town.

Palio dei Terzieri (15th)
Città della Pieve, paliodeiterzieri.it.
A day after Gubbio's medieval shenanigans, something very similar happens in Città della Pieve, though this time with only three teams. The town's fountain flows with wine as part of the celebrations.

Festival delle Nazioni
Corso Cavour, Città di Castello, T075-852 2823, festivalnazioni.com.
Run since 1968 in late August and early September, this is northern Umbria's foremost festival. A prestigious programme of classical music and dance focuses each year on a different country.

Cassandra Wilson concert, Umbria Jazz.

As well as offering some world-class chamber music, the festival features art and photography shows, and gives the public the opportunity to visit some great venues, including the Teatro degli Illuminati in Città di Castello, the courtyard of the Castello Bufalini in San Giustino and the Oratory of San Crescentino in Morra.

Rossini Opera Festival
Pesaro, T072-1380 0294, rossinioperafestival.it.
Works by Pesaro's favourite son are performed in his hometown.

September

Sagra Musicale Umbra
Perugia, T075-572 2271,
perugiamusicaclassica.com.
A long-running and well-respected season of sacred music in Perugia and other Umbrian towns, with international artists playing in churches and theatres.

Settimana Enologica
Montefalco, settimanaenologica.it.
A week-long celebration of Sagrantino di Montefalco, with tastings of the new wine, released three years after the grapes were harvested.

Todi Festival
todiartefestival.net.
With everything from 'Todi Rock' – a rather tame attempt to bring heavy metal to the town's piazza – to ballet and classical music, Todi's annual arts festival has a bit of something for everyone.

October

Marcia della Pace
tavoladellapace.it.
Every odd-numbered year, on a Sunday near the beginning of October, around 200,000 people walk the 24 km from Perugia to Assisi to call for peace in the world.

Eurochocolate
Perugia, eurochocolate.com.
What ought to be a great celebration of chocolate tends to lack much in the way of cocoa soul: the commercial massively outweighs the interesting. But it does have its attractions, such as the chance to buy massive amounts of chocolate, or to play giant chocolate chess in front of an audience in piazza IV Novembre.

Altrocioccolato
Gubbio, altrocioccolato.com.
Gubbio hosts its own chocolate festival, in opposition to Perugia's, and though it's a much smaller event, it does things that Eurochocolate fails to do: emphasizing fair trade and promoting alternatives to the Nestlé-Perugina mainstream.

Percussionistica
Città di Castello, percussionistica.it.
A world rhythm festival held in and around Città di Castello – some events also take place in Montone.

Gubbio Biennale
From October to December in even years, Gubbio hosts a season of contemporary sculpture exhibitions in the Palazzo Ducale and other venues around the town.

December

Christmas
Cribs and nativity scenes spring up everywhere. In Frasassi, along the route to the Tempietto del Valadier (see page 255), there are 'live' Christmas scenes, with costumed locals playing various parts. The so-called 'world's biggest Christmas tree', made up of lights, is lit on the mountainside behind Gubbio from 7 December to 10 January.

Sleeping

With an *agriturismo* or villa for rent on nearly every hillside, some old town hotels sprucing themselves up and ancient castles and abbeys reinventing themselves as places to stay, there are plenty of good accommodation options in Umbria and Marche. *Agriturismi* and villas are difficult to access without your own transport, though some will arrange to pick you up from a station. Staying in one of the major centres, such as Perugia, Spoleto or Orvieto, gives access to a good transport network, including trains north to Florence and south to Rome. Bear in mind, though, that train stations in the region tend to be down on the plain, often a bus journey away from the centres of hill towns. Wherever you are, a car gives you the invaluable freedom to explore, and none of the distances are enormous, though journeys can be slow. Rural accommodation just outside one of the smaller towns with your own transport might be the best of all worlds. Visit bellaumbria.net for some good accommodation listings.

Agriturismi

No longer a new phenomenon in Italy, the stay-on-a-farm concept is beginning to mature. Though there are still plenty of places where the accommodation is fairly plain – not much more than a room with a bed – others are moving up-market and branching out to specialize in cookery courses, wine tasting, horse-riding and even dog training. Vineyards are also beginning to get in on the act, with some offering accommodation as well as guided tours.

In order to qualify as an *agriturismo*, places have to produce a certain amount of their own food. Many are organic, and often this means that meals will include homegrown fruit and vegetables and hand-reared meat. Olive oil, wine and honey are almost always local and abundant. Rural accommodation that doesn't also produce its own food used to be called a country house, but has now been reclassified as *turismo rurale*. Prices for *agriturismi* are usually given per person, and start at around €30 per night – more like €45 for the smarter places. Half board is often a good deal: expect to add around €20 per person for a meal that would probably cost at least €30 in a restaurant.

Orto degli Angeli.

Torre di Moravola, in the northern Umbrian hills.

Many *agriturismi* close in the winter, and may impose a minimum stay in the summer. Increasing numbers have websites, but the small nature of these businesses means that they can be hard to find. A few of the best are in this guide, but there are hundreds of others: en.agriturismo.it, agrituristumbria.com/eng (Umbria only) or agriguida.com are good places to start a search. Local tourist information websites will usually have lists and links too.

Self-catering

Renting a villa gives you the option of more independence and privacy. Many also have swimming pools. For a family or a small number of people the option of a villa can work out cheaper than staying in a hotel; if you are a group of 10 or so, the savings are greater, and there are some spectacular places to stay.

Good websites to search on include holidaylettings.co.uk, which has plenty of choice in both Umbria and Marche; Le Marche Explorer specialize in Marche: le-marche-explorer.com.

Hotels

The region's hotels are often not especially stylish – whereas *agriturismi* have revitalized rural tourism, many town hotels have changed little in the last 30

Si sposa

Going to Italy to get married in Tuscany is now an old story, and a whole industry has grown up around it. In Umbria and Marche it's much more unusual, meaning that you may have to work a little harder to find a venue, but also that you may end up feeling more special.

It's not a cheap option, but you'll have a stunningly memorable venue and a backdrop to match. A handful of places are set up for foreign weddings, such as **Villa di Monte Solare** (see page 102), in the hills south of Lake Trasimeno, **Torre di Moravola** (see page 215), on a hilltop east of Montone in northern Umbria, and **Pietrarubbia** (see page 237) on the edge of the Sasso Simone e Simoncello regional park in Marche. Some venues have their own chapels, often centuries-old buildings that once served long-abandoned hilltop villages, and the best will organize everything for you – from the service to evening yoga and massage sessions. For some organizational assistance, try Love and Lord (loveandlord.com) in the UK.

years and are looking rather stale. Some are wonderful grand old relics, however, and others are bucking the trend and becoming chic and modern, using their old spaces in new and creative ways.

Some of the most interesting places to stay are converted buildings such as old abbeys: San Pietro in Valle (see page 157) in the Valnerina and San Domenico in Urbino (see page 236) both offer breakfast in the cloisters.

Hotels can be relatively expensive for what you get – expect to pay around €100 a night for a double room with a reasonable level of comfort. Try searching on wheretostayinumbria.com.

Eating & drinking

Umbria and Marche are known for their uncomplicated but delicious cuisine. Pasta and gnocchi, usually homemade, are delicious, often served with a simple tomato and wild boar sauce, or with local pecorino cheese. Landlocked Umbria has a proud tradition of cured meat and cheeses, which go excellently well with the crusty, fresh, saltless bread that is traditional here. Marche's coast means it offers more in the way of seafood, especially in seaside towns. Freshwater fish and eels from the lakes and rivers are sometimes found on menus too. Lentils are grown locally, especially in the Sibillini Mountains, and grains often feature in soups. Most ingredients are local, often supplied by small, sometimes organic producers. Tasty radicchio, the sweetest tomatoes and peppery rocket will make a fantastic salad, and if you're making a picnic there are plenty of great ingredients to buy.

Meals & menus

Most restaurants will offer an *antipasto* (a starter), followed by a *primo* (first course, usually pasta) and a *secondo* (second course, usually meat) with *contorni* (side dishes) and a *dolce* (dessert). Don't feel pressured into having everything, however, or even into sticking to the order – nobody will mind if you just have a second course, or a side dish without the meat, or a salad as a first course. And despite the preponderance of meat – often wild boar, Chianina beef or game – it's usually eaten as a separate course, so vegetarians won't have a hard time finding good food.

Pizzerias, often run by Neapolitans and serving excellent pizzas, are common and are often open later than standard restaurants – usually until 2400 or 0100. Most bars also serve food – Italians rarely drink without eating, and *enoteche* (wine bars) can be great places for a light lunch or supper.

Breakfast is usually a *cornetto* (a sweet croissant, often jam- or custard filled) grabbed at a café or bar. The standard of breakfast in hotels is usually poor, so you might be better skipping it and going to the local café. *Agriturismi* do much better. Locals eat lunch around 1300. Evenings often start with an *aperitivo* around 1900, followed by supper any time from 2000 or 2100 until around 2300.

Aperitivi

Increasingly common is the *aperitivo milanese*: an early evening beer, glass of prosecco or Campari and soda comes with a help-yourself buffet of meats, cheeses, and even plates of pasta. Most places will offer bowls of crisps and peanuts at least.

La Stalla, a rural restaurant near Assisi.

Wine

Umbria has 11 DOC wines, Marche another 13. In the west, Orvieto is known mainly for its white wine, which has undergone something of a renaissance in recent years. Montefalco is famous for its reds. Most prominent in Marche are whites, especially Verdicchio. There are plenty more varieties to look out for, however, and vineyards are increasingly opening their doors to visitors.

Montefalco The hills around Montefalco and Bevagna make some of the region's best red wine. The most sought-after is the expensive Montefalco Sagrantino, a rich wine, strong in tannins, that ages well.

Orvieto Wine has been produced here since Etruscan times: there are wine cellars carved into the rock beneath the town that have been in almost constant use for 2,500 years (see page 176). The white wine made here these days is crisp, dry and fruity, made mainly from Grechetto and

Tip...

You won't find Italians ordering a cappuccino after about 1000. If you want to fit in but don't fancy an espresso, go for a macchiato – a shot of coffee with a small amount of frothy milk.

Trebbiano grapes, unlike the sweet wine the town was once famous for. Some red is also made.

Torgiano South of Perugia, this little town is home to the Lungarotti family, who have set up an excellent wine museum (see page 83) with some of their viticulture millions. There's a big range of whites, reds and sparkling wines and they produce a total of 3 million bottles a year. The Rubesco red is rightly popular.

Conero Made up of at least 85% Montepulciano grapes and up to 15% Sangiovese, this wine from the hills near Ancona is dry and full-bodied.

About the region

Truffles

The product Umbria is probably known for above all others is truffles, and there are few restaurants where you won't find them on the menu in some form or other. They are shaved over pasta and used to flavour meat sauces and even liqueurs. Visit a farm in the country and you will probably see truffling tools, and perhaps meet a truffle hound.

The truffle is not just a way of life, but a potentially very lucrative commodity. By weight, truffles are some of the most valuable foodstuffs in the world, and the mystery surrounding them adds to their expensive allure. Nobody is quite sure how or why truffles grow, and they have not yet been successfully farmed. It is known that they grow in relationship with the roots of certain trees – usually oak – but little more.

In the past, male pigs were used to track them down, but this could lead to trouble: as the smell is apparently very similar to that of a female pig, there might be a fight at the end of a successful hunt over who got the truffle. These days, dogs are used, as they are easier to control.

Fresh truffles are difficult to transport, as well as being fiendishly expensive, but you can buy them in jars, under oil, to take home. Cheaper truffle sauces are also available, usually including some porcini mushrooms along with the truffles.

Meat & fish

The wild boar, once an endangered species in the region, has now become a pest in some areas, and even if you don't glimpse them around the wooded hills of the Apennines you will probably see the evidence of their snuffling for food on the ground. Wild boar meat features on many menus, often as sausages, or with *pappardelle* (pasta ribbons). Other cured meats are common too – a shop selling salami and other pork products is known all over Italy as a *norcineria*, after the town of Norcia, famous for its sharp-knived butchers, who once also had a sideline keeping boys' singing voices high.

Inland, you will probably also come across Chianina beef, from a strain of large white cattle, and freshwater fish. Eel is traditional, as is wood pigeon. On the Marche coast – especially in Ancona and Pesaro – there are some great seafood restaurants, where they serve fish straight off the boats.

Cheese

Cheese in Umbria and Marche is mainly pecorino, of which there is a large variety. Made from sheep's milk, or a blend of milk from sheep and goats, its strength varies depending on how long it has been aged. You may find it matured in red wine, to give flavour and a coloured rind. Moist when young, the matured cheese (*stagionato*) becomes increasingly crumbly.

The story goes that the first *formaggio di fossa* ('trench cheese') was created largely by chance, when pecorino was removed from harm's way in wartime and buried underground in the Talamello area of Marche. Not only does the cheese undergo a special kind of fermentation in these conditions, but in the few places where it is made yeasts have built up over the years that give it a unique flavour. The cheese is kept in straw-lined pits from August to November, when celebrations accompany its pungent unearthing.

Caciotta is a cows' milk cheese, usually milder than pecorino. White and crumbly, it is similar to English Cheshire cheese.

Tip...

When buying olive oil look for the expiry date, which by Italian law must be two years after it was made. The newer the oil the better – the best time to buy is in November or December when the new pressing has just arrived in the shops.

For the best cheese, you should buy either from small delicatessens or big supermarkets with dedicated counters. Some delis are designed more for tourists than locals, and quality can suffer. Watch where the locals go, and ask for a taste – a good shop will be happy to oblige.

Olive oil

Some of the best olive oil in Italy is produced in Umbria, and one of the best varieties of olive for oil is the clean, almond-flavoured Frantoio. For the highest quality, look for a fresh, green colour.

The reasons for the high quality of the oil here are mainly climatic. In the foothills of the Apennines, varieties survive that produce less fruit but more flavour. They are, however, also susceptible to the extreme cold weather that is possible here. At well-irrigated, warmer, lower levels, near to Lake Trasimeno, for example, yields are higher but quality may not be so good.

Biscuits & desserts

Umbria and Marche are not great for desserts, with a few exceptions. Most towns have a good ice cream maker or two, but in many restaurants desserts will not be homemade. There are, however, some excellent biscuits to look out for. Most commonly, *tozzetti*, a hard, heavy almond biscuit, similar to the Tuscan *cantucci*, are sold along with *vin santo*, into which they should be dipped. Spicy *mostaccioli*, which St Francis allegedly asked for on his deathbed, are another kind of hard biscuit to look out for. *Baci di Assisi* are softer, nutty confections.

A *digestivo* – a glass of something alcoholic to aid digestion – is commonly drunk at the end of a meal. Sweet dessert wines can be very good, and homemade grappa can sometimes be found, along with *amari* – bitter concoctions that supposedly once had medicinal uses. In and around Macerata and Ascoli Piceno in particular, age-old recipes are passed down and sworn by. *Nocino*, walnut liqueur, is another to look out for.

Bread

Traditionally made without salt, bread in the region tends to come in large loaves, which are sometimes still baked in a traditional wood oven (ask for *pane al forno*). Because it goes stale quickly, it is often bought in half, or even quarter loaves. Yesterday's leftovers are often used to make *panzanella*, a tomato and bread salad. Saltless bread can take some getting used to, but it can also be delicious, allowing the natural sweetness of the grain to emerge. The story goes that saltless bread developed as a reaction to the Salt War against the papacy in the 16th century (see page 32).

Above: Gran Caffè, Assisi.
Opposite page: Cheeses for sale at Dai Fratelli in Orvieto.

Menu reader

General

affumicato smoked
al sangue rare
alla griglia grilled
antipasto starter/appetizer
arrosto roasted
ben cotto well done
bollito boiled
caldo hot
contorni side dishes
coppa/cono cup/cone
cotto cooked
cottura media medium
crudo raw
degustazione tasting menu of several dishes
dolce dessert
fatto in casa homemade
forno a legna wood-fired oven
freddo cold
fresco fresh
fritto fried
piccante spicy
primo first course
ripieno stuffed
secondo second course

Drinks (bevande)

acqua naturale/gassata/frizzante still/sparkling water
birra beer
birra (alla spina) beer (draught)
bottiglia bottle
caffè coffee (ie espresso)
caffè macchiato/ristretto espresso with a dash
  of foamed milk/strong
spremuta freshly squeezed fruit juice
succo juice
vino bianco/rosato/rosso white/rosé/red wine
vin santo a dark, sweet, fortified wine

Fruit (frutta) & vegetables (verdure)

agrumi citrus fruits
anguria watermelon
arance oranges
carciofio globe artichoke
castagne chestnuts
ciliegie cherries
cipolle onions
fagioli white beans
fichi figs

finocchio fennel
fragole strawberries
funghi mushrooms
lamponi raspberries
legumi pulses
lenticchie lentils
mandorla almond
melagrana pomegranate
melanzana eggplant/aubergine
melone melon
mele apples
noci walnuts
nocciole hazelnuts
patate potatoes, which can be *arroste* (roast),
  fritte (fried), *novelle* (new), *pure' di* (mashed)
peperoncino chilli pepper
peperone peppers
pesche peaches
pinoli pine nuts
piselli peas
pomodori tomatoes
rucola rocket
spinaci spinach
tartufi truffles
zucca pumpkin

Meat (carne)

affettati misti mixed cured meat
agnello lamb
bistecca beef steak
carpaccio finely sliced raw meat (usually beef)
cinghiale wild boar
coda alla vaccinara oxtail
coniglio rabbit
involtini thinly sliced meat, rolled and stuffed
lepre hare
manzo beef
pollo chicken
polpette meatballs
polpettone meat loaf
porchetta roasted, stuffed suckling pig
prosciutto ham – *cotto* cooked, *crudo* cured
salsicce pork sausage
salumi misti cured meats
speck a type of cured, smoked ham
spiedini meat pieces grilled on a skewer
stufato meat stew
trippa tripe
vitello veal

Fish (*pesce*) & seafood (*frutti di mare*)

acciughe anchovies
anguilla eel
aragosta lobster
baccalà salt cod
bottarga mullet-roe
branzino sea bass
calamari squid
cozze mussels
frittura di mare/frittura di paranza small fish, squid and
   shellfish lightly covered with flour and fried
frutti di mare seafood
gamberi shrimps/prawns
grigliata mista di pesce mixed grilled fish
orata gilt-head/sea bream
ostriche oysters
pesce spada swordfish
polpo octopus
sarde, sardine sardines
seppia cuttlefish
sogliola sole
spigola bass
stoccafisso stockfish
tonno tuna
triglia red mullet
trota trout
vongole clams

Dessert (*dolce*)

cornetto sweet croissant
crema custard
dolce dessert
gelato ice cream
granita flavoured crushed ice
macedonia (di frutta) fruit salad
panettone type of fruit bread eaten at Christmas
semifreddo a partially frozen dessert
sorbetto sorbet
tiramisù rich dessert with cake, cream,
   coffee and chocolate
torta cake
tozzetti sweet, crunchy almond biscuits
zabaglione whipped egg yolks flavoured with
   Marsala wine
zuppa inglese trifle

Useful words & phrases

aperitivo a pre-dinner drink,
   often served with free snacks
posso avere il conto? can I have the bill please?
coperto cover charge
bicchiere glass
c'è un menù? is there a menu?
aperto/chiuso open/closed
prenotazione reservation
conto the bill
cameriere/cameriera waiter/waitress
che cosa mi consegna? what do you recommend?
cos'è questo? what's this?
dov'è il bagno? where's the toilet?

Other

aceto balsamico balsamic vinegar, always from Modena
arborio type of rice used to make risotto
burro butter
calzone folded pizza
formaggi misti mixed cheese plate
formaggio cheese
frittata omelette
insalata salad
insalata Caprese tomatoes, mozzarella and basil
latte milk
miele honey
olio oil
polenta cornmeal
pane bread
pane-integrale brown bread
panzanella bread and tomato salad
provola smoked cheese
ragù a meaty sauce or ragout
riso rice
salsa sauce
sugo sauce or gravy
strangozzi/strozzapreti a thick, Umbrian sort of spaghetti
umbricelli thick spaghetti
zuppa soup

Entertainment

With an interesting cultural mix of medieval traditions, jazz, classical music and theatre, Umbria and Marche usually have something of interest going on, often tied in to a vibrant calendar of festivals and annual events (see page 46).

Nightlife

Café life slides neatly into bar life come nightfall – usually without a change of venue. An *aperitivo milanese* is the increasingly common way to get the evening off with a swing – a pre-dinner glass of something with a generous (and free) buffet of snacks, which could just about keep you going all night if you're on a diet or a tight budget.

Drinking doesn't usually happen without food, which means that the difference between a wine bar and a restaurant with a wine list is sometimes imperceptibly subtle. Wine bars tend to stay open late, though (often until about 0200), and the emphasis is usually on the wine rather than the food. Bigger towns and cities, such as Perugia, have a lively bar scene, and live music, DJ bars, and other events such as poetry readings are common.

Nightclubs are rare, good ones even more so, though student-dense Perugia has a couple, and you will find seaside discos on the Marche coast.

Cinema

Most cinemas in the region show only films in Italian, often dubbed. One exception is the fabulous Teatro del Pavone in Perugia (see page 111) where films in English are shown on Monday evenings in an old opera theatre with four tiers of private boxes, allowing you to watch the latest Hollywood blockbuster in some style.

The little town of Montone (see page 212) is home to the annual summer Umbrian Film Festival, when a screen is erected in the main piazza.

Gay & lesbian

The gay scene in the region is decidedly low-key. The websites gayumbria.com and gaymarche.it (both in Italian) list upcoming club nights and other events in the region – these happen mostly in Perugia – and gayfriendlyitaly.com (in English) is another place to look for information on events, as well as general info on gay-friendly tourism in Italy.

Music

Some of the region's best music can be heard during its festivals. In fact it sometimes seems that one concert is enough for someone to announce a specially themed season. Umbria Jazz (see page 48), based in Perugia, is the biggest and most popular. It also has an offshoot in Orvieto in the form of Umbria Jazz Winter (see page 46). Spoleto's summer *Festival dei Due Mondi* (see page 48) features some top quality classical music, while the Macerata Opera Festival puts on spectacular performances in the distinctive Sferisterio. Smaller, more intimate pleasures are to be had year-round in churches and concert halls around the region.

Live music can also be heard in many bars – Perugia has the best scene (see page 111), but bars in many towns have pianos, and if you're lucky someone might strike up a tune. During the region's many traditional festivals, most of which happen in the summer months (see page 48), medieval music fills the streets.

Theatre & dance

Many towns in the region have spectacular old 18th- and 19th-century theatres, and even if you don't understand a word of Italian, going along to a performance is an experience. Teatro Nuovo in Spoleto has a high quality calendar, and there are also sometimes good things on at the Teatro Morlacchi in Perugia. Dance crosses linguistic boundaries more easily, and the more general arts festivals, such as those at Todi or Spoleto, usually include some dance performances, often in stunning settings.

Five of the best

People-watching spots

❶ **Corso Vannucci** Perugia (see page 71).
❷ **Corso Mazzini** Spoleto (see page 136).
❸ **Piazza del Duomo** Orvieto (see page 173).
❹ **Pesaro seafront** (see page 232).
❺ **Piazza del Popolo** Ascoli Piceno (see page 263).

Right: Puppet show, Corso Vannucci, Perugia.

Shopping

Books and wine for sale at La Bodega di Assu, Bevagna.

A region of little family-run delicatessens, *enoteche* and craft shops, Umbria and Marche have plenty of small-scale shopping opportunities but less in the way of high-street shops, except in the larger towns such as Perugia and Ascoli Piceno.

Art & crafts

Most towns in the region have a shop or two selling things hand-carved from olive wood, including kitchen items such as boards and wooden spoons. Among the tourist tat in Assisi is a place that sells good etchings of the town and its surroundings, printed on presses at the back of the shop (see page 113) and Spello has a craft shop with some inventive pieces made by a local sculptor (see page 165).

Books

Most towns have a bookshop or two, though only a few – in places such as Ancona and Perugia –

have much in the way of English-language books. Coffee-table photography books are easier to come by.

Ceramics

Deruta is the ceramics capital of the region, churning out enormous quantities of pots with bright yellow and blue designs on white backgrounds. For something a bit more individual, the organic market on the fourth Sunday of the month in Perugia has stalls with some good pieces, and there are some small studios around too.

Fashion

Corso Vannucci in Perugia is the nearest the region gets to high-end fashion. Ascoli Piceno is another place that offers plenty of choice in Italian clothes, dominated by Italian high-street names. Assisi has shoe shops, though they tend to specialize in sandals rather than stilettos – for shoe chic, Perugia has more options.

Food

The region's best souvenir is its food. It can seem that every little hamlet has a delicatessen, offering a profusion of cured meats and cheeses (see page 54). Picnic supplies are easy to come by: most places have a bakery selling fresh bread and a greengrocer with a good range of fresh fruit and salad. Supermarkets, or more often minimarkets, are convenient but seldom stock good fresh produce – markets are infinitely better. Check import regulations if you're thinking of buying meat or cheese to take home.

Olive oil is also available everywhere, though for the best experience – and often the best quality – it's worth trying to buy it straight from the producer. This is best done in the late autumn, just after the harvest.

Tip...

Many museums and restaurants in the region close on Monday – a good day for a picnic and a walk in the countryside.

Castelluccio is famous for its lentils, and specialities such as *baci di Assisi* or *tozzetti* – sweet, crunchy almond biscuits made for dipping in sweet wine – also make good gifts to take home. Baci, chocolates with hazelnuts inside, are Perugia's most famous export: they fill many a gap in the suitcases of tourists returning home, though you'll find better quality locally-made chocolate in cafés and shops.

Kitchenware

An Italian coffee pot, a corkscrew or some espresso cups make good gifts or souvenirs, and most towns have a shop selling shiny designer items for the kitchen. Wine glasses are another possible purchase, though they need careful packing.

Wine

Many wine bars double as wine shops, and most will be more than happy to pack up a case of wine to take home. Buying straight from a vineyard won't necessarily be cheaper, but it feels very satisfying to drink wine from a vineyard where you've seen it produced. The traditional wine-producing areas around Orvieto, Montefalco, Macerata and Cònero are the best places to find vineyards you can visit.

Activities & tours

With abundant breathing space and a rich culinary and viticultural history, Umbria and Marche have plenty of opportunities for doing more than just visiting churches and museums. So roll up your sleeves and make pasta, or throw yourself off a mountain attached to a sail.

Cycling

Given a sunny weekend, half of the men in central Italy don fluorescent lycra and hit the roads of Umbria and Marche, criss-crossing the Apennines on bikes.

Meal-time at The Hill that Breathes.

The twice-yearly bike tour of Umbria run by **The Chain Gang** (thechaingang.co.uk, from €1,685) actually starts just over the border in Tuscany before taking in Orvieto, Monte Castello, Todi, Montefalco, Assisi, Perugia and Lake Trasimeno on an eight-day circuit. Accommodation is in well-chosen hotels, where your luggage will arrive before you do.

If you fancy organizing your own cycling trip, or just doing a quick pedal across the hills, **bikeinumbria.it** has some excellent itineraries.

Food & wine

Many restaurants in the region offer cookery courses. In Perugia **Alter Ego** (see page 113) is a friendly and very good value option; **Enoteca Convento di San Giovanni** (see page 177) and **Zeppelin** (see page 191) also offer courses. **Country House Montali** (see page 110) runs vegetarian cookery courses, and many *agriturismi* and hotels (such as Villa di Monte Solare, see page 102) offer cookery courses to guests. For a great grounding in Umbrian food as well as cooking, **Madonna del Piatto** (see page 65) offers excellent food and cookery days to guests and non-guests alike.

Many vineyards run wine-tasting courses – **Montefalco** (see page 129) offers a particularly wide choice. In Orvieto, the **Enoteca Convento di San Giovanni** is also recommended.

Learning the fine art of pasta making at Madonna del Piatto.

Patrick Nicholas Photography course.

Hang-gliding & paragliding

As the gentle prevailing westerly winds hit the steep slopes of the Apennines, the resulting updraft creates some of the best conditions in Europe for hang-gliding and paragliding. **Monte Cucco** (see page 206), **Monte Subasio** (see page 124) and **Castelluccio** (see page 149) all have local clubs and qualified tandem fliers who will do most of the hard work for you. If you want to learn to go solo, week-long courses are also possible.

Photography

Photographer Patrick Nicholas (see page 195) runs courses from Orvieto that take participants out into southwest Umbria and across the border into Lazio.

Rafting

The higher stretches of the **Valnerina** are the best places in the region for white-water rafting. Centres near **Norcia** will guide you down the rapids. If you'd prefer, gentler rafting routes are also available.

Walking

Both Umbria and Marche offer fantastic walking country. You won't find many locals heading out into the hills for a weekend stroll, but the agricultural nature of the place and the region's religious traditions mean that there are some great paths to follow in the footsteps of monks and donkeys.

The **Apennines** are the region's most obvious walking territory, and generally the higher you go, the more paths there are, except in winter, when

Food, wine & a dog named Google

Agriturismo Alla Madonna del Piatto, via Petrata 37, Pieve San Nicolò, T075-819 9050, incampagna.com. Apr-Oct, Mon-Fri, from €110.

Letizia meets the small group of people attending her food and cookery course at 1000 in a delicatessen in Santa Maria degli Angeli. For the next hour and a half she talks through Umbrian oil, truffles, herbs, cheeses and meats, all with tastings provided by the deli. Truffles are discussed, as is her truffle-hunting dog Google ("Despite the name he hasn't found much yet"). And if you're lucky there may be some *mostaccioli* – biscuits that St Francis is said to have requested on his deathbed – and *nocino* – walnut liqueur.

Then it's up the winding roads to her house, and a glass of wine under the vine-covered pergola, with stunning views out across the hills to the Basilica of St Francis, while Letizia prepares her kitchen.

The cooking tuition is of the 'real kitchen' variety – there's no reluctance to use modern tools if it saves time – and Letizia is a mine of handy tips and facts about the best way to make pasta dough, or the ideal pastry mix for a *crostata* (a traditional Italian jam tart). You get a handout with recipes to take away, and if you want to go on drinking while you cook there's a ready stream of wine at all times. And, of course, at the end you get to eat the food you've made.

snow and ice make things more difficult. Other good walking areas include the steeply wooded **Valnerina** near Spoleto, and **Monte Subasio**, just to the east of Assisi (see page 124).

ATG Oxford (atg-oxford.co.uk, 8-day trip around €2,000) have several walking routes through the region (they also do cycle routes), including paths along Etruscan lanes to Orvieto, through olive groves to Assisi and across the hills to Urbino. Good food and good hotels are part of the fun.

Well-being

The Hill that Breathes (see page 230) offers a week's worth of yoga, letting go and fantastic food in a beautiful setting. **Le Muse** (see page 115) is a luxurious spa in the hills above Lake Trasimeno.

Areas for walking

❶ **Valnerina** A heavily wooded valley with a beautiful old abbey (see page 136).

❷ **Monti Sibillini** Straddling Umbria and Marche, fantastic upland and mountain walks (see page 148).

❸ **Parco Regionale di Monte Cucco** Huge beech forests, with mountains above (see page 206).

❹ **Valle del Carpina** Lots of well-marked trails through pre-Apennine rolling hills (see page 212).

❺ **Parco Naturale Sasso Simone e Simoncello** Little known, there are great views from the slopes of this regional park in Marche (see page 228).

Contents

Central Umbria

A giant poster of St Francis on the side of the Upper Basilica, Assisi.

Introduction

A heady mix of jazz, religion, history, art, hills and food: central Umbria has all of the region's signature features, though its most discovered quarter is also, in many ways, its least typical. Perugia, capital of the region and the area's only real city, is a buzzing place, where a cosmopolitan student population gives a sense of fun and energy to a stunningly unspoilt medieval centre, with winding streets and worn stone steps leading down from grand piazzas to Etruscan stone gates.

Not far away across the plain, Assisi, home of St Francis, is a holy town with plenty to offer believers and non-believers alike. Giotto's frescoes in the basilica are said to have rewritten the history of art, and aside from the saints and medieval churches there are also plenty of less obvious pleasures, such as great views across the Umbrian countryside. Even here – the one place in the region that tourism sometimes threatens to overwhelm – it's not hard to find everyday life going on in the back streets.

Lago Trasimeno, a huge glittering expanse of shallow water to the west of the area, has a distinctive cuisine based on its freshwater fish, as well as its own landscape, with ancient islands to explore and walks and cycle routes to blow the cobwebs away.

Medieval streets in the onetime foundations of Rocca Paolina, Perugia.

What to see in…

…one day
Pick either Assisi or Perugia and spend a day wandering their medieval streets. Assisi has the magnificent **Basilica di San Francesco**, and a wonderfully renovated archaeological museum, but also more tourists. Perugia has a stunning medieval centre, better bars and restaurants and, in the **Galleria Nazionale dell'Umbria**, some great Renaissance art. Also not to be missed in Perugia are its **medieval guilds**, and the views either end of its main street, **corso Vannucci**.

In Assisi, as well as the basilica and the **Museo e Foro Romano**, pop into the tiny but colourful **Oratorio dei Pellegrini** and the less visited **Catterdrale di San Ruffino**. If you have time, climb up to the **Rocca Maggiore** for its views down over the town and across the Valle Umbra.

…a weekend or more
A second day gives you the possibility of of heading into the countryside for a walk in the **Parco del Monte Subasio**, or around the shores of **Lago Trasimeno**. On the lake you can also kite-surf, or take a boat to one of the peaceful islands.

Perugia

Capital of the region, and its largest and best-connected city, Perugia is in many ways an anomaly. Its Italian and international universities give it a young, cosmopolitan and lively feel, and its status and size mean that the outskirts, at least, have some of the trappings of modernity. The old centre, however, is as impressive a collection of medieval architecture as you will find anywhere, and the views, when they are visible from the tall, arched streets, are stunning. The city tops several ridges of a hill, and from good vantage points you can see half of Umbria, including Monte Cucco, Assisi and the towns to the south – Trevi, Spello and Montefalco.

Perugia is an intoxicating mix. It's the home of Italy's most famous chocolate, its best jazz festival and one of its best Renaissance painters; it's less pastoral than many of its hill-town neighbours, but often more exciting too. Next to a wine and cheese shop you'll find the latest iPods for sale, and beside a smart wine bar there may be an artisan brewer, where wrinkled Italians mix with bright-eyed international exchange students.

Looking northeast from Via Prome.

Filled daily with people taking their evening *passeggiata*, and the focus of the Umbria Jazz festival, the stunning corso Vannucci is an elegant catwalk even in quieter times. From piazza Italia at the eastern end, across piazza della Repubblica to piazza IV Novembre, cafés spill out on to the wide pavements, and in summer restaurants set up tables in the middle of the street, which makes a great spot for people watching. For much of the time the street is closed to traffic, which greatly adds to the pleasures of window shopping in the smart boutiques and gazing at the extraordinary Gothic and Renaissance architecture.

At the northern end of the corso, on the western side, is the huge and oft-extended Palazzo dei Priori – one of Italy's most stunning town halls. Beyond is piazza IV Novembre, with the Duomo opposite. The centrepiece, between the two power bases of Church and State, is the Fontana Maggiore, a complex piece of medieval design with scenes depicting everything from the glories of the city to Aesop's fables.

Fontana Maggiore

Piazza IV Novembre.
Map: Perugia, E4, p72.

Symbol of the city, Perugia's Romanesque central fountain was built in the 13th century at the end of a long aqueduct. Designed and made by the father-and-son team of Nicola and Giovanni Pisano, it has mostly survived its 730 years remarkably well. It is one of the most important pieces of sculpture of its time – a beautiful and intriguing piece of work that repays close inspection. Three figures stand in the middle of two large concentric rings of bas-relief, and the whole thing is a mélange of idealism, romance, symbolism, mythology, religion and significant Perugian figures.

Essentials

❶ **Getting around** Other than getting to and from the station, buses and cars are of little use in the city centre, much of which is closed to traffic, or subject to tortuous one-way routes. There are paid car parks dotted around outside the city walls, where you may also be able to find some free parking. You can hire a scooter from **Scooty Rent** (via Pinturicchio 76, T075-572 0710, scootyrent.com) and get around Perugia's narrow medieval streets in style.

❷ **Trains** Perugia's new Minimetrò is a hi-tech piece of wizardry that slides passengers in space-age pods up the hill from Fontivegge Station into the centre of town every 2.5 mins (Mon-Sat 0700-2120, Sun 0830-2030, €1). It also goes to the Pian di Massiano parking lot, near the football stadium, where there are some free parking places.

❸ **Buses** City and long-distance buses depart from the APM bus terminal in piazza Partigiani (T075-506 7894), and most city services stop at piazza Italia, where there's an information and ticket kiosk. A single trip costs €1 (€1.50 if you pay on the bus), or 10 for €8.60; once validated, tickets last 70 mins. A 24-hr tourist ticket costs €3.60. Good information on all Perugia's transport options is available on apmperugia.it.

❹ **ATMs** There are plenty along corso Vannucci.

❺ **Hospital** Azienda Ospedaliera di Perugia, via Enrico dal Pozzo, T075-578 2861.

❻ **Pharmacy** 24-hr service at **Farmacia San Martino**, piazza Matteotti 26, T075-34024.

❼ **Post office** Piazza Matteotti, T075-573 6977.

❽ **Tourist information office** Piazza Matteotti 18, Loggia dei Lanari, T075-573 6458, daily 0830-1830. A useful guide to the city, in English, can be downloaded as a pdf from turismo.comune.perugia.it, which also has lots of other information on listings and festivals.

Tip...

If you can understand a little Italian, *vivaPerugia* is an invaluable monthly listings magazine, available from newsstands for €0.80.

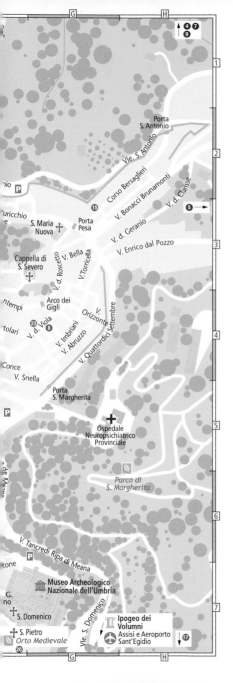

Perugia listings

❶ Sleeping

1 Anna *via dei Priori 48* D4
2 Azienda Agricola Biologica Torre Colombaia
   San Biagio della Valle A7
3 Brufani Palace *piazza Italia 12* E6
4 Castello dell'Oscano *strada Forcella 37, Cenerente* H1
5 Castello di Monterone *strada Montevile 3* H3
6 Fortuna *via Luigi Bonazzi 19* D5
7 Il Romitorio di Monte Tezio
   Località strada Colognola, Migiana di Monte Tezio H1
8 La Rosetta *piazza Italia 19* E6
9 Le Torri di Bagnara *Strada della Bruna 8, Pieve San Quirico* H1
10 Primavera *via Vincioli 8* D3

❶ Eating & drinking

1 Al Mangiar Bene *via della Luna 21* E4
2 Bottega del Vino *via del Sole 1* F3
3 Caffè di Perugia *via Mazzini 10* E5
4 Caffè MedioEvo *corso Vannucci 70* E5
5 Caffè Sandri *corso Vannucci 32* E4
6 Cinastik *via dei Priori 39* E4
7 Cioccolataria Augusta Perusia *via Pinturicchio 2* F2
8 Civico 25 *via della Viola 25* G4
9 Dal Mi'Cocco *corso Garibaldi 12* E2
10 Énonè *corso Cavour 61* F7
11 Frittole Vineria *via Alessi 30* F4
12 Gelateria Gambrinus *via Luigi Bonazzi 3* E5
13 Il Bacio *via Boncambi 6* E4
14 Il Birraio *via delle Prome 18* F3
15 La Lumera *corso Bersaglieri 22* G3
16 La Piazzetta *via Deliziosa 3* D4
17 L'Officina *borgo XX Giugno 56* H7
18 L'Opera *via della Stella 6* E4
19 Locanda Do' Pazzi *corso Cavour 128* F7
20 Nanà *corso Cavour 202* F7
21 Osteria del Bartolo *via Bartolo 30* E3
22 Osteria del Gambero *via Baldeschi 8a* E3
23 Osteria del Gufo *via della Viola 18* G4
24 Osteria del Tempo Perso *via Piacevole 13* E2
25 Pizzeria Etruschetto *corso Garibaldi 17* F2
26 Pizzeria Mediterranea *piazza Piccinino 11/12* F3
27 Porchetta stand *piazza Matteotti* E4
28 Trattoria del Borgo *via della Sposa 23a* C4

Decoding Perugia's fountain

Starting opposite the Palazzo dei Priori and working anticlockwise, the fountain's lower basin acts as a sort of calendar, with 12 pairs of reliefs each illustrating a month of the year, complete with signs of the zodiac:

January A man and a woman eat by a fire with a jug and a large wine flagon.

February Two fishermen, or perhaps one fisherman shown twice, fishing then going home with the day's catch.

March A figure takes a thorn from his foot and a tree is pruned.

April Ancient Roman figures stand around with branches and flowers.

May A man carrying a bunch of roses pursues a lady on horseback. Look for the dog beneath the woman's horse.

June Hard-working and rather tired-looking peasants gather crops.

July More hard work, this time threshing.

August On an especially decorative panel, two people gather figs.

September Grapes become the centre of attention. In the first panel a bare-legged man crushes them, while in the second another brings more from the vine.

October The wine-making process continues: one barrel is being filled while another is repaired.

November Ploughing and scattering seeds, gathered up in the folds of a cloak. Look for the braying oxen.

December A pig is hung upside-down to be slaughtered, and is subsequently carried away on a shoulder, closely watched by a dog, which tries to jump up.

After December come a lion and a griffin (the city's emblems), four pairs depicting the liberal arts – grammar and dialectics, rhetoric and arithmetic, geometry and music, astronomy and philosophy – and two eagles. The remaining seven pairs represent Adam and Eve, Samson and Delilah, a lion and a man (beating a lion cub), David and Goliath, Romulus and Remus, their she-wolf and Rea Silvia, and two of Aesop's fables: the wolf and the crane, and the wolf and the lamb.

On the fountain's upper level, various religious and historic figures mix with those from Perugia's history. Looking straight down corso Vannucci is **Perugia** herself, as a seated woman holding a basket. On either side of her are personifications of **Chiusi**, with corn, and **Trasimeno**, with some rather slippery-looking fish. Working anticlockwise from here are: **Herculanus** (bishop and patron saint of the city); the **traitor cleric**, who opened the city gates to the Goths in AD 547; **St Benedict**, with St Maurus clasping his thighs; **St John the Baptist**; **King Solomon**; **David** with a small harp; **Salome** with the head of John the Baptist; **Moses** with a tablet; **Matteo** (mayor of Perugia when the fountain was built); **Archangel Michael**; **Eulistes** (mythical founder of Perugia); the priest **Melchisedech**; **Ermanno da Sassoferrato** (*capitano del popolo*); **Victory**, portrayed as a woman holding a branch; **St Peter** with a key; a woman holding the **Church**; a woman seated and crowned representing **Rome**; a woman with a tablet representing **theology**; **St Paul**; and **St Laurence**, the city's other patron saint.

Finally, the figures at the top of the fountain are the three graces, from whom the water flows, just as it has done for centuries.

Above: Fontana Maggiore. Opposite page: Steps of the Duomo.

Cattedrale di San Lorenzo

Piazza IV Novembre, T075-572 3832.
Daily, approximately 0700-1300 and
1600-sunset, free.
Map: Perugia, E4, p72.

Perugia's 15th-century Gothic cathedral dominates
one side of piazza IV Novembre, its showiest and
most ornate decoration ostentatiously facing the
alternative, secular, power base of the Palazzo dei
Priori. As well as a 1555 statue of Pope Julius III,
there is a pulpit made especially for San Bernardino
of Siena when he addressed the city in 1425.

Best seats in town

The steps of the Duomo are the place to hang out in
Perugia in the summer months. It's a heady mix of
beautiful old Gothic architecture, beautiful young
Erasmus students and a sprinkling of wine and beer
drunk from plastic glasses. Mostly though, it's a
place just to chill – people meet, sit, talk, soak up the
atmosphere and ogle each other. Signs prohibit glass
bottles but otherwise just about anything goes.
If you want to go really leftfield, you could sit on the
steps of the Palazzo dei Priori opposite. Some even
sit on their own around the back of the Duomo, but
that seems to miss the point.

Both the front of the cathedral and its interior
fail to live up to the expectations raised by the
building's flank, though they are certainly not
without interest. The choir stalls and bishop's
throne at the front were partially destroyed by fire
in 1985, but the original intarsia work of 1486-1491,
by Giuliano da Maiano and Domenico del Tasso,
has since been carefully restored.

As well as the painted ceiling, the columns in
the Duomo are painted to give a marble effect –
look out for the popular shrine to the Madonna
delle Grazie on one of them.

In the Cappella di Sant'Anello is the Virgin's
supposed wedding ring, said to miraculously
change colour depending on who is wearing it.
Also here, in the Cappella di San Bernardino,
is the 16th-century *Descent from the Cross* by
Federico Barocci.

The **Museo Capitolare della Cattedrale
di San Lorenzo** (T075-572 4853, museiecclesiastici.
it, Tue-Sun 1000-1300, 1430-1730, €3.50/2.50
concession, free under 11) contains 26 rooms
of medieval and Renaissance art, including a
Madonna and Child with Saints by Luca Signorelli.
Downstairs, recent excavations have uncovered
some indistinct Roman remains.

Galleria Nazionale dell'Umbria

*Corso Vannucci 19, T075-574 1410,
gallerianazionaleumbria.it.*
Tue-Sun 0830-1930, audio tour available,
€6.50/3.25 concession, free for EU citizens
under 18 and over 65.
Map: Perugia, E4, p72.

The region's most important art collection
is housed in 40 rooms on the upper floors
of the Palazzo dei Priori. Good temporary
exhibitions are held here, and the highlights of
the permanent collection include many works by
Perugino and Pinturricchio, as well as an excellent
Piero della Francesca.

In chronological order, the collection starts at
the top of the building with elements of the town's
two 13th-century fountains, including the original

three water carriers from the Fontana Maggiore (see page 71). Room 2 has lots of early 14th-century Madonnas, heavy with gold leaf, influenced by Sienese art. In room 4, Maestro di Paciano's figures demonstrate what was to become one of the signature elements of Perugian art: expressive, exaggerated features and faces that are almost caricatures.

Domenico di Bartolo's smooth-faced 1438 polyptych demonstrates an early Sienese appreciation of Renaissance principles in his sense of perspective and the virtuoso way in which he paints the folds of clothes. There's a nice 15th-century dowry chest in room 6, decorated with the story of Tarquin and Lucretia, the former threatening a naked Lucretia with his sword. Also in this room, look for the tiny wild boar in Ottaviano Nelli's five-panel painting of 1403.

By the 1440s, the new figurative reality of the Renaissance had taken hold, and room 8 has pieces commissioned by Perugia's rich and powerful

Baglioni family. Fra Angelico's impressive 1448 altarpiece features a Madonna and Child surrounded by Sts Dominic and Nicholas on the left, John the Baptist and St Catherine on the right.

Gozzoli's 1456 picture features the Madonna with St Peter, John the Baptist, St Paul and St Jerome. Jerome was a cardinal (hence his red hat) who translated the Bible into Latin and, according to medieval stories, removed a thorn from a lion's paw, hence his depiction with a lion in many paintings of the time. The painting shows a three-dimensionality noticeably absent from earlier art – the treatment of the fabrics is especially tactile.

Piero della Francesca's dexterous altarpiece has room 11 to itself, and demonstrates typically virtuoso use of perspective, though the shadows seem strangely miscalculated. The figures on the left are Anthony of Padua and John the Baptist, while on the right are St Francis and Elizabeth of Hungary. The lower predella features the miracles of Sts Anthony and Elizabeth. Benedetto Bonfigli's

Frescoes by Perugino in the Collegio del Cambio.

pretty angels offering roses light up room 14, and room 15 has a large Perugino, *The Adoration of the Magi*, from 1523.

Some breaks from religious art are provided at this point, with some fascinating carved ivory mixed with gold pieces in room 17, and wafer irons lining room 20 – these long decorated tongs were used in various parts of Italy but only reached such artistic heights in Perugia, though the best collection of them is in the wine museum in Torgiano (see page 83).

The strongest part of the collection is room 22, where some of Perugino's best works are hung, rich in colour, costumes and light. The *Madonna della Confraternita della Consolazione*, painted in 1496, is particularly beautiful, depicting an especially pensive Virgin with Lake Trasimeno in the background. From here on, however, the Perugino paintings tend to become more formulaic, and it is the Pinturicchio altarpiece from 1495 in room 24 that really catches the eye, with its wonderful details such as the apples and walnuts on the floor and botanically observed studies of plants. The artist designed the whole ensemble, including the Romanesque arches.

The Perugino paintings in room 25 were once part of a huge polyptych, 8 m high, with 30 painted panels that are now scattered around the world. After these come a series of works by his followers, and the collection becomes a little less interesting, though there are some further highlights, such as Orazio Gentileschi's 1618 *Santa Cecilia che suona la spinetta*. Room 39 has historical significance for its images of the Rocca Paolina (see page 80) before it was destroyed.

Collegio del Cambio

Corso Vannucci 25, T075-572 8599.
Mon-Sat 0900-1230, 1430-1730 (closed Mon afternoons Nov-mid-Mar), Sun 0900-1300, €4.50.
Map: Perugia, E4, p72.

Extraordinary frescoes by Perugino and his assistants are the highlight of these three rooms off the corso, though there is intricate intarsia work

In the centre of the opposite wall, on the painted pilaster, is a self-portrait of Perugino himself, the ostentation of its positioning demonstrating the high regard in which he was held – or, perhaps, in which he held himself.

too. The guild of moneychangers was founded in 1259 and moved here in 1457, becoming an important part of city life and taking on the role of a tribunal in financial disputes. The guild still exists today, operating as a charity. They clearly weren't short of a florin or two, hence the expensively commissioned art.

After entering through a room panelled with carved walnut wood you come to the **Sala dell'Udienza**, or council room, frescoed by Perugino from 1498-1500 with the help of his pupils, perhaps including the young Raphael. Its richly colourful paintings, remarkably well conserved, are the Umbrian painter's masterpiece and among the finest Renaissance works in Italy. The schematic design of the paintings was devised by the humanist Francesco Maturanzio, and they pull together the central religious and secular themes of the Renaissance.

Classical figures are represented with personifications of Wisdom, Prudence, Justice, Fortitude and Temperance, while on the end wall the Transfiguration and Nativity are depicted. On the right-hand wall, in perhaps the most successful painting, God looks down on prophets and sybils set in a noticeably central Italian landscape. The figure of Daniel, third from the left, is thought to be a portrait of Raphael. In the centre of the opposite wall, on the painted pilaster, is a self-portrait of Perugino himself, the ostentation of its positioning demonstrating the high regard in which he was held – or, perhaps, in which he held himself.

Don't miss the door through to the **Cappella di San Giovanni Battista**, frescoed with stories of the life of John the Baptist by Perugino's pupil Giannicola di Paola in the early 16th century.

Collegio della Mercanzia

Corso Vannucci 15, T075-573 0366.
Mar-Oct and 20 Dec-6 Jan, Tue-Sat 0900-1300,
1430-1730, Sun 0900-1300, Nov-Feb, Tue and
Thu-Fri 0800-1400, Tue and Sat 0800-1630,
Sun 0900-1300, €1.50.
Map: Perugia, E4, p72.

Alongside the guild of the moneychangers, the
merchants' guild was another important element
of medieval Perugian life. This building became
its headquarters in 1390 and still oozes wealth and
prestige, though it lacks the headlining frescoes of
the moneychangers next door. The intricate

woodcarving and intarsia work that line the
guildhall were carried out in the early 15th century by
anonymous artists, perhaps from northern Europe.

Sala dei Notari

Piazza IV Novembre, T075-577 2339.
Tue-Sun 0900-1300, 1500-1900, free.
Map: Perugia, E4, p72.

From the piazza, stone steps curl up to the first
floor, where the large and impressive Sala dei
Notari was once used for lawyers' meetings. This
was the original Palazzo dei Priori, built in the 13th
century, before succeeding centuries expanded
the building down corso Vannucci. The assembly
hall is richly frescoed and beautifully vaulted. Today
it is occasionally used for seminars and concerts.

North of piazza IV Novembre

Pozzo Etrusco

Piazza Piccinino 1, T075-573 3669, sistemamuseo.it.
Apr and Aug daily 1000-1330, 1430-1800, May-Jul
and Sep-Oct Tue-Sun 1000-1330, 1430-1830,
Nov-Mar Tue-Sun 1100-1330, 1430-1700, combined
ticket with Cappella di San Severo and Museo delle
Porte e delle Mura Urbiche, valid for 7 days, €2.50.
Map: Perugia, F4, p72.

Perugia's oldest well is a dank, seeping, dripping
place, an enormous work of engineering but also
somewhat oppressive: inviting for potholers but
less enticing for others. Built in the third or fourth
century BC, it held as much as 450,000 litres of
water – enough to supply the whole city – and is
3 m in diameter at the bottom, 4.5 m at the top.
A chain of buckets on a rope would have been
used to collect the water, suspended from the
large stone beam across the top. These days water
is pumped out electronically to stop the well filling
up, and you can walk down slippery steps to stand
in the middle of it, on a newly constructed bridge.
The well would originally have been even deeper
than its current 37 m, but centuries' worth of
detritus has built up at the bottom.

Five of the best

Hidden medieval streets in Perugia

❶ **Via dei Priori** Through an arch of Palazzo dei
Priori, this street apparently once ran red with the
blood of medieval family battles.

❷ **Via dell'Acquedotto** A raised pedestrian
walkway created from a 13th-century aqueduct.

❸ **Via Roscetto** Down winding steps and through
arches of various eras.

❹ **Corso Garibaldi** One of the town's oldest streets,
leading out to the northern gate, with prettily
painted houses.

❺ **Via Volte della Pace** A narrow street leading
north from piazza Matteotti, this street has more
arches than sky.

Above: Priori Palace, Sala dei Notari. Opposite page: Via dell'Acquedotto follows the route of a medieval aqueduct.

Cappella di San Severo

Piazza Raffaello, T075-573 3864.
Apr and Aug daily 1000-1330, 1430-1800, May-Jul and Sep-Oct Tue-Sun 1000-1330, 1430-1830, Nov-Mar Tue-Sun 1100-1330, 1430-1700, combined ticket with Pozzo Etrusco and Museo delle Porte e delle Mura Urbiche, valid for 7 days, €2.50.
Map: Perugia, G3, p72.

Raphael's first documented fresco, painted around 1505 when he was in his early 20s, decorates this small and starkly plain chapel. Only the top half is Raphael's – he was called away to paint the Vatican and left the fresco unfinished. At the top of the painting God has almost completely disappeared, but underneath, to either side of Jesus, Sts Maurus, Placidus, Benedict the Abbot, Romuald, Benedict the Martyr and John the Monk are colourfully depicted, all with distinctively Raphael noses. After Raphael's death his one-time teacher, Perugino, completed the lower section in 1521, and the similarities and differences between the styles of student and teacher are interesting to study. At the back of the chapel, a 19th-century etching shows what the undamaged fresco once looked like.

Cassero di Porta Sant'Angelo & Museo delle Porte e delle Mura Urbiche

Corso Garibaldi, T075-41670.
Apr and Aug daily 1000-1330, 1430-1800, May-Jul and Sep-Oct Tue-Sun 1000-1330, 1430-1830, Nov-Mar Tue-Sun 1100-1330, 1430-1700, combined ticket with Pozzo Etrusco and Cappella di San Severo, valid for 7 days, €2.50.
Map: Perugia, E1, p72.

Porta Sant'Angelo, the biggest of the city's medieval gates, houses a rather dusty old museum dedicated to the fortification of Perugia, with dilapidated models of the city. It has some good views. Nearby, the unusual round **Chiesa di Sant'Angelo**, built in the fifth and sixth centuries, is the city's oldest church and incorporates 16 ancient Roman columns in its construction.

Around the region

Rocca Paolina

Entry from via Marzia, piazza Italia, via Masi or viale Indipendenza.
Daily 0800-1900, free.
Map: Perugia, E6, p72.

After the papal victory over the city in the Salt War of 1540, the not altogether placatory response by Pope Paul III was to build an enormous castle right over the top of the area of Perugia where the ruling Baglioni family lived. Hatred of this symbol of domination simmered for centuries until the Perugian population finally took their revenge by pulling the building down in 1859.

In using the existing houses as foundations for his giant fortress, what the pope's project succeeded in doing was preserving the streets below exactly as they were in the 16th century. Under the giant vaults built over the area, many can be walked around now: a sort of latter-day Pompeii, it's a dim, shadowy, atmospheric place that feels full of the ghosts of the past.

More of the fascinating history is told in the **Museo della Rocca Paolina e la Città** (T075-572 5778, sistemamuseo.it, Apr and Aug daily 1000-1330, 1430-1800, May-Jul and Sep-Oct Tue-Sun 1000-1330, 1430-1800, Nov-Mar Tue-Sun 1100-1330, 1430-1700, €1).

Palazzo della Penna

Via Podiani 11, T075-571 6233, sistemamuseo.com.
Apr and Aug daily 1000-1300, 1600-1900, May-Jul and Sep-Oct Tue-Sun 1000-1300, 1600-1900, Nov-Mar Tue-Sun 1030-1300, 1600-1830, €3.
Map: Perugia, E6, p72.

Perugia's 'modern art' museum has works from the 18th and 19th centuries, as well as a collection of six large sketches by German hero of the 1960s, Joseph Beuys. Bought at great expense by the city when Beuys came to visit in 1980, they are either incoherent doodlings or intriguing insights into his mind, depending on your point of view.

More interesting is the museum's collection of Futurist painting. Temporary exhibitions are held on the first floor.

Museo Archeologico Nazionale dell'Umbria

Piazza Giordano Bruno 10, T075-572 7141, archeopg.arti.beniculturali.it.
Mon 1000-1930, Tue-Sun 0830-1930, €4.
Map: Perugia, G7, p72.

Perugia's excellent archeological museum, in the cloisters of San Domenico, is a treasure trove of local finds, most of them pre-Roman. The ground floor, lined with various ancient stone carvings, can be visited without a ticket. For the best bits, however, climb the stairs in the corner to the first floor, where some beautiful carved stone funerary urns line the cloister, and other pieces are displayed inside.

Women in and around Perugia in Etruscan times seem to have been buried with the same dignity as men, and it is noticeable that many of the grander urns, with statues reclining as if for a banquet on the lids, are for women. Indeed the preponderance of single-sex tombs in the area has led to speculation that families may have been buried along matriarchal lines.

In rooms off to the left is a huge collection of amulets from around the world – an anthropological insight into superstition. More interesting are the rooms on the near side of the cloister, where you will find such pieces as a fourth-century-BC shield, coins, a prehistoric corridor complete with bones and flints, armour including some rather fetching knee and shin plates, some beautifully decorated funeral pots and delicate gold jewellery. A ceramic pair of breasts and a couple of uteruses would have been used as votive offerings, perhaps during prayers for fertility.

Beuys' pieces are either incoherent doodlings or intriguing insights into his mind, depending on your point of view.

Chiesa di San Pietro

Via Borgo XX Giugno, T075-34770.
Mon-Fri 0900-1300,
Tue and Thu also 1530-1830, free.
Map: Perugia, F7, p72.

An extraordinary ensemble of painting, colour and wood wizardry, the Church of St Peter, built in the 10th century, also has beautiful cloisters and is well worth the walk from the centre out to this corner of the city. Among the highlights is an extraordinary choir, where the intarsia work is said by some to be as good as any in Italy, and where each armrest is decorated with a different carved mythological creature. There is a *Pietà* by Perugino on the left wall.

The church's bell tower is one of the most distinctive elements of the city's skyline. San Domenico once had a similar spire at the top of its campanile, but it was demolished in 1540 as it interfered with the view from the Rocca Paolina.

Orto Medievale

Via Borgo XX Giugno, T075-585 6432.
Mon-Fri 0800-1700, free.
Map: Perugia, F7, p72.

The theory behind this little corner of greenery is that it follows medieval thought. In reality it's a slightly strange mix of cosmology, mysticism, numerology and claptrap about the way in which lilies represent 'cosmogonic ovulation', but it's certainly pretty enough to warrant a visit all the same. There's a waterfall, and butterflies and lizards flit between the flowers. The tree of eternal youth, however, is looking rather decrepit.

Galleria Miomao

Corso Cavour 120, T347-783 1708, miomao.net.
Tue-Sat 1500-2000.

A contemporary cartoon gallery, Miomao mounts exhibitions of cartoon art from Italy and around the world.

Museo Archeologico Nazionale dell'Umbria.

Ipogeo dei Volumni

Via Assisana, T075-393329.
Daily Jul-Aug 0900-1230, 1630-1900,
Sep-Jun 0900-1300, 1530-1830, €3.
About 5 km southeast of Perugia on SS75
towards ponte San Giovanni.

The most elaborate of a series of Etruscan graves
just outside Perugia, this is the burial place of a rich
and important family and dates from the third or
second century BC. It was discovered in 1840 while
a road was being built, and is the biggest of the 38
tombs found here. Underneath a busy road, it's
hardly in the most romantic of positions, and takes
some effort to get to, but is worth the trouble for
its impressive Etruscan sculpture and for the
Tutankhamun-esque feeling you get as you
descend the steps into the tomb.

There are seven urns – six Etruscan and one
later Roman one. Don't miss the phalluses (symbols
of good luck and fertility) at the top of the stairs
among a large collection of other urns discovered
in the burial ground outside. The earliest tombs
here, among the olive trees, date back to the sixth
century BC – ancient even in Roman times. There's
also an antiquarium containing more interesting,
and in one case rather erotic, Etruscan urns.

Perugina chocolate factory

*Via San Sisto 42, San Sisto, T075-527 6796,
perugina.it.*
Mon-Fri 0900-1300, 1400-1730 (Mar-Sep also Sat
morning), telephone to book a visit and tour in
English, free.
Leave E45 at Madonna Alta exit and drive
through San Sisto – the factory is on the right.

The source of all the world's Baci (the factory
produces 1.5 million a day, complete with their
characteristic multilingual axioms of love), a tour
of this huge Willy Wonka-style palace of chocolate is
an interesting and enjoyable experience, despite its
position in the ugly industrial hinterland of Perugia.

Il Bacione

The biggest chocolate ever made was created
specially for Eurochocolate in 2003. Taking 1,000
hours of work and eventually weighing 5,980 kg, it
was carried on a special convoy from the Perugina
factory to piazza IV Novembre, where it was
measured for entry into the Guinness Book of
Records. A model of it is in the chocolate museum at
the Perugina factory. The original was chopped up
and given away at Eurochocolate – it lasted less than
four hours.

Sweetness for sale at Eurochocolate.

One-hour visits start with a 15-minute
infomercial about chocolate in general and the
history of Perugina, plus some free tasters, before
heading to a museum, and then – the highlight
– along a raised walkway above the factory floor,
from where you get great views of the chocolate
process below, from vat to mould to wrapping.

Should you wish to get closer to the melted
chocolate, courses are available at a smart new
chocolate school in the building.

Museo del Vino

*Corso Vittorio Emanuele 31, Torgiano,
T075 988 0200, vino.lungarotti.biz.*
Daily summer 0900-1300, 1500-1900, winter
0900-1300, 1500-1800, audiotour available,
€4.50/2.50 concession, combined ticket with
Museo dell'Olivo e dell'Olio €7/4.50.
15 km south of Perugia off SS3bis.

Housed in a 17th-century building in the centre
of Torgiano, a sleepy place that is home to the
wine millionaires of the Lungarotti Foundation,
Umbria's best wine museum is a fascinating place,
densely packed with artefacts, art, ceramics and
paraphernalia relating to the great drink.
The museum's claim to be a testament to the
civilization of humanity may be a little grand,
but it does go far beyond simply demonstrating
the wine-making process. Some of the most
interesting pieces are the *beve se puoi* ('drink if you
can') glasses – complex and ancient novelties that
challenge the user to work out how to drink the
contents without spilling them. There are also
some beautiful ceramic wine jugs from nearby
Deruta (see below), some contemporary art
collected by the Lungarotti family and a
collection of intricately patterned wafer irons.

Museo dell'Olivo e dell'Olio

*Via Garibaldi 10, Torgiano, T075-9880 3300,
olio.lungarotti.biz.*
Daily summer 1000-1300, 1500-1900, winter
1000-1300, 1500-1800, €4.50/2.50 concession,
combined ticket with Museo del Vino €7/4.50.

Though it suffers slightly by comparison with its
more illustrious sibling, Torgiano's olive oil museum
gives an extensive background to everything
olive-related, going back to Roman times.

Deruta

19 km south of Perugia on E45/SS3bis.

Famed for centuries for its majolica, Deruta is the
place to come should you want a white-glazed

olive oil pourer entwined with colourful fruit. The
whole town can feel a little like a giant ceramics
bazaar, but once you're in the small centre, away
from the giant ceramics outlets near the motorway,
it's not an unattractive place, and in among the
gaudy replicas of age-old designs it's possible to
find some better quality pieces.

Just south of the town, the **Museo Regionale
della Ceramica** (largo San Francesco, T075-971 1000,
museoceramicaderuta.it, Apr-Jun daily 1030-1300,
1500-1800, Jul-Sep daily 1000-1300, 1530-1900,
Oct-Mar Wed-Mon 1030-1300, 1430-1700, €3)
illustrates the history of its principal industry.

The most bizarre use of Deruta's pottery is
2 km south at the **Chiesa della Madonna dei
Bagni** (daily, summer 0730-1230, 1430-1900, winter
0800-1230, 1430-1830). Here every wall is covered
with colourful glazed tiles commemorating
miraculous escapes from dramatic deaths, from a
man who fell off his horse in 1701, to someone who
was electrocuted while working on a pylon in 1971
and a motorway pile-up in 2000.

The whole town can feel a little like a giant ceramics bazaar, but once you're in the small centre, away from the giant ceramics outlets near the motorway, it's not an unattractive place

Monte Tezio

13 km north of Perugia.
Most of Perugia's immediate surroundings are
low-lying and rather built up. To the north, however,
961-m Monte Tezio offers a quick and easy trip into
rural Umbria. From Cenerente, 5 km northwest of
Porta Sant'Angelo, a road to the right climbs towards
Migiana di Monte Tezio. Just before you reach
Migiana, a waymarked but sometimes overgrown
path off to the left leads to the summit, a couple of
hours' walk. For better tended paths, turn left off
the road about 1 km before Migiana and follow the
route up the valley of the Fosso di Migliana via the
ex-hermitage of Romitorio.

A walk around the streets of Perugia

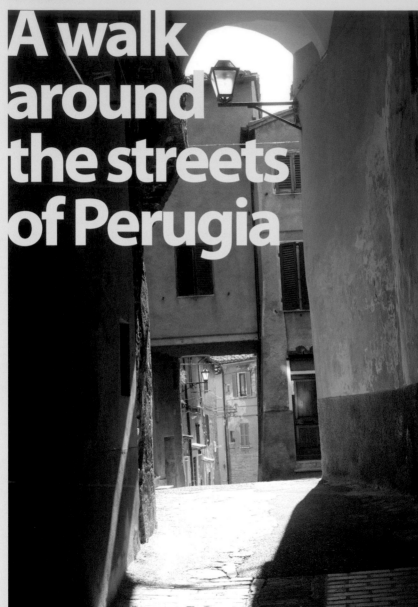

For a city of 160,000 people, Perugia has a remarkably unspoilt historical centre, with labyrinthine medieval streets full of relics of even earlier times.

This hour-long walk around the old centre starts in the heart of the city, **corso Vannucci**. Go under the **Arco dei Priori**, in the middle of Palazzo dei Priori. The street of the same name runs downhill through ancient medieval Perugia. This street is famous for the blood that reputedly ran down it in medieval times, when Perugia's leading families were, quite literally, always at each other's throats.

At the bottom of the street, the **Oratorio di San Bernardino** has a beautiful 15th-century multicoloured bas-relief façade. Next door, the large, pastel-coloured façade of the 13th-century **Chiesa di San Francesco al Prato** is just about all that has survived subsidence – the church is currently being restored and turned into a concert venue.

Turn back towards via dei Priori and take the steps on your left, which become via del Poggio. Don't miss the view over the churches to your left. Follow the road as it bends around to the right and becomes via Armonica, and cross a staggered junction past Teatro Morlacchi into **piazza Morlacchi**, named after Francesco Morlacchi, the Italian composer born in Perugia in 1784. The piazza is a favourite student hangout. Cross it and head down via Baldeschi. You'll soon come to wide steps leading down on your left towards **via dell'Acquedotto**.

A narrow pedestrian street that first runs underneath a bridge and then high above the ground between the surrounding buildings, the via dell'Acquedotto is a remnant of a 13th-century acquedut, 4 km long, that ran from Monte Pacciano to the Fontana Maggiore. It is also a great way to get out to this quiet part of the old centre.

Continue straight along via dell'Acquedotto, cross via Fabretti and continue uphill along the continuation of the old aqueduct, via Fagiano. Steps at the end lead up to via Benedetta –

Above: Tempio di Sant'Angelo.
Opposite page: Passages lead off corso Garibaldi.

branch right from here to join **corso Garibaldi**, one of Perugia's oldest streets. If you continue to the end of the corso you'll find on your right the **Tempio di Sant'Angelo**, a round church from the sixth century, built using 16 ancient Roman columns. Also here is **Porta Sant'Angelo**, the city's biggest medieval gate (see page 79).

Follow corso Garibaldi back south and you'll arrive in piazza Fortebracci, home of the Università per Stranieri and the **Arco Etrusco**. One of several ancient gates in the city, the hulking mass of the Arco Etrusco is the most famous. Originally built by the Etruscans in the third and second centuries BC, it was added to by the Romans 600 years later, when Emperor Augustus literally stamped his authority on the city. Having conquered – largely destroyed – and subsequently rebuilt the city, he had 'Augusta Perusia' inscribed on the gate, renaming the city after himself.

From here, climb up the steep via Ulisse Rocchi to arrive in piazza Danti, at the back of the cathedral. From the piazza, turn north, taking via del Sole and via Prome to the highest point in the centre of Perugia and a great viewpoint over the northern part of the town to the hills beyond.

Assisi

Perched high above the flat valley floor, on the flank of Monte Subasio, Assisi must have been a spectacular place even before the creation of so many extraordinary buildings and frescoes in veneration of its favourite son, St Francis. Cobbled streets wind across the hill, with occasional big views past geranium-filled window boxes to the valley below. Cats laze in the sun, nuns and monks climb stone stairs, and tour guides snake their parties through narrow streets. In high summer Assisi teems with tourists and pilgrims, but many of these arrive late and leave early, making the evenings and mornings relatively peaceful.

Below: Religious souvenirs on sale in Assisi. Opposite page: En route to the Basilica di San Francesco.

Basilica di San Francesco

*Piazza San Francesco, T075-819001,
sanfrancescoassisi.org.*
Daily, lower church Easter-Nov 0600-1845,
Nov-Easter 0600-1800, upper church, Easter-Nov
0830-1845, Nov-Easter 0830-1800, free.

Umbria's one truly unmissable sight, the Basilica of
St Francis is a many-tiered jewel box on the side of
a hill. Large yet intimate, bold yet intricate, it leaves
few visitors cold. And though there are many visitors,
it's surprisingly easy to avoid the worst crowds by
going early in the morning or later in the evening,
when the extraordinary beauty of the place is easier
to appreciate. Evenings have the advantage of great
sunsets over the Umbrian plains.

Frescoed with some of Italy's finest paintings
and lit through extraordinary stained glass, the
basilica is a colourful and uplifting place, and a
suitable celebration of St Francis – much more
so than the dour sterility of the huge Santa Maria
degli Angeli (see page 95) down on the plain.
Byzantine influences meld with Gothic and
Romanesque architecture to stunning effect, and
the restorations after the damage caused by the
1997 earthquake have left the church in fine fettle.

There are in fact two churches here – one on
top of the other. Construction of the lower church
started immediately on the canonization of St
Francis, just 18 months after his death in 1226. His
body was brought here in 1230. The upper church
was begun soon after, and was finished in 1253.
The hill on which the church sits was previously a
place where criminals were executed and buried
and was known as the Colle d'Inferno – the 'hill of
hell'; it was where St Francis had asked to be buried.

Basilica Inferiore Entered down stairs from
the main façade, through a beautiful double
doorway under a rose window, the lower church
is a sepulchral basilica. In the crypt here is the tomb
of St Francis himself.

The wooden doors are carved with stories
from the lives of St Francis, St Clare, St Louis and St
Anthony, added in the 16th century. Inside, chapels

Essentials

❶ Getting around Traffic is restricted in the
centre, and parking is limited to an hour. There are
car parks outside the walls, with free parking outside
Porta San Giacomo.

❷ Trains The train station, Santa Maria degli Angeli,
is around 3 km outside the city walls. A taxi into the
centre costs around €10.

❸ Buses You can get a bus from the station to piazza
Matteotti, in the city centre (buy a ticket in the bar
for €0.90 or for €1.50 on board, where you'll need the
correct change). Buses run half-hourly but sometimes
wait for incoming trains. Two other routes run from the
main car parks outside the walls into the centre.

❹ ATMs Banca dell'Umbria, piazza del Comune.

❺ Hospital Ospedale di Assisi, T0758-139227,
1 km southeast of Porta Nuova.

❻ Pharmacy Antica farmacia dei Caldari,
piazza del Comune 44, T0758-12552.

❼ Post office Largo Properzio 4, T0758-190711,
Mon-Sat 0800-1830.

❽ Tourist information office Piazza del Comune,
T0758-12534, Mon-Sat 0800-1400, 1500–1800, Sun
0900-1300.

Tip...

Cover up or take a large scarf or shawl with you
when visiting churches in summer. The Basilica di San
Francesco is especially strict and won't allow anyone
in with a bare back, shoulders or knees.

Around the region

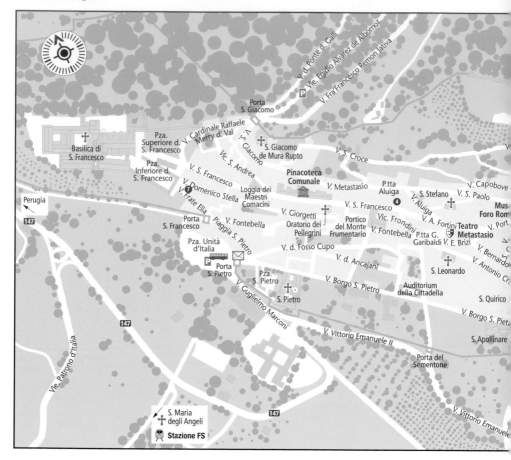

open off either side of a central nave with semicircular arches, richly patterned. The frescoes in the nave are by an unknown artist, known as the Maestro di San Francesco. Significantly, they illustrate five scenes from the life of Christ on the right side, and five scenes from the life of St Francis on the other: the juxtapositioning and the equal weighting constitute a deliberate move to equate one with the other.

The so-called *Madonna dei Tramonti* (*Our Lady of the Sunset*) by Pietro Lorenzetti, executed

between 1315 and 1330, is a beautiful painting that catches the evening light. It controversially seems to show Mary suggesting to Jesus that St Francis should be preferred to St John the Baptist.

Other highlights include the Chapel of Mary Magdalene, with frescoes by Giotto (1307-1308) illustrating her life, and Lorenzotti's pictures of Christ and St Francis in the presbytery and apse.

Tomba di San Francesco Down another level, the tomb of St Francis was never designed to be on

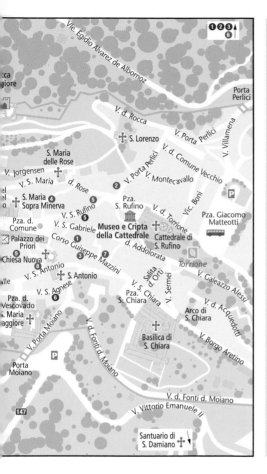

Assisi listings

❶ **Sleeping**

1 Agriturismo Alla Madonna del Piatto
   via Petrata 37, Pieve San Niçolò
2 Brigolante Guest Apartments   *via Costa di Trex 31*
3 Castello di Petrata   *via Petrata*
4 Il Palazzo   *via San Francesco 8*
5 Pallotta   *via San Rufino 6*
6 San Crispino   *via Sant'Agnese 11*
7 Subasio   *via Frate Elia 2*

❶ **Eating & drinking**

1 Caffé del Lion d'Oro   *corso Giuseppe Mazzini 11*
2 Caffé Duomo   *piazza San Rufino 5d*
3 Gran Caffè   *corso Giuseppe Mazzini 16a*
4 La Fortezza   *vicolo della Fortezza*
5 La Lanterna   *via San Rufino 39*
6 La Stalla   *via Ermeo delle Carceri 8*
7 MagnaVino   *corso Giuseppe Mazzini*
8 Medio Evo   *via dell Arco dei Priori 4*
9 Trattoria Pallotta   *vicolo della Volta Pinta 3*

public display, but the ground around it was dug out in the early 20th century, leaving a central column within which his body rests. It is a sombre but strangely modern place, and, though many clearly appreciate the opportunity to pay their respects, one can't help but feel that St Francis himself would not have wanted it this way.

Basilica Superiore After the relatively dark and sombre lower basilica, the upper church is a palace of light and colour. Giotto's 28 frescoes around the

nave, illustrating episodes from the life of St Francis, demonstrate a rare perception of emotion as well as of perspective, very different to other art of the time. With their backgrounds and their understanding of three-dimensional space, they broke new artistic ground and paved the way for the Renaissance.

Clockwise from the far north side (to the right of the altar), they depict: Francis being honoured by a man who lays down his cloak for him; Francis giving his cloak to a poor man; Francis's dream of a

St Francis

Environmentalist and patron saint of just about everything, from animals to Italy, St Francis's effect on Christianity has been enormous, and he is widely accepted as the most important of the pantheon of Christian saints; by Franciscans, he is revered on a par with Jesus.

One of seven children, Francesco di Bernardone was born to a wealthy cloth merchant of Assisi in 1181. His French mother Pica had him baptised Giovanni in his father Pietro's absence on business in France, but when Pietro returned he decided to rename him Francesco. At the age of 20, Francesco took part in an unsuccessful military raid on Perugia; he was captured there, and the meditative year he spent in prison probably had a profound effect on him.

Back in Assisi, while praying in the crumbling Chiesa di San Damiano (see page 95), Francis had a vision of Christ asking him to repair his house. Taking the instruction literally, he sold his possessions to help repair the church. His father was incensed by this and threatened to disinherit him, but Francis publicly renounced his inheritance and all his worldly goods, discarding even the clothes he was standing in, and embraced poverty as the way to godliness.

Never ordained as a priest, he lived a simple but cheerful life wandering through the woods, hills and mountains of Umbria, singing and preaching. Later, having met Pope Innocent III and received official recognition and permission to found a new religious order, he travelled to Egypt to intervene non-violently in the Crusades, and had an audience with Sultan Melek-el-Kamel, who was so impressed by his faith that he allowed him to preach to his subjects.

In the town of Greccio, near Assisi, Francis set up the first-known three-dimensional Nativity scene. But it is his poetry and writings, mostly written in Umbrian dialect rather than Latin because he believed in communicating with ordinary people, that have proved his most lasting epitaph. Often expressing his love towards the natural world, they offered a new path for Christianity at a time when it was increasingly tottering under the weight of corruption.

Above: A fresco representing St Francis.
Opposite page: The entrance to the Upper Basilica of St Francis in Assisi.

palace filled with arms; the image of Christ in the Church of St Damian asking Francis to repair his church; Francis stripping off and renouncing his worldly goods; Pope Innocent III dreaming that Francis is saving the church from collapse; the Pope confirming Francis's order; the vision of the fiery chariot; the vision of the heavenly thrones; Francis expelling the devils from war-torn Arezzo; Francis offering to walk through fire in front of the Sultan; the ecstasy of Francis; Francis creating his crib at Greccio – supposedly the world's first; the miracle of the spring; Francis preaching to the birds; the death of the knight of Celano; Francis preaching to Pope Honorius III; the apparition of Francis to the friars of the chapter at Arles; Francis receiving the stigmata; the death of Francis; Francis appearing in the visions of Fra Agostino and the bishop of Assisi; the recognition of the stigmata; Clare grieving over the body of Francis; the canonization of St Francis; the apparition of St Francis to Pope Gregory IX; the healing of John of Ylerda; the confession of a woman brought back to life; and Francis liberating a repentant heretic.

A plaque just inside the door commemorates the 1997 earthquake, which killed four people here in the basilica when large parts of the vaulting, some frescoed by Cimabue, collapsed.

Cimabue's work has also fared badly elsewhere in the upper church. The apse and western end of the transept feature frescoes painted in the late 13th century by the Florentine artist and his workshop. Due to deterioration caused by the use of lead oxide in his paint, which was probably applied to plaster that wasn't fresh enough, the paintings have a strange, ghostly, negative effect, rather like solarized photographs. Enough is visible, however, especially in his *Crucifixion*, to retain an impressive sense of drama.

The 13th-century Gothic windows, richly decorated with geometric patterns, are some of the finest in the region, and may have been made by a French, German or English artist.

The 1997 earthquake

When earthquakes shook Umbria and Marche in September 1997, many were made homeless and the cathedrals in Orvieto and Urbino were damaged. But it was scenes recorded on a video camera inside the basilica in Assisi that made the news headlines. A first earthquake struck, measuring 5.6 on the Richter scale. However, worse was to come – ten hours later a second quake, more powerful than the first, struck just as a group of experts were examining the earlier damage to the basilica. People inside the church described how they looked up and saw pieces of the building falling towards them. Four people in the basilica were killed by falling masonry.

The subsequent $50 million restoration was a painstaking two-year process, piecing together tens of thousands of tiny fragments of frescoes by Cimabue and Giotto. Some think the money spent on the basilica could have been better directed – many still remained homeless after. Even today, work continues to rebuild the nearby town of Nocera Umbra.

Via San Francesco

Winding its way from the basilica to the piazza del Comune (by which time it has become via Portica), via San Francesco is the nearest Assisi comes to having a main street. Dominated by over-priced ice cream and souvenir shops at the basilica end, it slowly takes on more of the medieval feel of the town, and it has a couple of worthwhile sights along its route – the art gallery and the sumptuously frescoed Oratorio dei Pellegrini.

The museum has been expertly spruced up – it is well lit and intelligently laid out, and it has good information boards in English.

Outside the Basilica.

Pinacoteca Comunale di Assisi

Via San Francesco 10, T075-812033, sistemamuseo.it.
Daily, mid-Mar-mid-Oct 1000-1300, 1400-1800, mid-Oct-mid-Mar 1000-1300, 1400-1700, €2.20/1.50 concession.

Assisi's picture gallery has a number of exceptional paintings, such as Giotto's *Virgin and Child Enthroned*, painted around 1305 and demonstrating a rare spatial awareness. Perugino's *Virgin and Child* of 1477 has a motherly tenderness, in marked contrast to the stylized and relatively primitive forms of the previous room.

Downstairs, changing exhibitions vary wildly, from the cutesy (nativity scenes) to the gory (the martyring of saints).

Oratorio dei Pellegrini

Via San Francesco 11, T075-812267.
Mon-Sat 1000-1200, 1600-1800, free.

A small square chapel built in 1457 for pilgrims coming to Assisi, the oratory contains some lovely, colourful 15th-century frescoes by Matteo da Gualdo, Pier Antonio Mezzastris and Andrea di Assisi, a student of Perugino. Nearly every inch of the walls is frescoed: da Gualdo's Mary and a baby Jesus are behind the altar, with St James to the left and St Anthony Abbot to the right. Angels around them play musical instruments and sing. Stories from the life of St Anthony Abbot are illustrated on the left wall, opposite stories of St James, including one about a roast chicken that came back to life to stand witness against a judge who had condemned an innocent man to death. The vaults above feature St Gregory, St Ambrose, St Jerome and St Augustine.

Museo e Foro Romano

Via Portica 2, T075-813053.
Mar-May and Sep-Oct 1000-1300, 1430-1800, Jun-Aug 1000-1300, 1430-1900, Nov-Feb 1030-1300, 1400-1700, €3.50.

One of the best archaeology collections around, Assisi's newly redesigned and renovated museum is displayed in the Roman Forum itself, under the town's central piazza and surrounding streets. The museum has been expertly spruced up – it is well lit and intelligently laid out, and it has good information boards in English.

Among the fragments of Roman inscriptions in stone in the first room is an arresting phallus, symbol of fertility and good luck. Also here, distinctive Roman funeral urns from Assisi display six-petalled flowers.

A glass-floored walkway runs over Roman paving and a drain, with archaeological finds displayed right and left.

The tribunal is a U-shaped limestone podium, probably used for public speaking. Holes in the surface would have held metal benches. Only the base remains of the aedicule, from the first century AD, but there are some beautiful inscriptions. Walking around it, on the paving stones worn down by thousands of pairs of Roman sandals, it's possible to imagine yourself in Roman Asisium 2,000 years ago. A magnificently engineered wall, with barrel-vaulted monumental fountains, runs along what would have been the northern side of the forum; on the eastern side are what would have been shops.

A projected video is well worth watching for its three-dimensional virtual reconstructions of how the centre of the Roman town once looked.

Santa Maria Sopra Minerva

Piazza del Comune.
Mon and Wed-Thu 0715-1900, Tue and Fri 0715-1400, 1515-1900, Sat-Sun 0815-1900, free.

Piazza del Comune, Assisi's central piazza, is usually filled with tourists leaving, arriving, trooping in and out of the tourist information office, or sitting having a drink at one of the cafés. The church here is remarkable for its portal, which is the front section of the ancient Roman temple of Minerva. The building features prominently in one of Giotto's frescoes in the Basilica di San Francesco (see page 87).

The temple was built here in the first century BC, financed by two private citizens of Assisi. From the sixth century it was used by Benedictine

Assisi's Roman temple is now incorporated into the church of Santa Maria Sopra Minerva.

monks, until in the 13th century it became the town hall. In 1539, Pope Paul III ordered that it should be restored as a church and dedicated to the Virgin Mary, and it was later entrusted to a Franciscan order. After the splendid façade, however, the baroque interior is a disappointment.

Opposite the church is a vaulted passage with some rather rude Roman frescoes on its underside. Recently restored, these once advertised the way to Assisi's brothels.

Basilica di Santa Chiara

Piazza Santa Chiara 1, T075-812282.
0700-1200, 1400 till sunset, free.

At the opposite end of Assisi to St Francis's basilica, his counterpart St Clare has a striking church, with a large rose window, flying buttresses, and a piazza at the front with great views across the Umbrian plain.

Inside there are many rather damaged, and not especially well-lit, frescoes, especially on the rib-vaulted ceiling above the altar. Note the two different depictions of Jesus on the cross, one calm, one very much suffering – these were the result of much religious debate and hand-wringing as to whether Jesus felt pain or not.

Down in the crypt, Clare's body can be seen in her tomb, and a glass cabinet displays her cloak and locks of her hair, together with the cloak of St Francis. Born in Assisi to a noble family, Clare renounced her wealth to follow the example of Francis, eventually setting up a convent at San Damiano and founding the order known as the Poor Clares.

Cattedrale di San Ruffino

Piazza San Rufino, T075-812283, assisimuseodiocesano.com.
Daily summer 0700-1300, 1430-1800, winter 0700-1300, 1500-1900, free.

The façade of Assisi's 12th-century cathedral, in three sections as is often the case in Umbria, is a fascinating storyboard, populated with weird and wonderful creatures – winged serpents, griffins, and lions in the process of devouring a sheep and a man. There's even a small dog trotting down the façade, to the right of the ornate rose window.

The large, pale interior of the cathedral is less interesting. Many come to see the font in which St Francis and St Clare were baptized, to the right

It's a fact...

Because of a miracle in 1252, when Clare, ill in bed on Christmas Eve, witnessed a vision of Mass being celebrated several miles away, in 1958 the pope declared her the patron saint of television.

inside the entrance, but more impressive is the large Roman cistern opposite, next to the exit. There are more, rather indistinct, Roman remains under glass down the centre of the aisle.

Rocca Maggiore

T075-812033.
Daily Jun-Aug 0900 till sunset, Sep-May 1000 till sunset, €5.

On the hill above Assisi, the town's castle has had many incarnations. There's almost certainly been some kind of fort here since pre-Roman times, but most of the current building dates from Cardinal Albornoz's construction on behalf of the papacy in the 14th century. It's not a beautiful building, but there are some great views from the top and a thrillingly long passageway between its two towers. You can climb the northwest tower by a new metal spiral staircase, but the best views are from the top of the polygonal tower, 105 m away, reached along a narrow corridor, lit by slit windows and lamps. Part of the castle is used as a temporary exhibition space.

Abbazia di San Pietro

Piazza San Pietro, T075-812311.
Daily 0730-1900.

A strikingly stark Romanesque church, San Pietro has an almost completely bare stone and brick interior, but its light and sense of open space means that it avoids seeming austere. It has hardly changed since the almost-square façade was completed in 1268. The three rose windows and a few slim stained-glass windows pinprick the walls with colour – look too for the fragments of mosaic on the ceiling buttresses. The early influence of Gothic architecture shows in the tops of its arches, which have the merest suggestion of points, and in the centre of the nave there is a splendid brick dome. At the front of the building, two rather weathered lions guard the handsome entrance.

Next to the church, the **Museo di San Pietro** (T075-815 5204, museiecclesiastici.it, Tue-Sun 1000-1300, 1500-1900) has a ceramics collection.

Chiesa di San Damiano

Daily Nov-Mar 1000-1200, 1400-1630,
Apr-Oct 1000-1200, 1400-1800, free.
Go through Porta Nuova and follow signs down
hill for about 1 km.

Outside Assisi's walls to the southeast, down a
flowery path flanked by olive groves, San Damiano
is a peaceful place. It was here in 1205 that St Francis
is supposed to have received the call to repair
the church, and here that St Clare lived, and died.
Francis came to church to visit her just once, though
his body was kept here for a while after death.

Above: San Damiano. Opposite page: Santa Chiara.

 The small cloister has flowers and a central well,
and you can lean over to see into the refectory, with
its original wooden benches and frescoed end wall.
Through the church you pass the Coretto (choir),
a small square room with an arched ceiling, and
up the stairs is the Oratorio, a small chapel, richly
frescoed. Beyond this is the dormitory – in the
corner a simple cross marks the site of Clare's death.

Basilica di Santa Maria degli Angeli

Santa Maria degli Angeli,
T075-80511, porziuncola.org.
Jul-Sep daily 0615-2000, Oct-Jun Mon-Fri
0615-1300, 1430-2000, Sat-Sun 0615-2000, free.
4 km west of Assisi, down on the plain.

When St Francis abandoned his possessions (and
his clothes) and left Assisi, he came here, to a tiny
chapel in the woods. The chapel survives, and if
you squint very hard it is just about possible to
imagine St Francis here, living a simple life and
talking to the birds. Open your eyes a little wider,
however, and you will see an enormous basilica
surrounding the cowering **Porziuncola**, which
looks like a dolls' house in comparison to the
gargantuan monstrosity built over its head.

 St Francis founded his order of friars here,
and died here in 1226, but it wasn't until the
16th century that Pope Pius V decided that
something more befitting the grandeur of the
church should be built around the popular
pilgrimage spot. Work began on the basilica in

1568 and was eventually finished in 1684. At 116-m
long it is one of the largest basilicas in the world.

 Despite the way in which a humble life
dedicated to simplicity is celebrated with such
ostentation and ornamentation, it's well worth a visit
to see Francis's chapel. The paintings, inside and out,
have been added since his death. The altar, notably,
was painted by Ilario da Viterbo in 1393.

 In the **Cappella del Transito** (Chapel of
the Transition), the infirmary of the friary where
Francis died, after having asked to be placed on
the ground, there is a statue of the saint by Andrea
della Robbia from 1490. The internal frescoes were
painted by Giovanni Spagna in 1520.

 The **Museo della Porziuncola** (T075-805 1430,
daily 0900-1230, 1500-1800) also has some
interesting exhibits, including a 13th-century
painting of St Francis and works by Tiberio d'Assisi.

Parco del Monte Subasio

T075-815 5290, parks.it.
Road open until 2100 in summer, 1900 in winter.

Winding up through Assisi's porta Cappuccini
and across the wooded slopes beyond, the
Monte Subasio road becomes a wide, stony track
that opens out on to the grassy uplands above the
tree line. Monks follow St Francis's paths, paragliders
step off the edge into the sky and visitors gulp at the
gargantuan views. Monte Subasio, wild and craggy,
snow-covered for much of the year, is a world apart
from the lace shops and postcards of Assisi below.

Lago Trasimeno

Italy's fourth biggest lake, Trasimeno, to the west of Perugia, is a shallow saucer of water surrounded by low hills. Its three wooded islands – Polvese, Maggiore and Minore – were all visited by St Francis and have ancient churches.

The lake retains some of its ancient fishing industry and has long had strategic significance – it was the site of one of the worst military defeats of the Roman Empire, when Hannibal, having led his troops, plus elephants, over the Alps, lured Flaminius's Roman army into an ambush and killed at least 15,000 soldiers.

Trasimeno is fed almost exclusively by rainwater, and there have been occasional plans to drain it, though the current threat is climate change: its level is already much lower than in ancient times, and it is in danger of drying out completely.

Castiglione del Lago is the most attractive lakeside town, with a regular ferry service to Polvese and Maggiore. Set back from the lake to the south, Panicale is a pretty hill town; beyond here, Città delle Pieve was the birthplace of Perugino and still has several of his works. Along the northern edge of the lake the motorway and railway spoil the peace somewhat, though there are some walking opportunities in the hills. A bike path along the water's edge gives a rare flat opportunity for cycling in Umbria.

Castiglione del Lago

With Etruscan and Roman origins, Castiglione del Lago is an obvious place for habitation, on a high spur jutting out into the shimmering water. Once, long ago, it was an island, but the lake has long since receded to leave the town, with its impressive castle, high and dry.

The town's eponymous fortress, the **Rocca del Leone** (T075-951099, hours variable, €4) was once fought over by Cortona and Perugia. The outside walls are well enough preserved to allow visitors to walk all the way around the ramparts and up a couple of the towers, from where there are great views of the lake past the stentorian signs. The castle keep reopened only in 2008 after sustaining damage in the 1997 earthquake. A ticket to the fortress also gets you into the **Palazzo della Corgna**, connected to the castle by a long fortified passage. The palace, where both Machiavelli and Leonardo da Vinci stayed in their day, is less interesting than the fortress, despite its large military frescoes.

The rest of Castiglione del Lago is a good place to wander, though without too much in the way of must-see sights. The main street is packed with food, wine and ice cream shops, and many of the delicatessens on and around the main piazza give out free tastes of their wares.

Panicale

13 km south of Castiglione del Lago.

A pretty little hill town just to the south of the lake, Panicale has good views to Castiglione del Lago and the distant lake itself. It also has the impressive sloping piazza Umberto I, dominated by the **Chiesa di San Michele Arcangelo**. Built in the 11th century, the church has a baroque interior containing the *Adoration of the Shepherds* (1519) by Gianbattista Caporali, a student of Perugino: €0.05 gets you 21 seconds of light and piped organ music.

Perugino himself is represented in the **Chiesa di San Sebastiano**, where his large fresco of the *Martyrdom of St Sebastian*, painted in 1505, can

Castiglione del Lago.

Città della Pieve.

be seen. A wander along quiet, concentric rings of streets will eventually bring you to the 14th-century **Palazzo del Podestà** at the very top of the town.

About 4 km to the west of Panicale, **Paciano** is another attractive hill village.

Città della Pieve

20km south of Castiglione del Lago.

South of Lake Trasimeno, this town was, despite his nickname, the birthplace of Pietro Vannucci (commonly known as Perugino) in 1446. Built mainly in red brick, the handsome medieval buildings have a diffferent feel to the pale stone structures in the rest of the region. Vicolo Baciadonne ('kissing ladies street') is claimed to be one of the narrowest streets in Europe – so much so that amorous contact with anyone coming the other way is almost inevitable. A ticket for the so-called Museo Diffuso (€4, from the tourist information office in piazza Matteotti, T0578-299375), covers five sights: the **Cattedrale**, the **Palazzo della Corgna**, the **Oratorio di Santa Maria dei Bianchi**, the **Chiesa di Santa Maria dei Servi** and the **Chiesa di San Pietro**. All except the Palazzo have Perugino frescoes from the beginning of the 16th century. In the Oratorio di Santa Maria dei Bianchi, Perugino's *Adoration of the Magi* is accompanied by a letter detailing the financial negotiations between the artist and the church.

Isola Polvese

The largest island on the lake, and also the most attractive, Polvese is a nature reserve, carefully protected. The island has 6,000 olive trees as well as oak woods, and had a population of around 500 people in medieval times, supported by fishing. Guided tours of the island are available from the information office (T075-965 9546, polvese.it) near the ferry landing.

The **Fortezza Medievale** dates back to the 13th century, when the lake was an important economic and strategic area and villagers needed protection

Tip...

The best view of sunset over Lake Trasimeno is from the eastern shores around Toricella. From the beach of Spiaggia Caloni there is a great view through fishing nets set up just off the shore across to Castiglione del Lago.

against attack. In summer it is used for occasional concerts as part of the Trasimeno Blues Festival (see page 111).

The **Monasterio di San Secondo** was built by monks who inhabited the island from the end of the 15th century. The island also has a garden of aquatic plants. A good walk follows a path around the edge of the island, taking an hour or so. There is a beach to the northeast of the landing point, from where it is possible to swim.

Isola Maggiore

The most easily reached of the lake's islands, Maggiore also has the most developed tourist infrastructure, with restaurants and shops vying for the trade of visitors the moment they step off the boat. Few visitors make it far from the quayside, however, leaving most of the island a rewarding place to explore.

Paths climb to the summit, where there are 360° views and the 13th-century **Chiesa di San Michele Archangelo** (daily 1000-1300, 1400-1745, combined ticket with Lace Museum €3). Frescoes here were painted between the 13th and 16th centuries and include a *Madonna and Child* from 1280. The four spandrels above the altar depict the four evangelists.

Another path around to the north of the island skirts the edge of the water, leading to places where you can swim, though if you're put off by the idea of lukewarm green murk it may not be for you. Also here is a shrine to St Francis, who spent time on the island. Higher up the hill you can visit the cave where he is supposed to have slept.

Nearby Isola Minore is privately owned and can't be visited.

Listings
Sleeping

Perugia

Many people come to Perugia to study, and there's an unusually good selection of short- to medium-term accommodation available. Prices for an apartment sleeping two range from around €500 per month up to about €850: studentliving.eu has listings.

Brufani Palace €€€
Piazza Italia 12, T075-573 2541, brufanipalace.com.
Map: Perugia, E6, p72.
One of the region's smartest hotels, the five-star deluxe Brufani is a large, old-fashioned place, with 94 rooms and a swimming pool with a glass bottom, under which are Etruscan remains. There's an expensive restaurant (€€€€) and a stylish bar, all leather and walnut, which is also open to non-residents and has seating outside in the piazza in summer. Rooms are furnished with sumptuous fabrics and all the comforts imaginable.

Castello dell'Oscano €€€
Strada Forcella 37, Cenerente, T075-584371, oscano.com.
A 19th-century faux-antique castle set on a wooded hill 7 km north of Perugia, the Castello dell'Oscano has a great restaurant and elegant rooms, though it can feel more like staying in a country house than a bona fide castle. There are

good views over the peaceful valley from the crenellated rooftop, a small pool, gym and sauna. There are also rooms in the neighbouring Villa Ada.

Castello di Monterone €€€
Strada Montevile 3, T075-572 4214, castellomonterone.it.
Less than 10 minutes outside Perugia, on the town's pretty eastern side, this is a castle with neo-Gothic touches but plenty of romance in its 18 rooms. Originally built in the 12th century, the castle was restored in the 1800s and is decorated with pieces such as an Etruscan urn, a 14th-century crucifix and a Roman bust. There's a smart restaurant in the ex-dungeon, an outdoor terrace, a bar with a huge fireplace, and a swimming pool. The beds and other furniture are all handmade in Umbria and the hotel has beehives, vines and olives. If money is no object, book the Camera delle Dame, with frescoes of damsels and windows looking out in three directions, from which you can watch the sun setting behind a great vista of Perugia.

Hotel Fortuna €€
Via Luigi Bonazzi 19, T075-572 2845, albergofortuna.it.
Map: Perugia, D5, p72.
This greenery-clad building just off piazza della Repubblica has 52 rooms, the best of which have 18th-century ceiling frescoes.

Standard rooms are plain but comfortable, with pale fabrics and wooden floors; 'executive' rooms have exercise bikes. There's an antique library and good views from the small roof terrace.

Il Romitorio di Monte Tezio €€
Località Strada Colognola, Migiana di Monte Tezio, T075-690859, montetezio.it.
Closed Feb.
In the peaceful hills of the Monte Tezio park, a 20-minute drive north of Perugia, the Romitorio is a converted 13th-century monastery, complete with a church and a vegetarian restaurant built from the old stables. There are seven bedrooms, plus two flats sleeping up to six people, all simply but elegantly furnished. The farm has animals, including horses, and riding lessons and treks are offered. Free transfer from Perugia airport.

La Rosetta €€
Piazza Italia 19, T075-572 0841, perugiaonline.com/larosetta.
Map: Perugia, E6, p72.
Big and central, the old-fashioned Rosetta has 18th-century ceiling frescoes in its grandest rooms and badly reproduced paintings elsewhere. Second floor rooms are more modern, with good black and white tiled bathrooms. Rooms overlook either the corso or a paved internal courtyard.

Le Torri di Bagnara €€

*Strada della Bruna 8,
Pieve San Quirico, T075-579 3001,
letorridibagnara.it.*

This converted 11th-century abbey 22 km north of Perugia has seven double rooms and suites, and four apartments of various sizes in a stone tower. The buildings are part of a large estate with mountain biking routes, woods and lakes. There's a large pool, and great views.

Anna €

*Via dei Priori 48, T075-573 6304,
albergoanna.it.*
Map: Perugia, D4, p72.

Friendly if occasionally eccentric, Anna is run by an elderly couple who know how to look after guests. Rooms are small and breakfast is best avoided, but the position – just a couple of minutes down the hill from the corso – is great, and you'll soon feel like one of the family. They also own Hotel Domus, further down the hill.

Azienda Agricola Biologica Torre Colombaia €

San Biagio della Valle, T075-878 7381, torrecolombaia.it.

One of the first certified organic farms in Italy, Colombaia is a set of converted hunting lodges in 80 ha of woods about 17 km southwest of Perugia. There are four more double rooms in the main house, where there's also an organic restaurant. There's good scope for bird watching,

and free yoga lessons in a meditation room.

Primavera Mini Hotel €

*Via Vincioli 8, T075-572 1657,
primaveraminihotel.it.*
Map: Perugia, D3, p72.

Near piazza Morlacchi, this friendly little family-run hotel is on the second and third floors of a building on a quiet side street. Eight rooms have TV, free Wi-Fi and minibars, and one, at the top, has a private terrace with great views across the Perugian rooftops. The rooms are plain but comfortable, with wooden floors and fairly modern furniture. It's popular, so book ahead.

Assisi

Castello di Petrata €€

*Via Petrata, T075-815451,
castellopetrata.com.*

Though it can sometimes feel a little too large for its own good, Castello di Petrata has a great position in the hills behind Assisi, a beautiful pool and other perks such as a billiards room, a restaurant and an open fire. You can hire mountain bikes, and in summer there is cooking outdoors.

San Crispino €€

Via Sant'Agnese 11, T075-815 5124, sancrispinoresidence.com.

Seven suites down the hill from Santa Chiara all have little kitchens cunningly disguised as dressers,

which open out to reveal a fridge and small cooker. The beds are draped with fabric and the biggest room has its own terrace, with sun loungers and fantastic views. There are mod cons too – rooms come with flatscreen TVs and internet-equipped computers. The same people own a 'resort' 5 km outside Assisi with a pool and gym.

Subasio €€

*Via Frate Elia 2, T075-812206,
hotelsubasio.com.*

Charlie Chaplin and Italian royalty once stayed here, right next to the Basilica di San Francesco. These days the hotel has lost some of its polish, but it reopened in 2008 under new management, and enough of the early to mid-20th century touches have been preserved to retain some style.

Walnut furniture and carpets are the order of the day, and some rooms have small baths and even smaller balconies.

Agriturismo Alla Madonna del Piatto €

Via Petrata 37, Pieve San Nicolò, T075-819 9050, incampagna.com.

You will be exceptionally well looked after at this beautiful little place high in the hills above Assisi. There's a minimum stay of two nights, three in high season. Homemade printed guides to local day trips are offered, as is a good library of guidebooks. A vine-entwined pergola has views across the rolling countryside to the back of the Basilica di San Francesco, as does one of the guest bathrooms. The oldest part of the house dates back to around 1500, when it may have been a watchtower, and two rooms downstairs have stone barrel vaulting. Upstairs, slightly more modern rooms are cosy, with underfloor heating, and all are attractively but soberly decorated, with iron-framed beds. Letizia runs cookery lessons (see page 65) every week in season, for both guests and non-guests.

Hotel il Palazzo €
Via San Francesco 8,
T075-816841, hotelilpalazzo.it.
A friendly place in the centre of Assisi with 12 rooms, all different. There are original 16th-century ceilings with wooden beams, art on the walls, and a cool, private courtyard. The bathrooms are white tiled and spotless. A suite is much bigger, with a frescoed ceiling and the top floor has panoramic views.

Pallotta €
Via San Rufino 6, T075-812307,
pallottaassisi.it.
A homely little B&B up the hill from piazza del Comune. Terracotta-tiled bedrooms have large reproductions of oil paintings from the gallery down the road, and tiny bathrooms. Upstairs there is a beautiful 'belvedere', with comfy

seats and huge windows looking out over Assisi. There's a washing machine, Wi-Fi and even umbrellas that guests can use for free. Guests get a 10% discount in the excellent Trattoria Pallotta, across the piazza.

Self-catering
Brigolante Guest Apartments
Via Costa di Trex 31,
T075-802250, brigolante.com.
Three self-catering apartments on a farm in the hills to the north of Assisi, sleeping two to four people. Nice touches include handmade soap, a wood-burning fire and a balcony overlooking Monte Subasio. Bedrooms have metal-frame beds and there are kitchen facilities as well as satellite TV. Sometimes available for two-night stays in low season, €475 a week in high season.

Villa di Monte Solare €€€
Via Montali 7, Colle San Paolo,
Panicale, T075-832376,
villamontesolare.com.
One of Umbria's most elegant hotels, the Villa di Monte Solare has 25 rooms high in the hills to the south of Lake Trasimeno among olive groves and vines and sweeping views south. There's a formal garden with lemon trees, breakfast comes with cooked eggs and sparkling wine, and there are two (soon to be three) swimming pools, with great views. The state-of-the-art spa (see page 115) is luxurious, and there's a cookery school for guests. From May to October, classical music concerts are held in the small chapel. Built in 1780, the main building is the most desirable,

with painted wooden ceilings and antiques-filled rooms.

Capricci di Merion €€
Via Pozzo 21, Tuoro sul Trasimeno, T075-825002, capriccidimerion.it.
A romantic *stile Liberty* house in the peaceful hills to the north of the lake, this square villa was built for Lady Merion by her lover Baron Rondò. Rooms, named after poets, composers and artists, are individually decorated, with plenty of antique character and colour; some have metal-framed four-poster beds. There is a swimming pool in the gardens, a sunbed and sauna, and the restaurant (see page 110) is excellent.

Casa Bruciata €€
Locale San Bartolomeo dei Fossi, Preggio, T075-941 0277, casabruciata.com.
Isolated in the hills to the north of the lake, Casa Bruciata is a collection of buildings with apartments sleeping between two and six people, which can be rented by the night or the week. There's a swimming pool with great views, a restaurant, and lots of home-grown produce that guests usually have access to.

Il Cantico della Natura €€
Case Sparse 50, Montesperello di Magione, T075-841699, ilcanticodellanatura.it.
An ecologically-minded place to the east of Lago Trasimeno,

Il Cantico has 12 beautifully designed rooms, each named after a month of the year, with dark wooden beams and draped beds. They run a good range of themed weekends 'for those who love' or for those who fancy a trip in a hot air balloon.

Fattoria Il Poggio €
Parco Naturale Isola Polvese, T075-965 9550, fattoriaisolapolvese.com.
The accommodation may be fairly basic, but the opportunity to stay on Isola Polvese and have the island more or less to yourself after the last boats have gone is worth giving up a few luxuries for. There are apartments and rooms, and films, fishing trips, canoeing and yoga courses can all be organized.

Il Torrione €
Via delle Mura 4, Castiglione del Lago T075-953236, il-torrione.com.
One of Lake Trasimeno's best deals, Il Torrione's two nicest rooms open on to a geranium-filled garden built right into the top of one of the ancient towers in the town's protective walls. Colourful modern art decorates the walls of the five simple, square rooms, which are equipped with fridges. There's also an apartment with a kitchen.

Lillo Tatini €
Piazza Umberto I 13, Panicale, T075-837771, lillotatini it.
A beautiful little medieval apartment in Panicale, owned by the restaurant of the same name. Bare stonework and arches retain the original feel, but there are newer, more personal touches too, such as the coloured tiles around the cooking area. Ask about special weekends such as a wine and food package, where for €160 per person guests get accommodation plus two full suppers in the restaurant with wine, plus *aperitivi* in Caffè della Piazza.

Miralago €
Piazza Mazzini 6, Castiglione del Lago, T075-951157, hotelmiralago.com.
From the pastel shades to the bronze dog statues, Miralago has a slight 1980s feel. It is, however, plum in the centre of Castiglione del Lago, and most of its 19 light, comfortable rooms overlook the lake or the piazza or both.

Eating & drinking

Perugia

Nanà €€€
Corso Cavour 202, T075-573 3571.
Mon-Sat 1300-1430,
2000 till late.
Map: Perugia, F7, p72.
In a large, yellow, high-ceilinged room, Nanà is a smart and serious restaurant with friendly and very efficient service. There are some tasty starters, such as carpaccio with walnuts and celery, the homemade pasta is delicious and the meaty seconds are generous. Try the thali-style cheese and fruit selection, with 10 different cheeses, and leave some room for one of the exceptional homemade desserts, especially the crème caramel ("done properly"). The wine list could be used to prop a door open, but is thin on local wines.

Osteria del Gambero €€€
Via Baldeschi 8a, T075-573 5461, osteriadelgambero.it.
Tue-Sun 1930-2300, Sun also 1230-1430, closed 2 weeks in Jan, 2 weeks in Aug.
Map: Perugia, E3, p72.
One of Perugia's most sophisticated restaurants, Gambero is smart but never stuffy, and has a nice personal, human touch. Delicious tasting menus focus on fish or meat, and there's also a rare vegetarian menu. Dishes are imaginative and full of interesting flavours: try the black lasagne with mussels and saffron, or duck with

pistachios and plum sauce. The bread is good too – homemade and with inventive flavourings – and there's a great choice of cheeses, though you should save some room for the peach strudel with cinnamon ice cream and red wine sauce. The friendly staff are very knowledgeable about the extensive wine list. Jazz plays, Paul Klee posters give a touch of contemporary style, and there's even a collection of books to browse should conversation falter.

Ristorante l'Opera €€€
Via della Stella 6, T075-572 4286.
Tue-Sun 1230-1430, 1900-2330.
Map: Perugia, E4, p72.
High quality cuisine in a deceptively plain restaurant: opera music plays and there are contemporary paintings around the walls, but there's little to prepare you for the rich and inventive food that emanates from the kitchen. The menu concentrates on fish – try the warm octopus, potato and green bean salad for a starter, followed by black macaroni with mussels and saffron. And unless you're really hungry, it is worth skipping the second course to leave room for a meltingly exquisite *torta cioccolata*.

Al Mangiar Bene €€
Via della Luna 21, T075-573 1047, almangiarbene.com.
Mon-Sat 1220-1600, 1930-2300.
Map: Perugia, E4, p72.

Down a steep stepped lane from corso Vannucci, Al Mangiar Bene is a warmly welcoming place with an entirely organic wine list and food to match. In an air-conditioned, rib-vaulted space they serve wood-fired pizzas as well as excellent traditional Umbrian food. The vegetarian choices are especially good, and wide-ranging, and even the chocolate mousse is unusually tasty. The mixed antipasti are good and plenty for two, and for *primo* you can choose a type of pasta and a sauce, or go for the homemade gnocchi, then follow it up with some more expensive meat options.

Bottega del Vino €€
Via del Sole 1, T075-571 6181, labottegadelvino.net.
Mon-Sat 1200-1500, 1900-2400, closed Aug.
Map: Perugia, F3, p72.
Overlooking piazza Danti, this atmospheric and genial wine bar serves some of Perugia's best food to hip young locals and a smattering of in-the-know tourists. The pasta menu changes daily, and there are some excellent salads. A bicycle hangs from the ceiling, jazz plays (with live performances on Wednesdays), the place is decorated with candles, old photos of Perugia and Umbria Jazz posters, and the staff are knowledgeable and friendly.

Civico 25 €€

Via della Viola 25, T075-571 6376.
Mon-Sat evenings only,
closed Aug.
Map: Perugia, G4, p72.
On a quiet back street, this
wine bar and restaurant attracts
a good mix of genial drunks and
smart young Perugians. A bar at
the front is a good spot to drop
by for a quick glass of wine,
while the tight, colourfully
modern tables on two levels
at the back are food-centred.
The *degustazione* starter –
a mix of whatever the chef
fancies giving you, is generous
and exceptionally good, and may
include tasty delicacies such as a
stuffed chilli pepper, a cheese
tart and *panzanella* (bread and
tomato salad). Service is very
professional and you can see
into the semi-open kitchen.
There are also a few outdoor
tables across the road.

La Lumera €€

Corso Bersaglieri 22,
T075-572 6181, lalumera.it.
Wed-Mon 1900-0100.
Map: Perugia, G3, p72.
Just outside porta Pesa, La
Lumera is a local restaurant with a
loyal clientele. Inside are wooden
tables, a tiled floor and old photos
covering the walls, but in summer
it mostly moves outside, with
tables haphazardly scattered in
an alleyway. The menu features
an excellent sardine tart, an
unusual variety of bread and a
good range of traditional

Umbrian classics, such as
umbricelli (thick spaghetti) with
pecorino cheese. Their support
for the Slow Food movement
can go too far, however, with
service that sometimes moves
at a glacial pace.

La Piazzetta €€

Via Deliziosa 3, T075-573 6012.
Wed-Mon 1200-1500,
1900-2300.
Map: Perugia, D4, p72.
This is an Umbrian restaurant
with a rare international focus.
There's a 'creative' menu and a
fish menu alongside the more
standard choices – try the apricot
with marinated salmon and
spring onion, or the beef with
courgette flowers and truffles.
And if you're having trouble
choosing, the *antipasti della casa*
are a great mix of inventive
starters. Service is friendly,
multilingual and eager to help,
and the restaurant is equally
popular with locals and visitors,
despite being hidden away on a
side street off via dei Priori. Six
tables outside under a pretty

vine-covered arbour are first
choice in summer, but there's
also a brick-vaulted interior.

L'Officina €€

Borgo XX Giugno 56,
T075-572 1699, l-officina.net.
Mon-Fri lunch and dinner,
Sat-Sun evenings only.
Map: Perugia, H7, p72.
One of Umbria's most
intelligent, metropolitan
eateries, sophisticated l'Officina
is a cultural centre, mounting
excellent contemporary art
exhibitions, as well as a wine bar
and restaurant. Dishes are not
simple, but well thought through,
and without fail delicious.
The beef tartar antipasto is
beautifully presented, with an
exquisite rocket pesto, a quail's
egg, Parmesan and red onion
chutney. Rabbit and tripe feature
in some meaty first and second
courses, but don't miss out on the
wonderful desserts, including a
spectacular raspberry soufflé.
A glass-fronted kitchen means
you can see the performance art
of food preparation going on.

Osteria del Bartolo €€
Via Bartolo 30, T075-571 6027.
Thu-Tue evenings only,
closed most of Aug.
Map: Perugia, E3, p72.
Small, barrel-vaulted and sunk
down from the street, eating at
Bartolo feels like dining in a wine
cellar, and the wine list is suitably
long, with lots of bottles on
display at each end of the room.
Chianina beef (bred in the region
for centuries) is a speciality –
you can have it in a stew or
as carpaccio. The 'fright' fish is
also excellent: tasty and in a
satisfyingly herby batter.

Osteria del Gufo €€
*Via della Viola 18, T075-573 4126,
osteriailgufo.it.*
Tue-Sat 2000-0100, closed Aug.
Map: Perugia, G4, p72.
On a winding back street, Gufo
is well worth seeking out for its
buzzing atmosphere and great
home cooking. Friendly and down
to earth, it mixes Umbrian tradition
and good, seasonal, local
ingredients with a touch of
imagination to make just about
the perfect osteria. There's a good
wine list too, though many will
be happy with the house wine –
fantastic value at €1 a glass.
The menu changes regularly but,
if they're available, try the delicious
maccheroni with smoked sausage
and the wild boar with fennel.
Unusually, the homemade
desserts, such as a much-better-
than-it-sounds potato and almond
pudding, are also very good.

Trattoria del Borgo €€
*Via della Sposa 23a,
T075-572 0390.*
Mon-Sat 1930-2400, closed Aug.
Map: Perugia, C4, p72.
Just off the bottom of via dei
Priori, this popular and friendly
place, with white walls and
wooden beams, is run by a
former butcher and his wife.
Everything is homemade,
from the excellent pasta to
the tasty desserts. In addition
to the traditional menu, daily
specials make good use of
seasonal ingredients. As you
might expect, the meat is very
good, but there are plenty of
vegetarian options too.
Arrive early or book ahead.

Dal Mi' Cocco €
Corso Garibaldi 12, T075-573 2511.
Tue-Sun 1300 onwards,
2015 onwards.
Map: Perugia, E2, p72.
A simple, traditional and popular
place, this offers choice only in
the sense that you can choose
which day to go on. Tuesday is
rice, Thursday gnocchi, but
there's always pasta, and the
second course is usually mixed
grilled meat. €13 gets you very
generous portions and side
dishes and a dessert too.
Wheat sheaves, brick vaulting
and old jazz add some style
and, as you might expect, it's
popular with students, though
it also fills up with Italian families
and businessmen.

Il Bacio €
Via Boncambi 6, T075-572 0909.
Daily 1200-1530, 1900-2430.
Map: Perugia, E4, p72.
You'll need to allow an hour or
so to read through all the pizza
choices, which include turnip
tops. In summer there are tables
outside in the middle of corso
Vannucci for the best front row
seats in town. Service can be
less than attentive, but the
good-sized, tasty pizzas and
the views are well worth it.

Locanda Do' Pazzi €
*Corso Cavour 128, T075-572 0565,
locandadopazzi.it.*
Mon-Sat 1200-1500, 2000-2300.
Map: Perugia, F7, p72.
A cosy trattoria decorated
with an extraordinary chandelier
resembling a sort of upturned
Venus flytrap, and lots of clocks,
none of which tell the right time,
in brick-vaulted rooms on
a corner of corso Cavour.
Do' Pazzi offers bargain
lunches, with two courses
from €9, and tasty fresh
homemade pasta, as well as
traditional meat dishes such
as sausages and broccoli.

Osteria del Tempo Perso €
Via Piacevole 13, T075-572 9831.
Mon-Sat 2030-0300.
Map: Perugia, E2, p72.
One of Perugia's best-value
restaurants is hidden away
near the Università per Stranieri:
take the steps to the right off via
Piacevole and look for the door

under the streetlamp. Slightly self-consciously old-fashioned, it serves wine in pottery cups. Candles and bare stone walls add to the atmosphere, as does the slightly strange mix of ancient Italian pop, jazz and 1970s disco. There is a concise menu of tasty daily specials, or you can book paella in advance.

Pizzeria Mediterranea €
Piazza Piccinino 11/12, T075-572 1322.
Wed-Mon 1230 onwards, 1930 onwards.
Map: Perugia, F2, p72.
A real pizzeria, selling nothing other than pizzas, Mediterranea does the simple things very well, and buzzes for most of the year. There are two rooms, with wooden tables, high, barrel-vaulted ceilings and stone walls, and the big pizza oven is a prime feature. There's plenty of choice, with tasty toppings and lots of fresh ingredients, and both the pizzas and the house wine are excellent value.

Pizzeria Etruschetto €
Corso Garibaldi 17, T075-572 9230.
Mon and Wed-Fri 1200-1430, 1800-2330, Sat-Sun 1800-2400.
Map: Perugia, F2, p72.
Proper Neapolitan pizza, and a proper Neapolitan atmosphere to boot. Eat in or take away, either in traditional rounds or by the metre. Expect a long wait on Friday or Saturday nights if you turn up without a reservation.

Two small rooms are decorated with photos of Naples, and a noisy crowd crams the wooden tables. Drinks are cheap and the pizzas are the some of the best in town.

Porchetta stand €
Piazza Matteotti.
Map: Perugia, E4, p72.
Perugia's cheapest lunch is about as near to fast food as you'll get in the *centro storico.* Most mornings, a van will arrive in piazza Matteotti with a stuffed and roasted pig, and pork rolls will then be sold until the pig has all gone, usually by about 1400.

Cafés & bars
Caffè di Perugia
Via Mazzini 10, T075-573 1863, caffediperugia.it.
Wed-Mon 0730-2400.
Map: Perugia, E5, p72.
Though it can't match the bijou stylishness of Caffè Sandri, Caffè di Perugia is a smart, big, brick-vaulted place in a medieval building that carries off its chandeliers and peach tablecloths with aplomb. There are seats outside, but the cosy interior is

especially suited to winter. You can also eat here, or try some local wines in the *enoteca*

Caffè MedioEvo
Corso Vannucci 70, T075-572 4129.
Fri-Wed 0800-2400.
Map: Perugia, E5, p72.
A place to see and be seen, pricey MedioEvo is the pick of the corso Vannucci cafés. Its tables have pride of place on piazza della Repubblica, and there are good pastries for breakfast and decent snacks on wooden boards at *aperitivo* time. If you don't mind missing the Perugian parade on show outside, the interior is beautiful, with decorated arches and subtle green and red walls.

Caffè Sandri
Corso Vannucci 32, T075-572 4112.
Thu-Tue 0800-2200.
Map: Perugia, E4, p72.
There's old-fashioned elegance and style in abundance here, with glass-fronted wooden cabinets and red-jacketed staff. It's worth having a coffee just to stand at the bar and marvel at the frescoed, vaulted ceiling, but you may also be tempted by the homemade sweets.

Cinastik
Via dei Priori, 39, T075-572 0999, myspace.com/cinastik.
Mon-Sat 1230-1500, 1900-0230.
Map: Perugia, E4, p72.
Perugia's hippest bar, laid-back Cinastik serves cocktails and

wine in a bohemian setting with plenty of Latin charm. There are comfy wicker chairs, a decrepit wooden floor and fantastically eclectic Italian jazzy tunes. Upstairs there's a piano and even the toilet features a candelabra. The mojitos are good and they have Tennents Super on tap. Live music from around 2230.

Cioccolateria Augusta Perusia

Via Pinturicchio 2, T075-573 4577, cioccolatoaugustaperusia.it.
Map: Perugia, F2, p72.
Some of Perugia's best ice cream, and homemade granita – especially good for hot summer afternoons.

Énonè

Corso Cavour 61, T075-572 1950, enone.it.
Wed-Mon 1900-0100.
Map: Perugia, F7, p72.
With dark wood, chrome and disco beats, Énonè is a funky, modern wine bar, with a ceiling wave lit by halogen lights, a long wine list and more than 25 different grappas. The food is also excellent, with a good range of antipasti and dishes such as fusilli with prawns and courgettes, tuna steak with caper berries and cherry tomatoes, or a meat and cheese 'wallet'. Even the coffee menu has several choices. A Sunday brunch buffet from 1100 makes it a great weekend destination.

Frittole Vineria

Via Alessi 30, T338-274 6070.
Tue-Sun 1830-0230.
Map: Perugia, F4, p72.
Whereas other wine bars may be places to be seen, this is a place to drink wine. The atmosphere is amenable and cosy, and the free early evening bar snacks are original and tasty – watch out for the extremely spicy Calabrese paté. The small interior is rib-vaulted and there are nice design touches such as hanging lamps over the bar. Wine racks and old wine boxes line the walls.

Gelateria Gambrinus

Via Luigi Bonazzi 3, T075-573 5620.
Map: Perugia, E5, p72.
Off piazza della Repubblica, the place to go for your *passeggiata* ice cream. Queues testify to the high regard in which this place is held.

Il Birraio

Via delle Prome 18, T075-572 3920, ilbirraio.net.
Tue-Sun 1930-0230.
Map: Perugia, F3, p72.
You walk past the huge vats to enter this microbrewery with a great, relaxed atmosphere and two types of its own beer. It's a surprisingly light, open place, with Arabic influences and a playfulness that combines brightly coloured bird boxes, carefully scratched bar stools, sculpture, dried chillies and lots of cushions. Six international

beers on tap augment the homebrew and there's usually sangria on the go too. *Piadine*, generously big *crostone* and fondue fill the gaps if you're peckish, jazz and blues play, and breastfeeding mothers mix with trendy students.

La Fortezza €€
Vicolo della Fortezza, T075-812418, lafortezzahotel.com.
Tue, Sat-Sun 1230-1430, 1930-2130, Mon, Wed, Fri 1930-2130.
Grilled duck with wild fennel, rabbit with apple sauce, and guinea fowl with truffles are some of the options at this refined restaurant up stairs from piazza Comune near the centre of Assisi, which has barrel-vaulted brick ceilings and a stuffed boar's head to keep you company.

La Lanterna €€
Via San Rufino 39, T075-816399.
Tue-Sun lunch and dinner.
Up a narrow side street off via San Rufino, La Lanterna has candlelit tables outside under big white canvas umbrellas. Pizzas, cooked in a real wood-fired oven by a Neapolitan *pizzaiolo*, are excellent, and there's a three-course pasta and meat menu. Inside it's surprisingly spacious, with white walls and open stonework.

MagnaVino €€
Corso Giuseppe Mazzini, T075-816814.
Tue-Sun 1200-1530, 1800-0200.
With a rare touch of youth in Assisi, this wine bar has put a new spring in the step of the town's evenings. The bar has green pinpricks of light and there

are low, comfortable seats, with a few metal chairs outside too. There are lots of antipasti options, some excellent and generously sized salads (try the radicchio with walnuts and pecorino) and very good pasta too, such as the locally made *taglierini* (thin noodles) with cherry tomatoes, and a very tasty gnocchi with Gorgonzola. The wine list, organized by region, is extensive, with 32 different sparkling wines and even more dessert wines.

Medio Evo €€
Via Arco dei Priori 4, T075-813068, ristorantemedioevoassisi.it.
Tue-Sun 1230-1500, 1900-2245.
A smart, vaulted place down the hill from piazza del Comune, with suited waiters, pristine white tablecloths and low lighting, Medio Evo has a high quality traditional Umbrian menu. There's homemade pasta such as the ubiquitous *strangozzi* with truffles and a good choice of *secondi* such as baked goats' cheese with tomatoes and rosemary, or rabbit cooked in Montefalco wine.

Trattoria Pallotta €€
Vicolo della Volta Pinta 3, T075-812649, pallottaassisi.it.
Wed-Mon 1215-1430, 1915-2130.
With arches and barrel vaults, this is an elegant but good value restaurant off piazza Comune opposite the Minerva Temple. A mix of in-the-know tourists

and locals fill the small tables and are served by exceptionally friendly staff. Unusually for Umbria, there are some excellent choices for vegetarians, with a tasting menu for €24 consisting of three courses of inventive little dishes. There's plenty of choice for carnivores too, with pigeon and veal featuring strongly among the second course options. Ask for a look in the wine cellar below, which dates back to Roman times.

La Stalla €
Via Ermeo delle Carceri 8, T075-812317.
Tue-Sun (daily Jul-Aug) 1230-1430, 1930-2200.
In the roughly converted old stalls of a barn 1.5 km east of Assisi, with walls graffitied and blackened by age and smoke, La Stalla is a rather unlikely success story, but it has remained almost completely unchanged for decades and is clearly doing something right. Waitresses in red aprons work the meat on an open fire, while pasta and bean dishes appear from the kitchen behind. Try the trademark *bigoli*, made from ricotta and spinach.

Cafés & bars
Caffè del Lion d'Oro
Corso Giuseppe Mazzini 11, T075-816420.
Daily 0800-2300.
A good range of ice creams, including a couple of gluten-free options.

Caffè Duomo
Piazza San Rufino 5d, T075-813794.
Just up from piazza San Rufino, Caffè Duomo has round ceramic tables under a giant canvas shade, with jazz and Wi-Fi to go with your *aperitivi*.

Gran Caffè
Corso Giuseppe Mazzini 16a, T075-815 5144.
Summer daily 0800-2300, winter daily 0800-2000.
Few people manage to walk past the spectacular window display of biscuits and pastries – surely Assisi's most photographed – without at least a glance. Inside, its grandness is done in a cartoon fashion, but it's worth putting up with for the cakes.

Lago Trasimeno

Country House Montali €€
Via Montali, 23, Tavernelle di Panicale, T075-835 0680, montalionline.com.
Apr-Nov, dinner served at 2000, reservations required.
One of Umbria's few vegetarian restaurants is in a secluded spot high in the hills to the south of Lake Trasimeno. They take their cuisine very seriously here – this is most certainly not a brown bread and sandals sort of place, but rather a smart restaurant and hotel, which has just launched its own cookery book and also runs cookery classes. Try the saffron risotto, or the aubergine tart with a caper and parsley sauce.

Strangely, vegans pay 20% more. Should you wish to stay, there are also 10 guest rooms, a pool, and great views.

Da Sauro €€
Via Guglielmi 1, Isola Maggiore, T075-826168.
Daily 1200-1500, closed Nov-Feb.
The island's most popular restaurant, at the left-hand end of the main street coming off the boat, Da Sauro has a beautiful shaded garden, but struggles to cope when it gets busy. Dishes include tagliolini pasta with smoked tench and other lake fish. Phone ahead or run from the ferry. If it's full, **Ristorante l'Oso** (T075- 825 4255), at the other end of the street, is a good alternative. Da Sauro also has some rooms to rent.

I Capricci di Merion €€
Via Pozzo 21, Tuoro sul Trasimeno, T075-825002, capriccidimerion.it.
Daily, lunch and dinner.
If the weather is good, the best seats at Capricci di Merion are under the lime trees in the garden, with views down to the lake. Inside, live harp music accompanies meals. The food is Umbrian with a twist – the 'fantasia', for example, features chocolate gnocchi. Pork is served with grilled fennel and all the dishes are artfully presented.

La Cantina €€
Via Emanuele 93, Castiglione del Lago, T075-965 2463, castiglionedellago.eu/cantina.
Daily 1200-1500, 1900-0100.
Despite its huge vaulted interior, most people choose to eat in La Cantina's little garden courtyard, complete with views down to the lake. The food is a draw too – tasty dishes such as roulade of trout and rice pudding with saffron and peach sauce are beautifully presented, and there's a very good-value lunch menu, complete with wine and water, for €13. Don't miss the toilets, which you enter through a giant barrel.

Entertainment

Lillo Tatini €€
Piazza Umberto I 13, Panicale,
T075-837771, lillotatini.it.
Tue-Sun 1230 onwards,
1930 onwards.
At the top of the piazza in
Panicale, the tables in front of
Lillo Tatini have great views of
everything going on below.
The food is imaginative Umbrian,
with dishes such as ravioli with
quails' eggs and ricotta, smoked
tench with rocket, or cannelloni
with lake fish, broccoli and lentils.

Vinolento €€
Via Vittorio Emanuele 112,
Castiglione del Lago,
T075-952 5262, vinolento.it.
Tue-Sun 1230-1430, 1900-0100,
closed 2 weeks in Nov and 2
weeks in Jan.
Castiglione del Lago's most
sophisticated eatery offers daily
specials such as duck breast with
Gorgonzola sauce or *taglierini* (thin
noodles) with spinach and goose
egg. There are tables set back off
the main street in summer, or a
cosier set up, with small square
wooden tables, inside.

Cafés & bars
Caffè della Piazza
Piazza Umberto I 13, Panicale,
T347-994 2530.
Tue-Sun 1000-2000.
On Panicale's piazza, this hip
little café has an enormous
menu of speciality coffees
and teas, as well as cocktails
and *aperitivi*.

Cinema
Teatro del Pavone
Piazza della Repubblica 67,
T075-572 4911,
teatrodelpavone.it.
English language films Mon,
usually at 1800 and 2100, €4.
Umbria and Marche have many
fine old theatres, often with
private boxes and ornate
detailing, but few are as
accessible as Perugia's most
central cinema, in a stunning old
theatre right on corso Vannucci.
Grab an ice cream from **Gelateria**
Gambrinus, a couple of doors
down, or microwave some
popcorn in the machine in the
foyer and choose your own box
for a Monday night showing of
an English language film.

Clubs
Domus
Via del Naspo 3.
Tue-Sun 2300-0500.
Near piazza Morlacchi, this is the
only nightclub in the centre of
Perugia. An intimate, brick-
vaulted place, popular with
students, it has two bars and
a small dance floor.

Loop Café
Via della Viola 19.
Daily 0800-0200.
Effortlessly hip and Perugia's best
spot for live music, Loop is also a
friendly, cosy and alternative bar,
frequented mostly by young
Italians who haven't been
dressed by their mothers.
The music, in a room at the back,
is an international and eclectic
mix – from a Nirvana tribute
band one night to electronica or
gypsy folk the next. Gigs on
Friday and Saturday evenings
and often Wednesdays and
Thursdays too. In the daytime
Loop doubles as a student-
friendly café with added art.

Lunabar Ferrari
Via Scura 6, T075-572 2966,
lunabarferrari.it.
Daily 0800-0200.
Despite the corny name, this is
a hip cosmopolitan cocktail bar,
with DJs playing sets after 2300.
Oversized lamps hang over the
red-lit bar and there are several
rooms for chilling with a young
Perugian crowd. Watch out for
the rocking chairs.

Music
Panicale (T075-837 9531,
panicaleturismo.it) has a good
calendar of baroque and classical
music in its theatre and churches.

Trasimeno Blues
trasimenoblues.it
A week-long programme at
the end of July features
international blues artists
performing in various
locations around the lake.

Listings
Shopping

Perugia

Art & antiques
Mario Cardinali – Rigattiere
Via della Viola 10, T075-572 4639.
Hours vary.
A junk shop of the finest order, Mario has a wonderful treasure trove of everything that the residents of Perugia don't want. If you're looking for a battered old cuddly reindeer, an infrared receipt printer or a stylish 1930s clock, this is the place for you. Ask to see the photo of Mario in 1961, when he was a scooter champion.

Books
Feltrinelli
Corso Vannucci 78/82, T075-572 6485, lafeltrinelli.it.
Mon-Sat 1000-2000; Sun 1000-1330, 1600-2000.
Perugia's best bookshop is right in the centre of the *centro storico*, perfectly placed for air-conditioned browsing.

There are some English-language books, CDs and a decent range of guidebooks among the 40,000 titles.

Clothing
Le Cose di Rita
Via della Viola, T340-493 6889.
Mon-Fri 1600-2000, Sat 1030-1300, 1630-2000.
Well-chosen and attractively displayed vintage clothes at knockdown prices.

Food & drink
Eredi Bavicchi
Via dei Priori 15, T075-572 2633.
Fri-Wed 0900-1300, 1600-2000, Thu 0900-1300.
Many leave Perugia with Perugino Baci chocolates, but much better options are available at this mouth-watering little shop, which has a fine range of artisan, handmade chocolate, alongside other local specialities.

Markets
Mercato Biologico
Piazza Piccinino.
1st Sun morning of each month.
Perugia's monthly organic market has a good range of local fruit and veg, as well as cheese, artisan bread and a few stalls of crafts and handicrafts.

Mercato Coperto
Off piazza Matteotti.
Daily.
What is now piazza Matteotti was once the location for Perugia's market, but a new, purpose-built, three-level covered market has now been constructed outside it. The stalls at piazza level sell bags and shoes – you have to descend to the two lower levels to find meat, fish, fruit and vegetables, usually locally grown, high quality and economical.

Picnics

Head downstairs in the covered market (go through the arch marked '18a' next to the Co-op in piazza Matteotti) to find the best in local fruit and veg. For anything you can't find here, the Co-op upstairs will probably fill the gaps, and next door **Ceccarini** (Mon-Sat 0730-1930, Sun 0900-1330) is an excellent bakery, with a great range of bread, cakes and biscuits – get there early for the best choice.

Photographic supplies
Foto Ottica Fratticcioli
Piazza Italia 10, T075-572 6126.
A proper photography shop,
not a peddler of film and tourist
tat, this has an excellent stock
of cameras, lenses and
equipment plus a wide range
of spare batteries and chargers,
and friendly staff who know
their stuff.

Assisi

Art & antiques
Artestampa
Via San Francesco 10c, T075-815115.
Daily 0930-1300, 1530-1930.
Several cuts above your average
print shop, Gastone Vignati
works here in the back of his
shop, where you can see the
presses on which he prints lino-
and woodcuts of Assisi.

Clothing
Brunelli Felicetti
Vla Arnaldo Fortini 18, T075-816039.
Mon-Sat 0930-1330, 1530-1930,
also Sun from 1030, Easter-Oct
and Dec.
Once upon a time, all Assisi's
shops were like this – rough
wooden floors, a large counter
at the back, goods piled at the
sides. The owner of this excellent
shoe shop will tell you that the
only change since 1922 has
been to replace the original
light fitting. And that they're
planning to change it back.
Aside from nostalgia, they offer
a fine selection of shoes,
especially sandals.

Food & drink
Alimentari
Via San Rufino, T075-816154.
Bread, cheese and ham and just
about everything you might
need for a picnic.

Souvenirs
Arte Legno
Via Arnaldo Fortini 20, T075-815 5219, artelegnospello.com.
Daily, summer 1000-2000,
winter 1000-1900.
Most souvenir shops around
Umbria have a few olive wood
chopping boards, but Arte
Legno has nothing that isn't
made out of the intricately
veined wood, from wooden
spoons to chess sets, including
some beautiful pieces.

Activities & tours

Perugia

Food & wine
Alter Ego
Via Floramonti 2a, T075-572 9527, ristorantealterego.it.
Excellent half-day cookery
courses in English or Italian,
especially in the art of pasta
making. Michele will also
show you how to make a great
tiramisù, and for the bargain
price of €30 you get to cook
and eat everything you've made,
with wine thrown in.

Language courses
Perugia is a popular place to
come to learn Italian. The
Università per Stranieri means that
the infrastructure is good – it's not
too hard to find a flat, and there are
plenty of others to learn with. The

Perugia Calcio

perugiacalciospa.it
After a stint in Serie A, AC Perugia
were relegated in 2004; the
following season, 100 years after
the club was founded, they were
declared bankrupt and ceased
to exist. They were reborn in the
lower divisions as Perugia Calcio
and are currently playing two
levels below the top division in
Serie C. In their prime, local boy
Fabrizio Ravanelli was a big star for
AC Perugia, and Colonel Gaddafi's
son Al-Saadi Qadhafi played for
the team, as did Ahn Jung-Hwan
of Korea, who is famous for
scoring the goal that knocked Italy
out of the 2002 World Cup.

university doesn't do courses less than a month long, however.

Comitato Linguistico
3rd floor, largo Cacciatori delle Alpi 5, T075-572 1471, comitatolinguistico.com.
Corner of piazza Partigiani, between Banca dell'Umbria and Infotourist point.
Courses for all levels, minimum two weeks, €356.

Lingua in Corso
Via del Persico 9, T075-374 5044, linguaincorso.com.
Near north end of Corso Cavour.
One-week courses from €143 for 20 hours, or €209 for 30 hours of tuition.

Università per Stranieri
Piazza Fortebraccio 4, T075-57461, unistrapg.it.
Founded in 1921, when Mussolini wanted to spread Italian culture around the world, Perugia's university for foreigners is now cemented as an important part of the city and teaches language and Italian cultural courses to 7,500 students from around the world every year. Month-long intensive Italian courses run during the summer, €400.

Running
Athletics track
Santa Giuliana, via Orsini, near piazza Partigiana
Perugia has few good running routes – roads out of town are mostly steep and lack much in

the way of pavements – but the athletics track is open to all for €1.50.

Assisi

Language courses
Accademia Lingua Italiana
Via Tiberio d'Assisi 10, T075-815281, aliassisi.it.
Group courses and intensive courses in Italian, including library access, walks and a programme of social events.

Lago Trasimeno

Cycling
There is a 24-km cycle path around the lake, currently from Castiglione del Lago to Torricella, though it may be extended in future. Rent bikes from **Cicli Valentini** (via Firenze 68b, Castiglione del Lago, T075-951663, ciclivalentini.it, Mon-Sat 0900-1300, 1600-2000).

Food & wine
Lago Trasimeno vineyards
There are several Colli del

Trasimeno wine routes that can be driven, cycled or walked around to visit the lake's vineyards and wine cellars. Contact the **Associazione Strada del Vino Colli del Trasimeno** (T075-847411, stradadel vinotrasimeno.it) for maps and further details.

Walking
Tourist information offices around the lake have maps and suggested walks by the lakeside and in the surrounding hills.

Watersports
Kite surfing
Trasimeno's warm, still waters make it a good spot for kite surfing. Lessons are available from **Scuola Kitesurf** (Lido di Tuoro, T346-798 2249, scuolakitesurf.it).

Sailing
Club Velico Castiglionese (via Brigata Garibaldi 48, T075-953035, cvcastiglionese.it) run sailing lessons on the lake.

Transport

Well-being
Le Muse
Villa di Monte Solare, Via Montali 7, Colle San Paolo, Panicale, T075-835 5818, villamontesolare.com.
Daily 0900-1900.

High in the hills to the south of Lake Trasimeno, the location of Le Muse spa and beauty centre has a peaceful and relaxing effect before you walk in the door: it's set in the villa's garden in an old *limonaia*, where lemon trees were once kept in winter. Inside are eight beautifully designed rooms, smiling staff and some great treatments that combine the latest products and trends with Umbrian traditions, such as full-body massages with honey or chocolate. Check the website for good deals that combine spa treatments with meals and accommodation in the Villa di Monte Solare hotel.

Perugia

There are two train lines that serve the city. From Stazione Sant'Anna, to the south of piazza Italia, trains on the privately run Ferrovia Centrale Umbria line serve stations north to Umbertide and Città di Castello, and south to Todi. For mainline trains, the main Fontivegge Station (usually just called Perugia – don't get off at Perugia Ponte San Giovanni, or Perugia Università) is further outside the centre, at piazza Vittorio Veneto (1.5 km southwest of piazza Italia); from here the Minimetrò is useful for getting to and from the centre, there are frequent buses, or you could get a taxi.

Assisi

There are trains every hour or so from Perugia to Assisi (20 mins).

Coming from the south, main line trains from Rome to Ancona stop at Foligno, where you can change for Assisi (15 mins).

Lago Trasimeno

Regular ferry boats leave Castiglione del Lago for **Isola Maggiore** (eight a day in summer, €6.60 return) and San Feliciano, on the eastern shore, for **Isola Polvese** (10 a day in summer, €4.80 return). There are fewer boats in winter – check apmperugia.it. For more luxury, and freedom from the timetable, you could charter your own boat, with the option of strawberries and prosecco on board, from **Navilagando** (T333-570 9373, navilagando.com). Passignano, on the train line at the northern edge of the lake, also has ferries to the islands, but there is less reason to visit the town itself.

Contents

Reserved front row seats in the street, Bevagna.

Introduction

Almost all of Umbria is hilly, which explains the strategic and historical importance of its only sizeable area of flat land – the Valle Umbra, stretching south from Assisi. Once a lake, it is now fertile land, and around its edges is an extraordinary wealth of beautiful walled medieval towns, most built on Roman foundations and little altered for hundreds of years. All repay exploration, with narrow and often cobbled streets leading to ancient churches and sleepy piazzas. The focus point of the area, Spoleto itself has a prestigious classical music festival as well as some great contemporary art, and in the surrounding countryside there are other attractions – Roman remains, ancient springs, abbeys and waterfalls.

To the south and east, the landscape rises towards the high ridge of the Apennines. Here, Norcia is a mountain town famed for its truffles and its butchers. Lentils are grown around nearby Castelluccio, even more remote and surrounded by a swathe of wild flowers in spring. From here the hills of the Sibillini national park stretch east over the border into Marche. This is the wildest part of the region, and boar, wolves and even a bear roam free on mountains that are topped with snow for a good part of the year.

San Francesco, Montefalco.

What to see in...

...one day
Spoleto Is the most obvious centre, and here you could take in some great Renaissance and contemporary art as well as the beautiful **Cattedrale di Santa Maria Assunta** (pause for a drink in the wonderful piazza outside) and the impressive **Roman amphitheatre**. The town's 14th-century **bridge** leads across to wooded hills – a good spot for a stroll. If all this leaves you with any spare time, the surrounding area has diverse attractions, including a man-made waterfall, an isolated abbey and some dusty mummies.

...a weekend or more
A second day in the area would allow a visit to one of the other medieval hill towns: **Spello**, **Montefalco**, **Bevagna** and **Trevi** all have their fans and there are nearby vineyards to explore too. Or, for a taste of a more rugged, upland version of Umbria, head to **Norcia**, at the edge of the Monti Sibillini National Park and on to **Castelluccio** for mountain walks, beech forests and wild boar.

Spello

Like Assisi, Spello is a medieval hill town sitting under Monte Subasio, but with the advantage that it has views both over the Valle Umbra and to the east, over much quieter, more bucolic rolling countryside. There are Roman arches, quiet winding streets, walks up the mountain (and, for the enthusiastic, all the way to Assisi), some stunning Pinturicchio frescoes, and lots of great eating and drinking possibilities.

Most of Spello's sights are near to the main north-south route through the town: from Porta Montanara in the north to Porta Consolare in the south, along via Giulia and via Cavour. Unusually for an Umbrian town, the cobbled streets of the old centre are not closed to traffic, so you'll need to dodge some cars and mopeds. The central piazza della Repubblica is the focus of the old town, but an anomalous disappointment as two of its sides are taken up with ugly 20th-century buildings. The rest of the town is more beautiful, criss-crossed with sloping, stone-paved streets and built in the pastel-shaded limestone of Monte Subasio.

Roman arches & amphitheatre

Around town are a number of ancient Roman arches, in various states of decay. The Roman town of Hispellum was an important base – the religious centre of Umbria under Emperor Constantine. The **Porta Consolare** is the main gateway, at the bottom of town, with three Roman statues decorating its exterior. These were added in the 17th century, having been taken from Spello's **amphitheatre**. The **Porta Venere**, west of piazza della Repubblica, is the most impressive, with two pale limestone dodecagonal towers flanking the arch. Also worth a look is the **Arco dei Cappuccini** (also known as the Porta dell'Arce), just below the highest point of Spello – small but with two complete arches. You can make out the grooves cut into the side by the portcullis that would once have been raised and lowered here. Just to the south you can look down on the ruins of the Roman amphitheatre, suitably juxtaposed with a modern running track.

Chiesa di Santa Maria Maggiore

Piazza Matteotti.
Daily 0830-1900, free.

Pinturicchio's exquisite frescoes in the **Cappella Baglioni** lift Spello's most famous church from being a relatively unremarkable building in a hotchpotch of styles, overlaid with baroque extravagance. It's hard not to be drawn in to the painter's masterpiece, which is colourful and full of energy and intriguing details. Watched over by four expressive Sybils on the ceiling are depictions of (from left to right) the *Annunciation*, the *Nativity* and the *Dispute with the Doctors*. There is a self-portrait in the far corner of the *Annunciation*; other details to look out for include ships sailing on a distant sea and an obstinate donkey being pulled across a drawbridge.

Essentials

⟳ Getting around Traffic is restricted in the centre: there's a small, free car park outside Porta Montanara, the gate at the north of the town.

⊜ Buses Buses run from Perugia and Assisi, but the train is usually a faster option.

☺ Trains From Spello station (often unstaffed) it is a relatively easy, if uphill, walk into the town.

⊕ Hospital Via Massimo Arcamone, Foligno, T0742-339 7408.

✛ Pharmacy Bartoli, via Cavour 63, T0742-301488.

⌕ Post office Piazza della Repubblica, T0742-300811.

❶ Tourist information office Piazza Matteotti 3, T0742-301009, comune.spello.pg.it, summer 0930-1230, 1530-1730, winter 0930-1230, 1530-1730.

Around the region

Chiesa di Sant'Andrea

Via Cavour.
Daily 0930-1900, free.

Built in the 13th century, the Church of Sant'Andrea has another Pinturicchio masterpiece, painted in 1507 and 1508, depicting the *Madonna and Child with Saints*: Lorenzo, Francesco, Ludovico, Andrea and, below, a young John the Baptist. Look for the light switch to the right, with a request for donations. Pinturicchio's father was a wool carder, and his well-observed interest in textiles and fabrics is obvious. Also in the church is a beautiful but badly lit 1565 painting by Dono Doni, reminiscent of Raphael.

Pinacoteca Civica

Palazzo dei Canonici, piazza Matteotti, T0742-301497.
Tue-Sun Apr-Sep 1030-1230, 1530-1800, Oct-Mar 1030-1230, 1530-1730, €2.60.

Spello's picture gallery, next to Santa Maria Maggiore, has a beautiful wooden *Madonna*, seated and waving, with her baby on her knee, from around 1240. Other highlights include Andrea d'Assisi's 1503 fresco from the Chiesa di San Bernardino, and a 16th-century terracotta *Pietà*, possibly of German origin. A wooden Christ from the early 14th century has movable arms, which allowed the same sculpture to be used as a crucified and a deposed figure. It was discovered in a storeroom in Santa Maria Maggiore in 1974.

Villa Fidelia

Via Flaminia 72, T0742-651726.
Jul-Aug daily 1030-1300, 1600-1900, Apr-Jun and Sep Thu-Sun 1030-1300, 1530-1800, Oct-Mar Sat-Sun 1030-1300, 1500-1800, €3/2 concession.

Just outside the town to the north, inside the yellow walls of early 19th-century Villa Fidelia, is the eclectic **Straka-Coppa Collection** of 19th- and 20th-century art and furniture. There are beautiful formal Italian gardens too, built on an ancient Roman site, and the villa sometimes hosts events – in 2008 Nick Cave played here.

This page: View down the hill, Spello. Opposite page: *Saint Joachim meets Saint Anne* by Dono Doni.

Monte
Subasio

Rising high above the Valle Umbra between Spello and Assisi, Monte Subasio is one of Umbria's most easily accessed bits of highland countryside. Within a couple of minutes of leaving Spello's northeast gate, Porta Montanara, you are in the midst of olive groves, with great views over the surrounding countryside and the Valle Umbra. Higher up, beyond deciduous woods, you come out on to bare hillside, where the only things that break the vast grassy landscape are a few grazing cows and the occasional monk bent earnestly against the slope. In winter the summit is usually snowbound, but in spring it is covered in wild flowers. St Francis used to come up here to meditate, and it's easy to see why – it seems a place detached from the world below.

The walk uphill is fairly hard going, though the woods are beautiful, especially in spring and autumn. It's possible to reach the top of the mountain in a car – the road into the regional park closes after dark, but during the day it's an exhilarating drive up above the tree line. At a certain point the road becomes gravel, but you can keep going all the way up and down the other side to Assisi, where you arrive at the Porta Cappuccini.

Various parking spots along the way also mean that you can drive some of the way up and then leave the car and continue on foot. To do the whole walk (about 20 km, or 6 hrs), you'll need Kompass map 663, or another good map of Subasio. The tourist information office in Spello provides a photocopied map, but it's fairly indistinct.

Leaving Spello through Porta Montanara, the road continues northeast – if you're driving, continue along here for about 4 km before turning left up a steep and winding road, signposted to Subasio Camping. For the walk, take the second right, via Bulgarella, towards Collepino, and you will soon come across a board on the left with a map of Monte Subasio detailing cycling and walking routes. Take the straight path up through the olive groves, following waymarked path 50, bending left and then right again after about 1 km and entering the Subasio

park just under the peak of Monte Pietrolungo. Keeping the peak on your right you leave the olives behind and cross a rocky part of the hillside before entering oak and beech woods. Branch left when you reach a junction in a clearing. From here the path continues to the spring of Fonte Bregno (around 3 hrs) with occasional expansive views through the trees across the Umbrian plain far below. After the spring you emerge from the trees and climb diagonally across the mountain towards the summit.

Subasio is a loaf-shaped mountain, and it's not always clear where the exact summit is – to reach it, branch right off the path towards the radio masts, crossing the road (which is unsurfaced by this point). At the very top is a trig point, and map boards identifying the various mountains on the horizon. Just below here is the place from which paragliders fling themselves off the mountain: if you're lucky you'll see them taking off.

Return to the mountain bike path, which follows the contours around the slope of the hill to Rifugio Vallonica (around 4 hrs 30 mins) and then bend left down a valley towards the **Eremo delle Carceri** (T075-812301, eremocarceri.it), a Franciscan hermitage set up by St Francis himself. It is now home to friars and Poor Clares and open to visitors – ask one of the friars for a guided visit.

From the hermitage, follow the road to the right (west) for about 1 km before branching off to the left on a rocky path that leads down through woods to Porta Cappuccini at the top of Assisi. Just down the road from Porta Cappuccini is piazza Matteotti, from where you can get a bus to the train station for the return to Spello.

Bevagna

A rare flat Umbrian town, Bevagna loses no charm through its lack of slopes. Originally Umbrian, then Etruscan, it became the Roman town of Mevania, on the via Flaminia, which reached here in 220 BC. Much of its current structure is medieval, and it has largely intact walls that still enclose almost the whole of the contemporary town. At its centre, piazza Silvestri is a beautiful spot, with two notable Romanesque churches and the Palazzo Consoli, the consul's building, adapted to contain a theatre in the 19th century.

The town's Roman past can be seen in a stunning mosaic, and the structural outline of an amphitheatre is also visible. A summer festival revives medieval trades, and hand paper-making can be seen in action throughout most of the year. Bevagna's position in the middle of wine-growing country means it has good *enoteche*, and the food is also excellent. It remains a quiet, relatively undiscovered town, with plenty of scope for peaceful wandering.

Piazza Silvestri

Bevagna's central point has a great ensemble of medieval buidings. Palazzo dei Consoli, dating back to 1187, was once the seat of the town magistrate. Following earthquake damage, when the interior of the building was destroyed, the Teatro Francesco Torti (see below) was built inside.

San Silvestro is a beautiful 12th-century Romanesque church built in pale stone, with sturdy convex columns and a raised chancel. Above the door to the right, an engraved stone shows the date of completion of the church – 1195. The column just inside the door on the right was once the foundation for a bell tower above. On the walls down to the light and airy crypt there are some fragments of frescoes.

The Chiesa di San Michele Arcangelo, built in the 12th and 13th centuries, dominates the piazza with its square façade, triple frieze arch around the door and big round window. Inside it's less impressive, with more modern elements mixing with the Romanesque columns and arches.

Museo & Mosaico Romano

Corso Matteotti 70, T0742-360031.
Daily Jun-Jul 1030-1300, 1530-1900, Aug 1030-1300, 1500-1930, Apr-May and Sep 1030-1300, 1430-1800, Oct-Mar Tue-Sun 1030-1300, 1430-1700, €3.50 including tour of mosaic and theatre.

Bevagna's museum and art gallery has a collection of mainly 17th-century art and an archaeological section (closed at the time of writing) that includes some pre-Roman pieces. Both are overshadowed, however, by the nearby mosaic floor of the one-time frigidarium of the Roman public baths. Visitable only by guided tour from the museum, it features sea monsters, octopuses and lobsters. A ticket for the museum also entitles you to a tour of the Teatro Francesco Torti (T0742-361667), a tiny but perfectly formed theatre built in 1886 inside the medieval Palazzo dei Consoli: it has a busy calendar of drama and music.

Essentials

❶ Getting around Three or four buses arrive daily from Foligno, the nearest train station. There is free parking just outside the gates at the northern edge of the town.

⊕ Hospital Via Massimo Arcamone, Foligno, T0742-339 7408.

❷ Post office Corso Matteotti, T0742-361568.

❶ Tourist information office Piazza Silvestri, proloco.bevagna@infinito.it, summer 0930-1300, 1500-1900, winter 0930-1300, 1500-1800.

Above: Teatro Francesco Torti.
Opposite page: Paper museum.

Circuito culturale dei mestieri medievali

ilmercatodellegaite.it.
Apr-Nov, Tue-Fri 1030-1230, 1600-1800, Sat-Sun 1000-1230, 1600-1830, €3 for all 4 trades, or €1 each.

During the last week in June, Bevagna's summer festival, the Mercato delle Gaite, revolves around the revival of medieval trades, and some of these can also be seen in action during the rest of the year. The highlight is the medieval paper factory on the square, where handmade paper is still made more or less in the way it was at the time when the first copies of Dante's *Inferno* were printed in nearby Foligno. A waterwheel turns a wooden pulping machine and the whole process is enthusiastically explained. Elsewhere in town there is a candlestick maker, a weaver and a painter.

Montefalco

Marketed as the 'balcony of Umbria', medieval Montefalco sits on a hill on the western side of the Valle Umbra. The 360° views advertised may be a little hyperbolic, but there are certainly some spectacular vistas. There is more exaggeration in the signs at the outskirts of Montefalco: 'wine city, oil city', it says, but in fact it's a small place, not much more than a village, though it has produced six saints in its time, and countless bottles of wine. The most respected wine centre in Umbria, the town is surrounded by vineyards growing the Sagrantino grape, and there are plenty of places to sample and buy the tasty red stuff.

The supernumerary Montefalco saints mean that the town has some impressive, and well-frescoed, churches, though the best are reserved for Assisi's St Francis, who gave his famous sermon to the birds nearby. The Church of San Francesco is now a part of the town's worthwhile museum, which also exhibits contemporary art, archaeology and some wine paraphernalia.

Below: Onion seller, Montefalco. Opposite page: Paolo Bea Vineyard, near Montefalco.

Compleso Museale di San Francesco

Via Ringhiera Umbra 6, T0742-379598.
Daily Aug 1030-1300, 1500-1930, Jun-Jul
1030-1300, 1500-1900, Mar-May and Sep-Oct
1030-1300, 1400-1800; Nov-Feb Tue Sun
1030-1300, 1430-1700, €5.

Combining the frescoed Church of San
Francesco, the town's museum and art gallery
and a contemporary art space, San Francesco is
Montefalco's one proper sight.

There is no shortage of art in the church,
including Perugino's colourful, pastoral *Nativity*,
but Benozzo Gozzoli's *Scenes from the Life of
St Francis* in the apse steal the show. Gozzoli's rich
and intriguing stories were painted in 1452 and are
considered to be one of the most important cycles
of Renaissance frescoes.

Downstairs, the so-called monks' wine cellar
contains various old utensils and equipment for
the manufacture of wine, though the opaque
translations into English are less than informative.
Also here are fragments of engraved stones and
pilasters and a handsome first-century AD Roman
funeral altar. Finally downstairs, the *spazi espositivi*
are three large barrel-vaulted spaces devoted to
temporary – and often good – exhibitions of
contemporary art.

Upstairs, in the Pinacoteca, look out for works
by local Renaissance artist Francesco Melanzio,
including a downcast *Virgin with Six Saints*.

Favourite things

Fine winery

Cantina Paolo Bea
Località Cerrete 8, Montefalco,
T0742-378128, paolobea.com.
Visits and tastings by appointment, €50 per person
(€40 per person for groups of 3 or more).

The Cantina Paolo Bea is truly the best winery
to visit in the region. It's an expensive day out,
but you get not only the individual attention of
the winery's architect and enologist, but all his
passion and enthusiasm too.

You also get to taste some very fine wines
indeed, including a Sagrantino and a Sagrantino
passito. The processes here are not just organic, they
go further: avoiding the use of nutrients, using only
natural drying, cultivating only indigenous varieties,
sourcing new plants only from existing ones, and
doing everything possible to work with natural
processes rather than against them. This may
sound a little like new-age winemaking, but
it is actually very hi-tech, and very effective.

Giampiero, son of the titular Paolo, is an architect
as well as a wine enthusiast, and the new cantina
they have built just outside Montefalco is a prime
example of creative, sustainable, imaginative
industrial architecture, with special ducts to bring
in air from outside and water channels to regulate
the humidity.

On a tour of the winery they explain not just
the processes, but also the philosophy behind the
company. Giampiero says that he doesn't like to
analyse too much: "I don't want to know what sort
of flower I can taste in the wine," he says, "I'm more
interested in how it makes me feel."

The whole process from grape to bottle is
slower and more thoughtful here than in the average
winery – the wine is bottled, not on a fixed schedule,
but once it is ready. The Paolo Bea process feels a
little like a religion, with the grape as the object
of worship and the new cantina as its chapel.
Such devotion, coupled with the latest technology,
creates some superlative results. Once you've been
here, you may not be able to look at a bottle of wine
in the same way again.

Around the region

Piazza del Comune

The centre of Montefalco life, and home to some good wine bars and shops, piazza del Comune is dominated by the town hall, the **Palazzo Comunale**, with an arcaded façade. Look out too for the ex-church of **San Filippo Neri**, now a theatre.

Chiesa di Sant'Agostino

Via Ringhiera Umbra.

A church with a cloister built in the 13th century, Sant'Agostino is notable for its enormous permanent nativity scene, and, bizarrely juxtaposed, a macabre collection of three mummified bodies of holy pilgrims. Flick the switch to turn on the nativity lights and to set the windmill turning and the angels flying, before studying the desiccated faces and wizened toes of the church's oldest residents. Beato Pellegrino, the first of the three, had apparently come to worship the other two, Illuminata and Chiara, when he died in the church. It is said that his body did not decay for 100 years. Should three dead bodies not be enough, you can also visit the cadaver of one of the local saints, Chiara of Montefalco, in the nearby church dedicated to her.

Five of the best
Local wines

❶ Orvieto Classico.

❷ Montefalco Sagrantino.

❸ Verdicchio.

❹ Rubesco di Torgiano.

❺ Sagrantino passito.

Visiting vineyards

Ask at Montefalco tourist information office (piazza del Comune 17, T0742-378490, stradadelsagrantino. com, daily 0900-1300, 1400-1800) for maps and information on local vineyards to visit. The office specializes in vineyards and wine tastings, but can also supply other info. Vineyards are usually open 0900-1230, 1500-1800, but ring ahead to check.

Vineyard near Bevagna.

Trevi

Perched high above the valley floor, Trevi is in many ways the archetypal medieval Umbrian hill town. Almost entirely closed to traffic, the old centre – enclosed within Roman and medieval walls – is remarkably quiet; during siesta you might think it uninhabited.

Much of the town's magic is to be found wandering up and down the narrow cobbled streets and steps: happening upon fragments of ancient fresco, glimpsing views of the valley below and watching angular shadows move across the walls. There are also some sights – notably the cathedral, a convent converted into a museum complex, a couple of out-of-town churches that contain significant Renaissance frescoes by Perugino and Lo Spagna and a good contemporary art centre.

Trevi is surrounded by swathes of olive groves, and oil is everywhere in its shops and restaurants. The town is also proud of its 'black' celery, harvested and sold in autumn, though other than its marginally darker green leaves, you may struggle to notice much difference from conventional celery.

Nearby, ancient springs flow out of the ground at Clitunno, a beautiful spot where Roman emperors once held parties; there are good walks and cycle rides in the surrounding countryside.

Complesso Museale San Francesco di Trevi

Largo Don Bosco 14, T0742-381628.
Apr-May and Sep Tue-Sun 1030 1300, 1430-1800,
Jun-Jul Tue-Sun 1030-1300, 1530-1900, Aug daily
1030-1300, 1500-1930, Oct-Mar Fri-Sun 1030-
1300, 1430-1700, €4.

The ex-convent now contains a complex of
museums under one roof. One ticket admits you
to the **Museo della Civiltà dell'Olivo** (Museum of
Olive Culture), the paintings in the **Pinacoteca** and
archaeological finds in the **Antiquarium**, as well as
the **Chiesa di San Francesco** itself.

The most extensive and interesting section is
the olive oil museum, downstairs. In places it is a
strange mix of dense text on the organoleptic
qualities of olives and childish interactive trivia
quizzes, but it's a well-designed museum, and
there is enough of interest to make it worth a visit.

The highlights of the art gallery are works by
Perugino, Pinturicchio and Lo Spagna, whose 1522
Coronation of the Virgin also features, on the predella,
St Francis receiving the stigmata and St Martin
sharing his cloak. The church has a frescoed cloister
and a beautiful, elaborately decorated 14th-century
organ. The archaeological section is less impressive,
despite a Roman sarcophagus and the skeletal
remains of a seventh-century Umbrian inhabitant.

Cattedrale di Sant'Emiliano

Via della Rocca.
Daily 0900-1200, 1600-1800, free.

In the very centre of the town, Trevi's Duomo,
dedicated to local saint, Emiliano, was built in
the 12th century and extended in the 15th.
The 19th-century rebuilding of the interior left
little of beauty, apart from an elaborate stone
altar from 1522, on the left of the nave. Just to the
right of this, look out too for a framed fragment of
original fresco by Melanzio. Opposite, if the door is
open, you can enter a small, dim, frescoed space
labelled 'Antica Abside'. Walled off by the baroque
restoration, it gives a tantalizing glimpse of the
original church.

Tip...

Getting to Trevi by public transport can be
challenging. The train station is about 4 km from the
town centre and there are few buses to get you up
the steep hill into the old town. If you're coming by
car there's parking around piazza Garibaldi, to the
east of the walls.

Steps lead up the steep Trevi slopes.

Above: Cattedrale di Sant'Emiliano. Opposite page: Fonti del Clitunno.

Palazzo Lucarini

Via Beato Placido Riccardi 11, T0742-381021, officinedellumbria.it.
Tue-Sun 1600-1900, free.

Opposite the Duomo, the bare white walls of the Palazzo Lucarini make a good exhibition space for contemporary art. The temporary shows here are often of high quality and make a refreshing change for anyone tiring of a diet of Gothic and Renaissance religious art.

Chiesa della Madonna delle Lacrime

Via Madonna delle Lacrime, 1 km south of Trevi.
Opening hours vary.

In 1485, so it is claimed, tears of blood flowed from the eyes of a painted Virgin in a shrine in a wall on this site. A huge church was subsequently built here, completed in 1522 and frescoed by Perugino (*Adoration of the Magi*, 1521, on the right of the nave) and Lo Spagna (*The Carrying of Jesus to the Tomb*, 1520, in the left transept). To get to the church, leave town by the Porta del Cieco or the Porta della Strada Nuova and head downhill through the olive groves.

Chiesa di San Martino

1 km north of Trevi.

Overlooking the valley, the convent of San Martino has more frescoes by Lo Spagna. Walk along viale Augusto Ciuffelli from piazza Garibaldi for about 10 minutes to reach the church.

In 1485, so it is claimed, tears of blood flowed from the eyes of a painted Virgin in a shrine in a wall on this site.

Fonti del Clitunno

*Via Flaminia 7, Località Fonti del Clitunno,
T0743-521141, fontidelclitunno.com.*
Daily Jan-Feb 1000-1300,1400-1630, 1 Mar-15
Mar 0900-1300,1400-1800, 16 Mar-31 Mar
0900-1300, 1400-1830, 1 Apr-15 Apr 0900-1930,
16 Apr-30 Apr 0900-2000, May-Aug 0830-2000,
1 Sep-15 Sep 0830-1930, 16 Sep-30 Sep
0900-1930, Oct 0900-1300, 1400-1800,
Nov-Dec 1000-1300, 1400-1630, €2.
About 8 km south of Trevi, off SS3 to Spoleto.

The springs of Clitunno have been a well-known
beauty spot for centuries, and Roman Emperor
Caligula used to come here for parties. Several
springs flow out from the rocks and into large,
clear pools, where ducks swim among the rippling
reflections of the trees. A bar, café and shop have
sprung up since Roman times, but it remains a very
pretty spot, peaceful despite the traffic on the road.

Tempietto sul Clitunno

Campello sul Clitunno.
Apr-Oct 0845-1945, Nov-Mar 0845-1745, €2.

About 500 m north of the springs, this early
Christian temple is well hidden (and badly
signposted) off the main road. Turn left off the
SS3 and then immediately right. The temple is a
further 400 m or so along this road.

A small building set in lush grass above the water
that flows down from the springs, the temple was
built using ancient Roman pillars and stones and
there are disagreements about its age – estimates
range from the fourth to the 13th century.

Spoleto & the lower Valnerina

While Perugia swings along to its summer jazz festival, Spoleto has a more sedate, but equally high quality, classical music festival. Which seems fitting for a town with such a refined air, famous for its elegant 14th-century bridge and its Duomo. Spoleto's arts credentials run deep – not only does it have some great Renaissance art, it has had a long and happy relationship with modern sculpture, and its contemporary art gallery is excellent.

Across Spoleto's spectacular 14th-century bridge, the Ponte delle Torri, to the east of the town, wooded hills and the lower reaches of the Valnerina are an area of semi-wilderness, with a spectacular ancient abbey and where waterfalls created by the Romans are now turned on and off at the flick of a switch. River walks and a museum of mummies are other attractions in the area.

Below: Cattedrale di Santa Maria Assunta, Spoleto. Opposite page: Rocca Albornoziana.

Cattedrale di Santa Maria Assunta

Piazza del Duomo, T0743-231063.
Daily Apr-Oct 0830-1230, 1530-1900,
Nov-Mar 0830-1230, 1530-1900, free.

The beautiful façade of Spoleto's Duomo, which forms the backdrop to the finale of the Spoleto festival, has eight rose windows and a newer Renaissance portico. The cathedral was built in the 12th century; the portico was added in 1491. The long piazza makes a fine concert venue, as well as a marvellous approach. Inside, there are some great works of art: Fra Filippo Lippi's frescoes of the *Life of the Virgin* on the wall behind the altar are spectacular, and there's an excellent Pinturicchio *Madonna and Child* in the Cappella Eroli. There's also some impressive intarsia (inlaid wood) work in the side chapel at the end on the right, and a beautiful ancient marble floor. Look too for a letter from St Francis in a chapel on the left-hand aisle.

Filippo Lippi, one of the great Renaissance artists, died in 1469 in Spoleto, and the frescoes in the apse of the duomo were his last work. Stories abound that he was poisoned – there seems little evidence for this, though he did make enemies during his life. He was buried in the south transept. In the scene of the *Transition of the Virgin* in the centre of the cycle, the man in a white monk's habit and black hat is Lippo Lippi himself – the angel in front of him is his son Filippino, who would become a famous painter.

Rocca Albornoziana

Piazza Campello, T0743-223055, sistemamuseo.it.
Rocca: Jul-15 Sep Mon 1000-2000, Tue-Sun 0900-2000, Apr-14 Jul and 16 Sep-31 Oct Mon 1000-1800, Tue-Wed and Sun 0900-1800, Thu-Sat 0900-1930, Nov-Mar Tue-Wed and Sun 0900-1700, Thu-Sat 0900-1745; Museo Nazionale del Ducato di Spoleto: Apr-Oct Tue-Wed and Sun 0900-1330, Thu-Sat 0900-1930, Nov-Mar Tue-Wed and Sun 0900-1330, Thu-Sat 0900-1930, €6/3 concession, free EU citizens under 18 and over 65.

High above the town and one of the most impressive of the Albornoz fortresses that dot the

Around the region

hilltops of the Valle Umbra – built to exert papal control in the 14th century – Spoleto's castle has been undergoing restoration ever since it ceased to be a prison in 1982. Mehmet Ali Ağca, the would-be assassin of Pope John Paul II in 1981, was held here.

These days it is home to the **Museo Nazionale del Ducato di Spoleto**. The museum has early Christian and monastic exhibits and some rare artefacts from the Duchy of Spoleto in the sixth, seventh and eighth centuries. A beautifully carved Romanesque stone panel, in which two angels emerge from what were once ancient Roman columns, is among the highlights of the Romanesque and Gothic section. The influence of Giotto is visible in the Piccolomini Apartment, which contains Gothic paintings and sculpture and Renaissance art that was once held in Spoleto's now defunct Pinacoteca.

When the Rocca is open but the museum closed, visitors can access the Cortile d'Onore and the Camera Pinta, decorated with early 15th-century frescoes telling a tale of a rather sad-looking knight.

Ponte delle Torri

The Bridge of Towers, 250 m across and, at its highest point, 80 m tall, is Spoleto's must-see sight, and one of Italy's engineering wonders. Built as an aqueduct in the 14th century, possibly on Roman foundations, the bridge is a short walk east of town, just beyond the Rocca. It has spectacular views down into the wooded valley below and across to the Basilica of San Pietro, and makes a great entry point to the excellent network of paths and trails that wind through the woods around **Monteluco**.

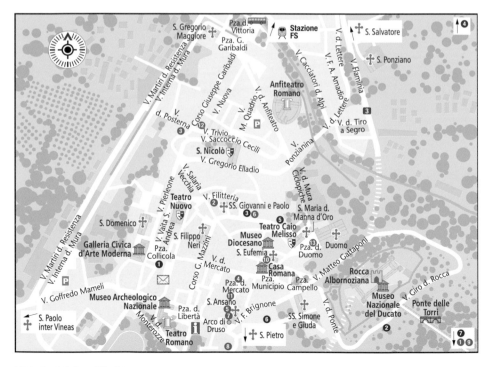

Basilica di San Pietro

Strade Statale Flaminia 3, T0743-49796.
Daily 1000-1200, 1530-1700, free.

A 15-minute walk down from the far side of Ponte delle Torri, or around 10 minutes from piazza della Libertà, the grand but isolated church of San Pietro has a fascinating storyboard of a façade, covered in 12th-century Romanesque bas relief. Grizzly highlights include a man dying a horrible death, helped on by two devils and abandoned by the Archangel Michael, second down on the left. Above, a presumably more righteous person passes away more pleasantly. There are various lions coming face-to-face with humans, and, in some cases, eating them, and there are illustrations of fables involving foxes, wolves, crows and dragons. It's a rich mix of legend and religion, and quite a contrast to the rather dull interior.

It's a rich mix of legend and religion, and quite a contrast to the rather dull interior.

Spoleto listings

❶ Sleeping
1 **Charleston** *piazza Collicola 10*
2 **Gattapone** *via del Ponte 6*
3 **Il Panciolle** *via del Duomo 3*
4 **Le Terre di Poreta** *Località Poreta*
5 **Palazzo Dragone** *via del Duomo 13*
6 **Palazzo Leti** *via degli Eremiti 10*
7 **San Pietro in Valle** *Ferentillo*

❶ Eating & drinking
1 **Al Cantico** *San Pietro in Valle*
2 **Cantina de'Corvi** *piazzetta S S Giovanni e Paolo*
3 **Emporio** *via Porta Fuga 22*
4 **Gelateria Primavera** *piazza del Mercato 7*
5 **Il Mio Vinaio** *via Arco di Druso 8*
6 **Il Panciolle** *vicolo degli Eroli1*
7 **Il Tempio del Gusto** *via Arco di Druso 11*
8 **L'Angolo Antico** *via Monterone 109*
9 **Osteria Baciafemmine** *vicolo Baciafemmine, Scheggino*
10 **Osteria dell'Enoteca** *via Saffi 7*
11 **Osteria del Matto** *vicolo del Mercato 3*
12 **Osteria del Trivio** *via del Trivio 16*
13 **Tric Trac** *piazza Duomo 10*

Museo Archeologico e Teatro Romano

Via Sant'Agata, T0743-223277.
Mon-Sat 0830-1930, €4.

The Roman theatre is still used for performances, especially during the Spoleto Festival (see page 48). Dating from the first century AD and excavated from 1954-1960, it is 70 m in diameter. The first two steps, at the bottom of the theatre, are lower and wider and were probably reserved for Roman VIPs.

Alongside the theatre, a well-laid-out and displayed archaeological museum has two engraved Roman stones forbidding the cutting down of trees in the holy woods of Monteluco, just outside Spoleto. Other highlights include a sensuous but headless female Roman statue revealing one breast, Emperor Augustus's marble head (with a missing nose) and some beautiful eighth-century BC bronze jewellery.

Casa Romana

Via di Visiale, T0743-234250.
Mid-Mar-mid-Oct daily 1000-1300, 1500-1830, mid-Oct-mid-Mar €2.50.

Built just above the ancient forum, where piazza Mercato stands today, a passage leads underground into what must have once been an important Roman house. Indeed it just might have belonged to Vespasia Polla, mother of Emperor Vespasian. A central courtyard has an *impluvium* –

The 14th-century Ponte delle Torri.

a basin for collecting water, which feeds into a cistern. Around this are seven rooms, all with beautiful black and white Roman mosaics of geometric patterns.

Arco di Druso

Via Arco di Druso.

Just off the piazza del Mercato, the Roman arch was built in AD 23 to mark the military victories of Drusus, son of Tiberius. Drusus was set to become emperor but died at the age of 36, probably poisoned by his wife and an accomplice.

Next to the arch are some stones signposted as a temple – for a better view of its remnants, go down into the medieval **Cripta di Sant'Isacco** under the **Chiesa di Sant'Ansano** (daily, 0730-1200, 1500-1830, free) next door, where St Isaac's carved stone sarcophagus is also well worth a look.

Galleria Civica d'Arte Moderna

Palazzo Collicola, Piazza Collicola, T0743-46434. Wed-Mon 16 Mar-14 Oct 1030-1300, 1530-1900, 15 Oct-15 Mar 1030-1300, 1500-1730, €4/1.50 concession.

In 1962 Spoleto held a sculpture festival, for which 104 pieces of contemporary sculpture were placed around the town. Some are still there, for example at the top of piazza del Duomo and outside the train station. The festival cemented a link between the town and contemporary art, and this museum, which opened in 2000, is one of the best in the region.

Alexander Calder's mobiles set the tone – colourful and playful, they compel the viewer to blow at them. Fifteen rooms of sculpture and paintings include work by Henry Moore, Pietro Ruggeri and a group of local artists, including Leoncillo, whose twisted, melting Roman column is memorable, and de Gregorio, whose thick,

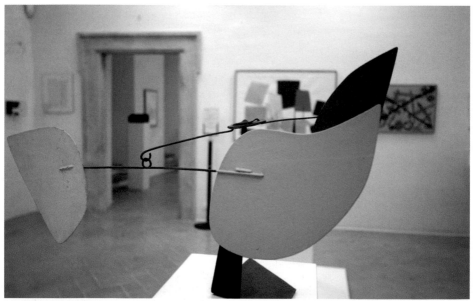

Galleria Civica d'Arte Moderna.

Walks in the hills

To the east of Spoleto a network of paths criss-crosses through the hills, thickly wooded with holm oak. The tourist information office in piazza Libertà has some basic free maps and guides.

To reach the paths, cross the Ponte delle Torri, turn right and go up the steps beside the tower. Here you may have to duck through the broken fence of a slow-going-on-abandoned restoration project, but after that the trails are well marked and well maintained. The path left from here heads past the outskirts of Spoleto, with good views back to the bridge and Rocca, before turning right up a beautifully peaceful wooded valley.

For mountain bikers there are tougher tracks up and down through the trees and for those in need of a little more exercise, the first couple of kilometres have exercise frames beside the main path.

heavily brush-marked canvases draw you in. Pino Pascali's lighthearted *Coda di Cetaceo* (whale's tail)won first prize in the 1966 festival, and Sol Lewitt's *Bands of Colour*, painted in 2000, fills an entire room with bright stripes.

Museo Diocesano & Basilica di Sant'Eufemia

Via Aurelio Saffi, T0743-231022, museiecclesisastici.it. Aug daily 1000-1800, mid-Mar-Jul and Sep-Oct Mon-Fri 1000-1300, 1500-1800, Sat-Sun 1000-1800, Nov-mid-Mar Tue-Fri 1030-1300, 1500-1730, Sat-Sun 1100-1700, €3/2.50/2 concession.

A small picture gallery, Spoleto's diocesan museum has some good religious paintings, such as Filippino Lippi's *Madonna and Child with Sts Montano and Bartolomeo* from 1485. Look for the tiny picture underneath that shows a bear helping to pull a plough, having killed one of the oxen – a story from the life of St Montano. Andrea da Caldaroa's *Annunciation* (1543) has echoes of Pinturicchio in its botanical detail.

The real star of the show, however, is the Church of Sant'Eufemia, one of the region's most beautiful Romanesque buildings, built in the 12th century and open only to visitors to the museum. You enter halfway up the church, on an unusual raised gallery that runs around three sides and was once reserved for women. A couple of the columns have faded frescoes, but for the most part it is bare, making it easier to appreciate the light, elevated structure of the church.

Basilica di San Salvatore

Piazza Mario Salmi 1, T0743-49606. May-Aug 0700-1900, Mar-Apr and Sep-Oct 0700-1800, Nov-Feb 0700-1700, free.

Outside Spoleto, at the bottom of the hill, is this weird and wonderful Romanesque church. It was built in the fourth and fifth centuries, primarily using Roman remains, and the higgledy-piggledy interior looks as if someone threw the Roman Empire up in the air and sat back to see how it landed.

Pieces of carved stone are built into the walls, upside-down Roman columns are haphazardly patched together and somehow, the whole thing doesn't fall down. The sun streams in on the pale stone structure, bare and strangely beautiful.

Around Spoleto

Cascata delle Marmore

T0744 62982, marmore.it. Waterfalls in action all year round, operating more frequently throughout summer. Check the website for comprehensive details. €5/2.50 concession. 16 km south of Spoleto on SS3.

The Marmore waterfalls, in the lower Valnerina, have a total drop of 165 m, making them among the highest in Europe. Originally created by the Romans, when they diverted the River Velino into the River Nera in 271 BC, the falls are now controlled by the Galleto hydroelectric plant upstream, and water is released according to a complex schedule.

It's a popular destination – especially on summer weekends, when the crowds can make the whole experience feel like an entertainment theme park. However, if you can manage to avoid the worst of the scrums, the falls are a spectacular sight, especially in the late afternoon as the sun streams down through the clouds of spray thrown up by the thundering water.

Chiesa di San Pietro in Valle

sanpietroinvalle.com.
Daily 1000-1600 but hours may change, free.
22 km southeast of Spoleto off SS209: look for one of two turnings to the right just before Colleponte.

In a serenely peaceful spot in the Valnerina, high above the valley floor, little has changed in the landscape that surrounds this abbey, and it seems somehow right that so much inside has also survived almost unchanged for so long. A restaurant and sympathetically-run hotel (see page 157) have done little to change the magic of the place.

At the end of a cypress-lined drive, the abbey nestles in a bend in the hills. From the front, follow the path around to the right to reach the entrance to the church. There has been a place of worship here since at least Roman times, and inside the door to the right is a small conical altar from the first century BC. Other Roman remnants are exhibited on the walls, and the eighth century Faroaldo, Duke of Spoleto and founder of the abbey, is buried in a Roman sarcophagus to the right of the altar, one of six ancient sarcophagi in the church. Most of the structure is Lombard, from the eighth century, or Romanesque, from the 12th century. The church and abbey were restored in the early 20th century, and inaugurated by Mussolini in 1931.

The church has one aisle ending in a three-bay apse, and is richly frescoed with ancient paintings. The 12th-century frescoes on both side walls depict Biblical scenes: the Old Testament is illustrated on the left wall, scenes from the New Testament on the right. The frescoes, by an anonymous Umbrian artist, are not complete, but all the same they demonstrate a remarkable sense of movement and expression, way ahead of their time. They predate Giotto by around 150 years, and compared to the flat, front-on Byzantine images that were the norm in the 12th century, they must once have seemed very modern. Highlights include Eve being born from Adam's rib, high up on the left side, and Noah receiving news of the flood.

The eighth-century altar is also well worth a look, with its geometric patterns and primitive figures, one of which has the sculptor's signature ('Ursus') on either side of his head.

The cloister is a pretty, two-tier, geranium-punctuated construction, which is now used by the hotel. Look for the statues of Sts Peter and Paul on either side of the door.

Opposite the abbey is the ruined **Rocca di Umbriano**, which once looked over the valley and protected the abbey from invaders. From the abbey to Umbriano is about an hour's walk, or you can walk up the steep hill above the abbey (follow the red and white waymarked path just to the south of the building) for some good views of the valley.

Ferentillo

26 km south of Spoleto on SS209.

The small town of Ferentillo is a climbing centre because of the sheer rock faces across the valley. It also has a weird museum of mummies.

Other villages in the lower Valnerina worth exploring include **Scheggino** and **Arrone**, both of which have narrow, steep streets winding up to views of the valley below.

Museo delle Mummie

Chiesa di Santo Stefano, Ferentillo, T0743-54395.
Apr-Sep 0930-1230, 1430-1930, Mar and Oct 0930-1230, 1430-1800, Nov-Feb 1000-1230, 1430-1700, closed Sun morning during mass, €3. Head across the piazza in the part of town to the east of the river – the ticket office is just down the road from the church.

When a new church was constructed in 1500, part of the previous building, put up 300 years earlier, was left underneath as foundations.

Ex-residents of Ferentillo in the lower Valnerina.

It served for a long time as the town's cemetery and, by a weird quirk of fate, the bodies that ended up there have been preserved, due to a micro-organism in the sandy soil below.

The museum is not for the faint-hearted. Anyone expecting cartoon mummies, carefully swaddled, will be disappointed – these are gruesome, naked, desiccated dead bodies, often painfully exhibiting the means by which they died. There are two French soldiers, one of whom was hanged, the other tortured; a Chinese couple who came to Italy for their honeymoon in 1750, caught cholera and never went back; and a bell ringer knocked off the tower by his own bell, his tongue still between his teeth. Children killed by the plague, mothers, and a murdered lawyer fill the crypt of the church, along with several hundred human skulls.

Best of the rest

Umbria and Marche have so many attractive towns, so much rolling countryside, that there are many places that couldn't be fitted into this book. Here are just a few tasters:

Foligno Bombed in the Second World War and much maligned since, Foligno is these days mostly known as a railway junction, but there are a few reasons you might want to stop for a little longer. Il Bacco Felice is a popular little restaurant, and there are villas to see and art to peruse.

Terni Umbria's second city, Terni is an ugly, industrial place, especially in contrast to the beauty that surrounds it. It has a few claims to fame though – the gun that shot JFK was made here, and St Valentine was born here. More recently it was used to shoot the concentration camp scenes in *Life is Beautiful*, which just about sums up its contemporary appeal. It does, however, have a good art gallery and an Easter music festival.

Monti Martani Between the E45 and the N3, to the south of Perugia, this sleepy area of hills is little visited, despite its wealth of little hill towns and villages.

Norcia

High in the hills in the southeast of Umbria, and right at the edge of the Monti Sibillini National Park, Norcia is a different sort of town from its counterparts down on the plain. Famous for its truffles, its butchers and St Benedict, who was born here in AD 480, it has a strong identity of its own and feels like a solid mountain town, braced against earthquakes and the cold wind.

Despite being surrounded by wooded hills and valleys, the town centre is, unusually, flat. It was probably settled by the Sabines in the fifth century BC; as Nursia, it was an ally of Rome in the second Punic War in 205 BC. The 14th-century walls surrounding the town remain more or less intact, despite several destructive earthquakes.

The surrounding countryside is some of Umbria's wildest, with the hills of the Monti Sibillini National Park coming right down to the eastern edge of the town. To the north, the isolated Valcastoriana runs up the edge of the park, with some good walking possibilities and easy access to some of the region's most spectacular landscapes.

'Mules' balls', a traditional Norcian delicacy, for sale in a Norcineria.

Piazza San Benedetto

Norcia's central piazza is an impressive if not entirely cohesive ensemble of buildings, consisting of a castle-turned-museum, a beautiful church and the 14th-century town hall. The information office for the Monti Sibillini National Park is also here. In the centre stands an 1880 statue of the town's most famous son, St Benedict (see page 146), founder of the Benedictine order and patron saint of Europe. The **Palazzo Comunale** has a portico that was added in 1492 and an attached chapel reached up steps from the piazza.

Basilica di San Benedetto

Piazza San Benedetto, T0743-817090.
Daily 0900-1800, free.

On the corner of the piazza, to the right of the Palazzo Comunale, the church that marks the birthplace of the first Western monk and the first nun, Benedict and his twin sister Scholastica, is a strangely downbeat place. The Gothic façade has an attractive rose window and statues of Benedict and Scholastica, but the interior has largely been rebuilt and has a disappointingly forgotten air. Downstairs it is more interesting, with a semi-excavated Roman house and some *opus reticulatum* Roman walls built into the crypt, which also has an ancient fresco.

Castellina & Museo Civico

Piazza San Benedetto, T0743-817030, artenorcia.net.
Wed-Mon 1000-1300, 1600-1930, €4.

Built by the papacy in 1554 to quell Norcian unruliness, the Castellina broods over the centre of the town and now holds its museum. There are medieval sculptures in stone and painted wood, and a terracotta *Madonna* by Luca della Robbia. Paintings include a rather feminine 15th-century *Risen Christ* and a Renaissance *Madonna and Child Enthroned* by Francesco Sparapane from 1530.

Right: A Norcia doorway.

Piazza San Benedetto, Norcia. Opposite page: Ploughed fields in Valcastoriana.

Benedict & Scholastica

St Benedict was born in Norcia in AD 480. The only source work about his life is the second book of Pope Gregory I, written 50 years after Benedict's death. It tells how he went to study in Rome but was so appalled by the state of life there, at the tail end of the Roman Empire, that he became a hermit, and then an abbot to a group of monks. After a while, they became fed up with his reforms and tried to poison him, at which point he left them and set up his own small monasteries, including one at Montecassino, where he wrote his 'Rule': a set of guidelines that has been adopted and used by monks and nuns ever since. Much less is known about his twin sister Scholastica, and some have suggested that she is merely a personification of the Benedictine love of study.

Duomo

Piazza San Benedetto.

Norcia's 16th-century cathedral, just off the main square, is a fairly dull church worth going into for the fresco of Sts Benedict and Scholastica, alongside the Madonna and a redheaded Jesus, in the Cappella della Misericordia.

Several of the town's other churches are worth a peek inside if they're open: **San Giovanni** has a Renaissance altar, and the **Oratorio di Sant'Agostinuccio** has a nice wooden ceiling. The **Tempietto** is a small, square 14th-century shrine with arches opening on to the street, decorated with bas-relief.

Valcastoriana

North of Norcia, this valley running along the edge of the National Park is an isolated slice of rural central Italy, punctuated by abbeys and small villages perched precariously on the hillsides. Shepherds steer their flocks of sheep around, tractors plough the fields, and not very much else happens.

The road to **Preci**, running through the valley, forms the western border of the park, with villages such as **Campi Vecchio** perched above it on the west-facing slopes of the mountains. Despite the altitude, the landscape here is rolling rather than craggy, pastoral rather than dramatic, but it is a beautiful, peaceful place – it's not hard to see why monks and hermits chose to live here.

The **Abbazia di Sant'Eutizio** (T0743-99659) is a good spot to aim for, about 20 minutes' drive out of Norcia. An important Benedictine abbey, it was built on an older Roman site in the fifth century. There's a restaurant here (T074-393 9319, Tue-Sun), a museum (Mon and Wed-Sat 1000-1300, 1500-1900, Sun 1000-1800, Sun only in winter, €2) containing the abbey's treasures and remnants of the days when it was a noted centre for medicine, plus doves and peacocks, caves, a garden with views and a church dating back to 1190.

En route, stop at the **Chiesa di San Salvatore**, below Campi Vecchio, for a look at its Gothic façade and 15th-century frescoes inside. A tree-lined road leads up the hill from here, with great views.

Monti Sibillini

The region's wildest and most beautiful landscapes are in the Monti Sibillini National Park (sibillini.net), spilling across the border between Umbria and Marche. One of the highest parts of the Apennines, it is home to boar, wolves and a bear, and the backdrop to many legends of witchcraft and sorcery. Huge upland plains stretch out beneath its high snowy peaks, carpeted in spring and early summer with wild flowers and farmed at other times for lentils. At the heart of this wilderness, Castelluccio is a remote hill town, often cut off in winter and a great centre for walking and hang-gliding.

The River Nera cuts a narrow valley – the Valnerina – into the hills, a beautifully wooded place winding down from the Sibillini Mountains, with occasional ancient churches along its banks.

Below: Beech woods in the Sibillini Mountains above Piano Grande. Opposite page: Houses in Castelluccio.

Castelluccio & the Piano Grande

Despite all the postcards and calendar shots, it's hard to be prepared for the Piano Grande. A gargantuan grassy basin between high mountains, it sprouts a profusion of wild flowers in late spring and early summer. Later, in autumn, as the beech woods turn a thousand shades of orange and rust brown, it is often filled with a sea of morning fog, out of which the hill village of **Castelluccio**, one of Italy's highest inhabited places, pokes into the bright sunshine. In winter it is often bitterly cold, and snow blankets the surrounding hills, some of which have gentle ski runs. Used mostly for grazing sheep and cows, and for growing lentils, it is a serene place, with occasional walkers and hang-gliders punctuating the vast open spaces.

Castelluccio is a tough, frost-bitten sort of place, with little or none of the cuteness found at lower levels. The views are extraordinary, and though there are no obvious sights, the village's situation alone is enough to make it a must-see. In 2008 every street was dug up to lay new cables and pipes, bringing fibre optics to houses that until recently had no electricity – it remains to be seen whether such progress will drag Castelluccio into the 21st century.

All around the Piano Grande there is fantastic walking territory. The Kompass 1:50,000 Sibillini map is one of the easiest to get hold of; the tourist information office in Norcia sells a rather flimsy alternative, or you may be able to find a 1:25,000 CAI map. There are paths, but it's also possible to walk just about anywhere across the unfenced mountains.

For those looking for a longer trek, there are plenty of routes following the Appenine ridge north from Castelluccio, and there's a circuit of the national park known as the **Grande Anello** ('big ring') – a nine-day, 120-km route. Information centres have a good booklet (in English) on the

The Sibillini Sibyl

The Sibyls were prophetesses in both Greek and Roman antiquity. Living in caves, they foresaw wars and the coming of Christianity and were consulted by emperors. Pictured on Michelangelo's Sistine Chapel ceiling, they may be the ancient forerunners of the relatively modern concept of the witch. Various myths put their number at 10 or 12. The so-called Apennine Sibyl, after whom the Sibillini Mountains are named, may not have been recognised as one of them during Roman times, though it's also possible that she was the Sibyl of Cumae, the most important Roman Sibyl.

Medieval tradition says that she was a prophetess condemned to live in a mountain cave until Judgment Day because she threw a wobbly at the news that Mary had been chosen rather than her to be the mother of Jesus. It was believed that a coterie of beautiful young women lived with the enchantress in the mountain and would sometimes come out at night to dance with local young men, returning to their cave before dawn. So strong were some of these myths that the papacy found it necessary to forbid people to approach the cave, and later blocked off its entrance.

Tip...

Before visiting the Sibillini, contact one of the **Case del Parco** (in Norcia, for example: piazza San Benedetto, T0743-817090) to pick up official guides and maps. There is an information centre in Castelluccio (piazza di Castelluccio, T333-384 2646), but it's only open in high summer – Jun-mid-Jul Sat-Sun 0930-1230, 1530-1830, mid-Jul-Aug daily 0930-1230, 1530-1830.

route and there are *rifugi* (refuges) on the way round. For mountain bikers, there's a longer, 160-km route, taking four or five days and also called the Grande Anello.

Lago di Pilato

Just below the ring of the Sibillini's highest peaks, the Lake of Pontius Pilate is said to contain his body. Some stories say that he drowned himself here, others that his body was driven by oxen into the lake. The rare freshwater crayfish that live here, and occasionally turn the water red, add to the mythology surrounding the place. At a height of 1,940 m, it is hidden between Monte Vettore and Cima del Redentore, but can be reached by walking from the end of the road leading northeast out of Castelluccio (12 km there and back). From the road, head east to the pass of Forca Viola before turning south up the Valle del Lago di Pilato.

Ulysses and his taste for honey

A rare Marsican brown bear, Ulysses has lived in the Monti Sibillini National Park since 2007, having arrived from Abruzzo to the south.

Adult Marsican brown bears weigh as much as 130 kg and are nearly 2-m tall when standing on their hind legs. Traces of Ulysses' presence have been found on six apple trees that he has climbed, and he has damaged a number of beehives in his search for honey. Photo traps have recorded him a number of times, and about 14 km of tracks have been followed. It is believed that his new Sibillini territory covers an area of over 330 sq km, though he has also ventured outside the park. He probably hibernates in a remote mountain cave.

His existence in the national park is likely to remain a lonely one, however. The Marsican brown bear is one of the most critically endangered of European mammal species and – apart from Ulysses – is believed to exist only in the Abruzzo National Park, where the total population numbers only about 40.

In 2007 and 2008 it's believed that four of the species were deliberately poisoned in Abruzzo.

Morning mist lingers over Piano Grande.

Outdoor activities in the Sibillini

The Monti Sibillini National Park is a great setting for year-round activities, from paragliding and hang-gliding, to cross-country skiiing, walking or kite flying.

Cycling

In Sarnano, on the Marche side of the park, **Sibillini Cycling** (T334-743 8418, or T+44(0)208-133 5441 in the UK, sibillinicycling.com, Apr-Oct) rent mountain bikes from €15 a day and offer free car cycle carriers and helmets. They also offer guided 'bike days' and short touring holidays.

Hang-gliding & paragliding

Prodelta, T339-563 5456, prodelta.it.
Hang-gliders and paragliders flock from all over Europe to Castelluccio and the **Piano Grande**, where the vast expanses of grassy slopes and a large, smooth landing site make it a perfect spot for flying, especially for beginners.

Throwing yourself off the top of a mountain and gliding down on the thermals must be one of the best ways to see the Sibillini. No experience is necessary, and a tandem flight with an experienced, licenced glider gives you most of the exhilaration, without some of the fear.

Ring in advance to reserve a flight – one day's notice may be enough during the week, but you

usually need to book at least three or four days ahead for weekend flights. It may sometimes be necessary to cancel flights because of bad weather.

Horse-riding

Centro Ippico Oxer, Paganelli, T339-533 4468, escursioniacavallo.it.
The Oxer Riding Centre, about 7 km from Norcia, offers excursions on horseback in the Sibillini, ranging from a gentle afternoon's walk to longer treks on ancient mountain tracks, camping or staying in refuges or on farms.

Rafting

Rafting Umbria, T348-351 1798, raftingumbria.com.
Gaia, Località Biselli di Norcia, T338-767 8308, asgaia.it.
On the edge of the Sibillini, near Norcia, there are opportunities for rafting downstream on the Corno River, both slowly and quickly. If a meandering journey is more your thing, the **Biselli Gorge** is a good route, with opportunities to swim.

There are also rapids that can be tackled by those after a little more adrenaline, and places where the brave can dive into streams from a 'natural diving board'.

Skiing

There are ski lifts on **Colle le Cese**, to the south of Castelluccio, as well as at **Monte Prata**, to the north, and you can do cross-country skiing across the plains. It's a stunningly beautiful place to ski, though the slopes are relatively short and not especially steep. The snow can be unreliable, however, even in the middle of winter, and there is little infrastructure except at weekends.

Walking

For a serious trek, the **Grande Anello dei Sibillini** (Great Sibillini Ring) is a 120-km, nine-day route. The park website (sibillini.net) also has details (in Italian) of many one-day walks you can do, or you can grab a decent map (see page 149) and strike out on your own. Especially up high in the

mountains it's possible to walk just about anywhere, but make sure you are properly equipped – it's quite possible for the weather to close in.

Monte Guiadone, near Castelluccio From the belvedere just above Rifugio Perugia, overlooking the Piano Grande to the south of Castelluccio (where there is parking), a good and fairly level 8-km walk winds around the contours of the mountains above the plain, passing through beech woods before ending either on a grassy spur of the mountain that juts north, or, if you feel like a short ascent, at the 1647-m summit. The views all along this route are stunning.

From the belvedere, follow the little-used road to the right that heads gently downhill toward the wood. Pass by ski lifts on your right before branching left along a path as the road descends to Piano Piccolo, another plain, to the right. Follow this path through small beech woods and along the sides of exceptionally steep grassy slopes high above the Piano Grande.

Alternatively, for a higher route, with views across the Piano Grande to the usually snow-capped Monte Vettore and Cima del Redentore, head northwest from the belvedere around the western edge of the plain below. This route, which can also be done by mountain bike, eventually takes you into Castelluccio.

Sleeping

Albergo del Teatro €€
Via Giulia 24, T0742-301140,
hoteldelteatro.it.
The breakfast terrace with great views is the highlight of this comfortable, mid-range hotel, with 11 rooms, in the centre of Spello. There are shiny wooden floors, tiled bathrooms (some with Jacuzzis), peach-coloured walls and big beds.

Il Sommelier €€
Via Porta Fontevecchia,
T0742-21410,
residenzailsommelier.com.
With four suites, each loosely themed around a wine, this B&B opened in 2008. Wooden rafters, bare stone walls, tiled floors and fireplaces add to the appeal; breakfast is served in the ex-wine cellar.

La Bastiglia €€
Via Salnitraria 15, T0742-651277,
labastiglia.com.
Closed 9 Jan-9 Feb.
Spello's most stylish accommodation, La Bastiglia, at the top of the town, has a beautifully landscaped swimming pool with great views over the Chiona Valley. There are three grades of room, the best ('not unlike royal residences') having private terraces; the junior suites also have hot tubs. Rooms in the new wing have less character but all have shiny wooden floors and comfortable,

modern furnishings. Half board at €35 extra per person, with dinner in the hotel's smart restaurant (see page 159), is a good deal.

Palazzo Bocci €€
Via Cavour 17, T0742-301021,
palazzobocci.com.
A 14th-century building decorated in 19th-century style: the best of the 23 rooms have frescoes and open fires, though most are much plainer. From June to September the buffet breakfast is served in the garden. Satellite TV and air conditioning.

Self-catering
Buonanotte Barbanera
Via Fonte del Mastro II 9,
T0335-354597,
buonanottebarbanera.it.
Exceedingly stylish, this townhouse-for-rent is halfway between an Umbrian hideaway and a Moroccan riad. There's a

beautiful walled garden and the three elegant double bedrooms have colourful fabrics and carefully chosen art. Wood, white walls, tiles and brick vaulting all contribute and there's a kitchen in a more rural style, with painted dressers. It's available for rent in its entirety for a minimum stay of a week (€500 per day in high season).

In Urbe
Via Giulia 97, T0742-301145,
inurbe.it.
Simple but attractive self-catering apartments in the centre of Spello, with wooden floors, some exposed brick, and good views across the countryside. Kitchens have fridges and gas cookers. Certainly not Spello's most luxurious accommodation but very good value, and they'll pick you up from the station too.

Orto degli Angeli €€€
Via Dante Alighieri 1, T0742-360130, ortoangeli.it.
A grand town house from the 18th century and a Renaissance palace make up this stunning hotel in the heart of the old Roman town. There is a pretty hanging garden built over the Roman theatre, which incorporates some of the original walls. The rooms in the 18th-century building are formal and smart, with frescoed ceilings, while the older building has a more relaxed, rustic feel. Everywhere there are generous public spaces, and thoughtful design infuses the hotel.

Genius Loci €€
Via Monti Martani 23, T0742-362111, geniuslociumbria.com.
Outside Bevagna, en route to Montefalco, Genius Loci is a handsome country house with a pool. They do cookery courses and wine tastings.

Il Chiostro di Bevagna €
Corso Matteotti 107, T0742-361987, ilchiostrodibevagna.com.
Set around a cloister just off the piazza, large wooden furniture and corny Alpine scenes decorate spacious, comfortable rooms. The whole place has a slightly down-at-heel feeling, but it's good value, and in summer the buffet breakfast is served in the cloister itself.

Villa Pambuffetti €€
Viale della Vittoria 20, T0742-379417, villapambuffetti.com.
Just outside the city walls, in tree-filled grounds, Pambuffetti has a pool and some great views of the surrounding countryside, especially from the sought-after tower bedroom, plus wood panelling, air conditioning and an outdoor summer restaurant under a gazebo. There are lots of books and a fire in the reception area, and cookery classes can be booked on site.

Camiano Piccolo €
Via Camiano Piccolo 5, T0742-379492, camianopiccolo.com.
About 1 km downhill out of town, this *agriturismo* has nine comfortable rooms and six apartments in ex-farm buildings around a pool and shaded by trees. In the summer you can

eat alfresco, whereas in winter there's a cosy wooden-beamed interior in country farmhouse style. The menu is traditional Umbrian with no real surprises, but service is friendly and the place has a nice relaxed air. Apartments are available to rent on a weekly basis, rooms by the night. Rooms in the house have more style than those in the outbuildings.

Hotel degli Affreschi €
Corso Mameli 45, T0742-379243.
A friendly, family-run place in the centre of town, with good views and badly reproduced frescoes. Neither modern nor especially old-fashioned, it won't be winning any design prizes any time soon, but it's comfortable and very well placed. Guests also get free access to the pool at the modern hotel Nuovo Mondo, outside the town.

Antica Dimora alla Rocca €€

Piazza della Rocca, T0742-38541,
hotelallarocca.it.

In a handsome 17th-century
building in the middle of Trevi,
the 34 rooms of this elegant and
friendly hotel are split between
the *piano nobile* – the first floor,
with frescoes and high ceilings –
and the old servants' quarters on
the less fussy second floor, with
wooden beams and a cosier feel.
Breakfast is served right on the
intimate piazza della Rocca.

During the festival Spoleto's
hotels fill up, and prices rise:
book well in advance.

Gattapone €€

Via del Ponte 6, T0743-223447,
hotelgattapone.it.

Elegant, arty and with an
undertone of decadence,
Gattapone has 15 rooms near
the Rocca, and great views over
the Ponte delle Torri and the
valley below. The American bar
has old festival posters and an
early 20th-century feel, while
downstairs in the lounge there
are deep red walls, leather sofas
and big windows. Rooms are
slightly plainer but very
comfortable. Free parking.

Palazzo Dragoni €€

Via del Duomo 13, T0743-222220,
palazzodragoni.it.

In an ancient town house
overlooking the Valle Umbra,
Palazzo Dragoni has a grand
sitting room with a piano, a
breakfast room with views all the
way to Assisi, and smart rooms
with parquet floors, arches, and
more vistas, for which it's
sometimes not even necessary
to get out of bed. Ask to see the
secret tunnels under the house,
which once led people to food
and safety in times of siege.

Palazzo Leti €€

Via degli Eremiti 10, T0743-
224930, palazzoleti.com.

At the top of town, Palazzo Leti
is an elegant hotel with a formal
garden overlooking the valley
(and, unfortunately, the road)
to the east. The 11 rooms are
warm, cosy and stylish, with
metal-framed beds, tiles,
antiques, old beams and modern
luxuries such as air conditioning

and, in some cases, Jacuzzis.
All rooms face the valley.

Il Panciolle €

Via del Duomo 3, T0743-45677,
albergopanciolle.it.

Generous and reliable rooms are
comfortable and well kitted out,
with TVs and mini-bars. Rooms
overlooking the street aren't very
bright – those facing the valley
are better. A simple breakfast is
included and there's a popular
restaurant downstairs.

Hotel Charleston €

Piazza Collicola 10, T0743-
220052, hotelcharleston.it.

Stylish and good value, the
Charleston has unusually high
quality contemporary art on its
walls. In a 17th-century building,
it has a bar and wine-tasting room,
a sauna and a good communal
space with a fireplace. In the rooms
the orange walls are a little garish,
but the tiled black and white
bathrooms are more muted and
some have views over the piazza.

Le Terre di Poreta €€
Località Poreta, T0743-521186, leterrediporeta.it.
11 km north of Spoleto.
A 17th-century organic olive oil estate, Le Terre have turned various buildings into guest accommodation – whether you want an apartment or a seven-bedroomed villa they have it. And all come with access to swimming pools, tennis courts, and a gym with a sauna. There is also the chance to join in estate activities such as pruning the olives or going truffle hunting.

San Pietro in Valle €€
Ferentillo, T0744-780129, sanpietroinvalle.com.
May-Oct.
22 km southeast of Spoleto.
Sympathetically restored rooms are grouped around the cloister of a beautiful abbey in the Valnerina. The 19 rooms and two suites have old tiled floors, wooden furniture and beams. Some of the larger rooms also have their own seating areas. A beautiful grassy garden faces across the valley towards the ruined village of Umbriano. The nearby **Santa Croce Agriturismo** (santacroceagriturismo.it), with seven apartments based around a 14th-century tower with a swimming pool, is under the same management.

Il Casale degli Amici €€
Vocabolo Cappuccini 157, T0743-816811, ilcasaledegliamici.it.
A lentil-growing farm with beautiful rustic rooms and apartments in a peaceful spot about 3 km east of Norcia. Rooms are very nicely kitted out with solid wood furniture and metal-framed beds, and the welcome is exceptionally warm, as is the underfloor heating. Half board is a good option, as the attached restaurant (see page 164) serves some of Norcia's best food; breakfast is special too, with lots of homemade produce. Larger rooms are worth paying the extra €10 for – well designed, they have fireplaces, seating areas and big wooden beds.

Palazzo Seneca €€
Via Cesare Battisti 12, T0743-817434, palazzoseneca.com.
Norcia's newest and most stylish accommodation, Palazzo Seneca, a *'residenza di charme'*, opened in 2008 after 10 years of rebuilding and redesigning. The result is an elegant hotel in a 17th-century palace with a jazz bar (concerts are usually held every Saturday night), a library, a refined restaurant and a stylish wellness centre in the cellar complete with sauna, marble massage parlour and a chromotherapy bath. Suites have black marble bathrooms, and there are nice touches such as antique phones.

Casale nel Parco €
Vocabolo Fontevena 8, T0743-816481, casalenelparco.com.
1 km outside Norcia on the way to Fontevena.
Catering for walkers, Casale nel Parco has a good swimming pool under the hills and some simply decorated and fairly rustic rooms and apartments, with plenty of space for a family, that open on to a central grassy area. There's a restaurant with a large fireplace, they offer traditional *prete* – bed warmers – and can organize horse-riding trips.

Grotta Azzura €
Corso Sertorio 24, T0743-816513, bianconi.com.
Should the Palazzo Seneca be full, or too expensive, this nearby hotel, owned by the same family, would be a reasonable fall-back, especially if you can get one of the better, bigger rooms with tented beds. Smaller, more modern rooms upstairs have balconies, but the style feels a little dated.

Monti Sibillini

Castelluccio's only 'proper' hotel is the basic Albergo Sibilla – the Locanda de' Senari is a much better option.

La Locanda de' Senari €
Via della Bufera, T0743-821205, agriturismosenari.it.
25 Apr-Oct, and weekends in winter.
On the edge of the village, with great views over the Piano Grande, Locanda de' Senari is a cosy *agriturismo* with five attractive rooms and a restaurant offering good, traditional meals using home-grown ingredients.

The menu changes regularly, but always includes lentils and local meats. Some rooms have four-poster beds and there are sloping, wooden-beamed ceilings and large showers. Downstairs there's a roaring open fire.

La Vecchia Stalla €
Astorara, T0736-41758, benale.net.
In a village on the Marche side of Monte Vettore, this is a thick-walled stone mountain B&B, 1,000 m up, with walks from the front door. There are just two double rooms. The family owns an organic farm, which supplies some of the ingredients for the home-cooked food.

Eating & drinking

La Bastiglia €€€€
Via Salnitraria 15, T0742-651277, labastiglia.com.
Wed-Mon 1300-1415, 2000-2230, closed Thu lunch and 9 Jan-9 Feb.
A swish but unexpectedly relaxed restaurant, with dark wooden ceilings and big contemporary art, which spreads out from its three rooms on to the terrace in summer. La Bastiglia offers set menus with extravagant titles such as 'a journey through the balanced senses'. If the name, the eight courses or the suckling pig seem a little over the top, you could go for the vegetarian menu, with more down-to-earth dishes such as chickpea flan with red turnip sauce.

Drinking Wine €€
Via Garibaldi 20, T0742-301625, drinkingwine.it.
Thu-Tue 1100-2400.
Sunk down from the main street, you can do as the name says at this modern wine bar, though they also serve coffee, pear and chocolate tart and some good light meals such as potato, rosemary and chicken salad. In summer there are more tables across the street under umbrellas.

Enoteca Properzio €€
Piazza Matteotti 8/10, T0742-301521, enoteche.it.
Daily 1000-2200.
One of Umbria's finest *enoteche*, Properzio stocks 2,200 different wines, and provides good food to go along with them. In the 12th- and 13th-century Palazzo dei Canonici in the centre of Spello, one of the wine-tasting rooms was once used as a studio by Pinturicchio. There are tables outside on the street, inside under brick-vaulted ceilings, and in a walled garden at the back. Try the exceptionally good bruschette selection, or the carefully sourced Mediterranean salad with 35-year-old balsamic vinegar. Wine tastings are available (in good English) – book in advance by phone or email and allow €40-60 per person for a couple of hours, food included.

Il Molino €€
Piazza Matteotti 6/7, T0742-651305.
Wed-Mon 1215-1430, 1930-2240.
An atmospheric spot, in a 14th-century oil mill, Il Molino has an open fire, brick-vaulted ceiling, white tablecloths and wooden chairs, and serves traditional Umbrian dishes such as grilled meats, pasta, and soups with wild asparagus and a certain amount of style.

La Cantina di Spello €€
Via Cavour 2, T0742-651775, oasiumbria.it.
Tue-Sun lunch and dinner.
Attached to a shop selling fine foods from the region, La Cantina uses the same local ingredients to good effect in its smart restaurant. The menu is seasonal but may include dishes such as swordfish 'bites' with capers and olives or Lake Trasimeno bean salad.

Osteria de Dadà €
Via Cavour 47, T0742-301327.
Mon-Sat 1230-1530, 1900-2230, Sun 1230-1530.
A friendly little place with simple wooden tables, where they're keen on doing things the right – and Umbrian – way. The locally sourced menu changes daily, and depends on what's in season. Specialities include *cinghiale sagrantino* (wild boar cooked in red wine), and pasta is always homemade, either tagliatelle or *strangozzi*. There's a set three-course menu for €18, but the owner is happy for you to order as little or as much as you like.

Cafés & bars
Bar Giardino Bonci
Via Garibaldi 10, T0742-651397.
Thu-Tue summer 0700-2400, winter 0700-2230.
As a restaurant it may not be especially exciting, but its garden, with superlative views, makes this a great spot for a drink or an ice cream.

come to a cavernous dining room. Try the fresh, homemade pasta with bacon and tomato, and save some room for pears marinated in Montefalco wine. There is a tasting menu for €38.

Caffè Farfalle
Piazza Garibaldi.
Good homemade ice cream in summer.

Il Coccorone €€
Largo Tempestivi, T0742-379535, coccorone.com.
Thu-Tue 1230-1430, 1930-2200.
A smart place with a handful of outdoor tables with geraniums, and white tableclothed tables inside under brick arches and wooden beams. The open fire is lit even in summer to cook the meat that dominates the menu. There's a cheaper 'tourist menu' as well as the extensive *menu degustazione*. Truffles, guinea fowl and snails all feature and, though it can feel a little dated, standards are high.

L'Alchimista €€
Piazza del Comune 14, T0742-378558, montefalcowines.com.
Wed-Mon 1230-1500, 1900-2145, Tue 1230-1500.
With wooden tables right on the central piazza, l'Alchimista is a cool, chic, family-run wine bar with exceptionally good food. There's a good range of salads,

La Bodega di Assù €€
Corso Matteotti 102, T0742-360978.
Thu-Tue 1130-2100, closed 10 Jan-end Feb.
Just off the main square, Assù's bodega is a friendly, chirpy, effortlessly cool place, tiny but packed with interesting things to look at, with arty photos, piles of books, colouring pencils on every table, handwritten menus and wine bottles lining the walls. There are also two or three tables outside on the street. The food is great too – try a fresh, succulent, wild leaf salad, or a hearty fennel and celery soup. You can also buy produce to take home: wine, olive oil, and even the ceramic jugs that water is served from.

Ottavius €€
Via Gonfalone 4, T0742-360555.
Tue-Sun 1230-1430, 1930-2230.
Sunk down below the level of the piazza, Ottavius is famous for its *gnocchi al sagrantino*, but you might also go for the mixed grill with broad bean purée. It has bare walls and a friendly atmosphere.

Redibis €€
Via dell'Anfiteatro, T0742-360130, redibis.it.
Thu-Mon 1230-1430, 1930-2200, Wed 1930-2200.
Built into the structure of the ancient Roman theatre, Redibis is a large, grand place, with elegant hanging lights and plenty of style. From the entrance you circle around what would once have been the stage until you

such as radicchio with grilled pecorino, pear and walnuts, and a fine selection of polenta made from various grains. Unusually good vegetarian options include *lasagne alchimista* – stuffed crêpe with radicchio, porcini mushrooms and cheese. Jazzy Italian music comes from an iPod-dock, and a vine climbs up the cooling pergola. It's popular and hardly a secret, so arrive early or reserve a table.

Spiritodivino €€
Piazza Mustafà 2, T0742-379048, spiritodivino.net.
Tue-Sun 0900-0100, daily in Aug.
A chic sort of wine bar, Spiritodivino cultivates a tastefully sinful atmosphere, with contemporary styling such as chilli plants on the outdoor tables and a large black and white photo of naked women drinking wine on one of the

Montefalco tavernas

Opening only for special festivities such as the summer **Agosto Montefalchese**, the town's four *quartiere* each lay on good-value traditional meals outdoors in the evenings, with plenty of atmosphere. Served on shared benches around town, the best is probably **Taverna Sant'Agostino**, which takes over the cloister of the ex-convent.

---

inside walls. Dishes such as honeyed cod on sliced tomato and Chianina beef are well matched with the wide selection of Umbrian wines.

Il Verziere €
Via Goffredo Mameli 22, T0742-379166, ringhieraumbra.com.
Tue-Sun lunch and dinner.
Minimalist interior design has yet to reach Il Verziere, where every inch of wall and ceiling is covered in pictures, signs and musical instruments. Service and cuisine is straightforward rather than inventive, but there are wood-fired pizzas, as well as pastas, risottos and plenty of local wine.

Trevi

Gustavino €€
Piazza Mazzini 7, no phone.
Tue-Sun 1030-2300.
A wine bar with pretty slatted folding wooden tables under umbrellas outside. Chic styling includes wine-based axioms written on the tables, pink-on-black handwritten menus and orange water glasses. Excellent salads are served on large wooden platters with wooden cutlery and there's superb coffee too.

Gustavo €€
Via Salita San Francesco 13, T0742-78545, gustavogustavino.it.
Tue-Sun 1830-0130.
The elder brother of Gustavino, Gustavo is a little more serious, and stays up later. There are candles in wine bottles on wooden tables, live music and poetry, and homemade dishes, such as gnocchi with radicchio, and goats' cheese with strawberry compote, chalked up on a board. There's also a tasting menu for €25.

La Prepositura €€
Vicolo Oscuro 2a, T0742-381392, hotelallarocca.it.
Daily 1200-1400, 1945-2215.
La Prepositura offers an interesting menu in vaulted rooms just off the piazza. Dishes may include smoked turkey carpaccio and veal with lemon and there's a good value €14, three-course lunch menu.

La Vecchia Posta €€
Piazza Mazzini 14, T0742-381690, lavecchiaposta.net.
Fri-Wed 1230-1500, 1930-2200.
On the main piazza, La Vecchia Posta serves carefully presented traditional Umbrian food such as pappardelle with wild boar or capelletti with truffles, and good, homemade desserts. It's a cosy, friendly, yellow-walled place, with a few tables outside on the piazza in summer. Upstairs there are rooms for rent.

Cafés & bars
Caffè Roma
Piazza Mazzini.
In the corner of the piazza, Caffè Roma is where the locals come to chat and while away the day. It may not be the world's most atmospheric café, but its position, just under the tower, means it does a steady trade.

Spoleto

Cantina de' Corvi €€
Piazzetta Santi Giovanni e Paolo, T0743-44475, cantinadecorvi.it.
Tue-Sun 1230-1500, 1930-2230.
Tables outside on a wooden platform under cover, and a smaller, vaulted space inside. It's popular with Italians, and the four-course *'menu del territorio'*, including lamb, the traditional local *strangozzi* pasta and wine, is a good deal.

Emporio €€
Via Porta Fuga 22, T0743-47623. Lunchtime and Fri-Sun evenings.
A lively place, with a mix of old-fashioned rural style and playful modern colour. There are a couple of tables outside, as well as some metal picnic tables inside among the wine bottles and vegetables. The menu of the day gets posted on the door.

Il Panciolle €€
Vicolo degli Eroli 1, T0743-221241, ristoranteilpanciollespoleto.com.
Daily 1230-1430, 1930-2230 (closed Wed in winter).
Underneath the hotel of the same name, Panciolle has an open grill on which meat is cooked, and a large garden with palm trees and views. Popular with locals, it's decorated with greens and yellows and has open stonework and arches. There's a wide selection of wines, and they

are carefully matched to the food, which changes often – expect traditional Umbrian dishes with a degree of flair, excellent local cheeses and a good choice of breads.

Il Tempio del Gusto €€
Via Arco di Druso 11, T0743-47121, iltempiodelgusto.com.
Fri-Wed 1030-1500, 1800-2400.
The Temple of Taste has tables outside in summer on the piazza as well as intimate rooms inside. There are daily specials and good set options, including a vegetarian menu. The bread is warm, the waiting staff glamorous. Presentation is clearly important here, and antipasti come with artistically arranged elements on square black plates. Try the smoked trout and salmon or the delicious whole-wheat pasta with pigeon in a Sagrantino sauce. There are good homemade desserts too.

Osteria del Matto €€
Vicolo del Mercato 3, T0743-225506.
Wed-Sat 1100-1500, 1700-0200, Sun 1100-1500, 1700-1200.
A little like participatory theatre, at the Osteria of the Madman the eccentric and vivacious host will draw you in to an extraordinary piece of drama in which he is the protagonist. There's no menu – the only question is whether you want white or red wine: you'll get a series of small courses of delicious Umbrian dishes, from

green salad to pork with cheese sauce to fried courgette flowers. After a couple of courses you'll feel like an old friend and after a couple more you'll feel full. But there may be another half dozen to come, so pace yourself. All this comes in at a very reasonable fixed price, plus wine.

Osteria del Trivio €€
Via del Trivio 16, T0743-44349.
Wed-Mon 1230-1430, 1930-2200.
Decorated in Umbrian country-kitchen style, with red and white checked tablecloths, tiled floor, dresser and old weighing scales. Specials change daily and you'll probably be given a choice at your table rather than presented with a menu. The *strangozzi* pasta with broad beans, bacon and pecorino is excellent.

Tric Trac €€
Piazza Duomo 10, T0743-44592.
Daily 1200-1600, 1830 till late.
On the edge of the piazza facing the duomo, Tric Trac is a smart but not too formal *enoteca* and a good spot to sit with a glass of wine and appreciate the duomo. There are two menus – a lighter, faster *enoteca* menu and a restaurant menu; you can order from either or both. The Salad Caravaggio, with pear, white cabbage, chicory and fennel in a limoncello dressing, is especially good, and a whole section of the menu is devoted to black truffles.

L'Angolo Antico €
Via Monterone 109, T0743-49066.
Tue-Sun lunch and dinner.
A large Italian place with old festival posters and banknotes decorating the walls. The menu is extensive and includes decent if rather thin pizzas as well as main courses such as snails, wild boar casserole, and the ubiquitous pasta with spicy tomato *spolentina* sauce. The mixed bruschette are excellent and local families munch along happily to piped Italian pop.

Cafés & bars
Gelateria Primavera
Piazza del Mercato 7, T0743-48580.
A wide selection of homemade ice cream right on one of Spoleto's main piazzas. It fills up with locals in the evenings.

Il Mio Vinaio
Via Arco di Druso 8, T0743-49893.
Daily 0900-2100.
Just off piazza Mercato, this is a good spot for a lunchtime wooden platter of meats and cheeses with a glass or two of local wine.

Osteria dell'Enoteca
Via Saffi 7, T0743-220484, osteriadellenoteca.com.
Wed-Mon 1100-1500, 1900-2300.
Good traditional food as well as plenty of wine choices at this dark, atmospheric little spot.

Around Spoleto

Al Cantico €€€
Abbazia di San Pietro in Valle, Ferentillo, T0744-780005, ilcantico.it.
Lunch from 1200, dinner from 1800, closed Mon lunch and Dec-Mar.
22 km southeast of Spoleto. Under separate ownership from the neighbouring hotel, Cantico keeps its customers happy with high quality food. There are four different set menus from €50-60.

Osteria Baciafemmine €€
Vicolo Baciafemmine, Scheggino, T0743-618311.
Thu-Tue evenings only, except Sun lunch.
13 km southeast of Spoleto on SS209.
A newly renovated osteria in the pretty riverside village of Scheggino. The name comes

from the fact that the alley is so narrow that passers-by cannot help but kiss. It's a cosy place, using seasonal ingredients, and meat is roasted on the open fire.

Norcia

Granaro del Mo\nte €€
Via Alfieri 10, T0743-817551.
Daily lunch and dinner.
Norcia's most popular restaurant, underneath the Grotta Azzurra hotel, is a huge place, with cosy rooms inside, near the roaring fire, or tables outside. Meat cooked on the open fire is the speciality but there are plenty of truffle and lentil dishes too.

Five of the best

Traditional dishes to try

❶ **Cacio pepe** Plain and simple *cucina povera*: pasta with pecorino cheese and pepper.

❷ **Strangozzi alla cinghiale** Thick hand-rolled pasta with wild boar sauce.

❸ **Tartufi** Truffles, served in many forms, but at their best when they're simple, such as grated over bruschette.

❹ **Zuppa di lentiche** Hearty mountain fare, this soup is best eaten where the lentils grow, around Castelluccio.

❺ **Tozzetti e Vin Santo** A fine way to end a meal: dunk the crunchy almond biscuits into the dessert wine.

Il Casale degli Amici €€
Vocabolo Cappuccini 157,
T328 8612385,
ilcasaledegliamici.it.
1245-1500, 1945-2130; may be closed during the week in winter – ring ahead to check.
Up the hill out of Norcia, Casale degli Amici is an *agriturismo* (see page 157) with a fantastic restaurant. The lentils are home grown, the salami is of the highest quality, the pasta is melt-in-your-mouth fresh and the meat is expertly cooked. In a large, barrel-vaulted room with bare stonework and lights suspended from wires, it's also an atmospheric place, and one that is popular with locals. Well worth the trip.

Taverna de' Massari €€
Via Roma 13, T0743-816218,
tavernadeimassari.com.
Wed-Mon lunch and dinner.
This little place just off piazza Santi Forti has checked tablecloths and a 'typical' menu for €22, or you could splash out on a truffle menu for €34 or €46. A la carte dishes such as tortellini with cream and truffles, or Castelluccio lentils with grilled sausage, are hearty and typically Norcian.

Trattoria del Francese €
Via Riguardati 16, T0743-816290.
Sat-Thu (daily Jul-Sep) 1200-1430 (1500 in summer), 1930-2130.
A small place with an open fire on which the meat is cooked,

Trattoria del Francese makes few concessions to stylishness – the wood cladding is ugly, there are polystyrene tiles on the ceiling, and shields, plates and certificates decorate the walls. The food, however, is excellent, and it fills up with loyal Italians. There's a separate truffle menu and the *contorni* are unusually good.

Monti Sibillini

In Castelluccio, **La Locanda de' Senari** (see page 158) also has a good restaurant.

Panini allo Scarafischio €
What appears to be little more than a burger van in Castelluccio's piazza-cum-car-park is actually one of the best places around to buy fine sausages, cured meats and cheese, any of which can be made into great panini, hot or cold. Expect conversation about world economic problems and a plastic beaker of wine to go with your ham sandwich.

Taverna Castelluccio €
Via Dietro la Torre 8, T0743-821158, tavernacastelluccio.it.
Homely and simple, with blue and white tablecloths, and pictures on the walls inside and a couple of tables outside on the street, the taverna offers a traditional local menu using almost all local, natural ingredients such as lentils, beans, beef and pecorino cheese.

Shopping

Spello

Arte & Arte Applicata
Via Cavour 13, T0742-652022, cucciarelli.com.
Easter-Oct daily 1000-1300, 1500-1800 (but if you phone to request a viewing in winter they'll be happy to open up for you).

Whereas many 'galleries' in the region try to sell tourist tat with an artistic veneer, this little place is full of imaginative and inventive pieces in wood made by local sculptor Angelo Cucciarelli. Some of his large sculptures are displayed here (ask to see the catalogue) among the charming chess sets, coat hooks and lamps, all beautifully crafted and with a playful sense of fun.

Food
Hispellum (corso Cavour 35, T0742-651766) has a great selection of local wine, cheese and meat, but **La Tavola dell'Umbro**, right on piazza della Repubblica (T0742-651340, Mon-Sat 0700-1330, 1530-1930, Sun 0900-1300, 1530-1900) is better for picnic provisions, with fruit, bread and a wide range of drinks as well as cheese and other regional produce.

Bevagna

La Casereccia
Corso Matteotti 56, T0742-361969.
Delicious homemade pasta is made at the back of this little shop on the main street.

L'Orto di Porta
Piazza Garibaldi, T0742-360584.
Good local fruit and veg.

Enoteca di Bevagna
Corso Matteotti 65, T0742-362107, edoardomondi.com.
Daily 0930-1300, 1400-1930.
Free wine tastings, and a good range of bottles to take away.

Trevi

Kappa Market
Via Lucarini 35, T0742-781145.
Mon-Sat 0900-1300, 1630-2000.
A little supermarket with bread, a deli counter, excellent fruit and veg and lots of good picnic fare, as well as locally produced olive oil in industrial-size cans.

At the sign of the boar's head

Norcia is dominated by *norcinerie* – shops selling local meat, cheese and other products. Many have stuffed boars' heads outside them, and, in some cases whole stuffed boar, as well as various cured meats hanging from their doorways. All will happily sell you some Norcian sausage, or, if you find the hairiness a little off-putting, a jar of local truffles.

Spoleto

Il Libro
Corso Mazzini 63, T0743-46678.
Mon-Sat 0930-1300, 1630-2000, Sun 1130-1300, 1800-2000.
An excellent selection of books on Spoleto and Umbria – coffee-table photography books as well as guide books. Also some maps and English-language novels.

Mobilia
Via Sahara Vecchia 30, T0743-45720.
Daily 0900-1300, 1530-1930.
A good mix of old-fashioned metal toys, globes, mobiles, antique magnifying glasses and furniture.

Activities & tours

For activities in the Monti Sibillini National Park, see page 148.

Children

Parco Avventura Nahar
Vocabolo Rosciano 25, Arrone, T320-275 6657, lacollinafiocchi.com.
Jul-Aug daily 1000-1900, Mar-Jun and Sep-Nov Sat-Sun 1000-1 hour before sunset, €15, junior trail €10.
8 km from the Cascate delle Marmore on road to Polino.
Helmeted and attached to a wire, you clamber high up through the trees of the Valnerina on this adventure trail.

Cycling

A 60-km route along the banks of streams and rivers, the **Spoleto-Assisi cycle path** starts at its highest point, in the village of Arezzo (not to be confused with the Tuscan town) near Spoleto. There is a dam on the River Marrogia here. Tourist information in Spoleto can provide you with a booklet detailing the route. Another cycle path runs along the valley floor on the far side of the main roads below Trevi.

Rafting

Centro Canoa e Rafting Le Marmore
Via Carlo Neri, T330-753420, raftingmarmore.com.
You can try white-water rafting from just below the Marmore Falls, or a more gentle punt downstream from Ferentillo. Both trips last around an hour; neither requires any rafting experience, though you should be a good swimmer. All clothing and equipment is provided.

Walking

Trevi tourist information offers a free town map with walking routes in the area on the back. The **Cammino di San Francesco** goes through the town, and you could combine a walk along this with the **Sentiero degli Ulivi** to make a satisfying circuit of two or three hours, with some good views.

Spoleto Galleria
Via Arco di Druso 7, T0743-225873, spoletogalleria.it.
Closed Thu morning.
The sort of shop that Spoleto does very well: high quality crafts, sculpture and furniture with a touch of imaginative eccentricity.

Norcia

Antica Norcineria
Piazza del Comune 11.
Daily 0700-1330, 1600-2000.
A decent range of bread, cheese and fruit right in the middle of town. And there's an *enoteca* next door should you want a bottle of Sagrantino.

Tip...

The swimming pool at **Hotel Nuovo Mondo**, outside Montefalco on the way from Bevagna, is open to non-residents 0830-1900, €5.

Transport

Valle Umbra

Spello is on the same train lIne as Assisi, and there are also four to six buses daily from Assisi and the same number from Perugia. Trains from Rome on the main line to Ancona call at Foligno (about 90 mins), and also at Spoleto and Trevi. For stations beyond Foligno towards Perugia, it's often necessary to change.

Norcia

There are seven buses a day to Norcia from Spoleto, the nearest station. A car is useful, especially for getting out into the hills, though the winding roads can be slippery and dangerous.

Monti Sibillini

Castelluccio is almost impossible to reach without a car. There are once-in-a-blue-moon buses from Norcia, but you might never get to leave. If you have no transport, a better bet might be hitching.

Contents

Southwest Umbria

Duomo, Orvieto.

Introduction

O n a spectacular plug of volcanic rock rising like a huge wedding cake from the valley floor, Orvieto is a magnificent sight. And towering over the town is its biggest building: from miles away the cathedral dominates the landscape, its enormous façade covered with alarming depictions of sin and sinners. It's as near to Rome as to Perugia, and cosmopolitan weekenders have helped to keep an unusual number of good restaurants in business and give the town a less provincial feel than many places in Umbria. The local crisp white wine is another draw, and there are some interesting shops and a couple of good museums; you can also descend into the honeycomb of tunnels and wells dug into the tufa over the centuries.

Along a winding road to the northeast, Todi is another popular destination, at least in part for the self-perpetuating notion that it has the highest quality of life in the world. Whatever the truth in such a story, it's worth a visit for its beautiful piazza and the awesome engineering of the ancient Roman cisterns underneath.

To the south there is a prehistoric forest, beautiful Roman remains at Carsulae, and Narni, an under-visited hill town with alarming underground remains and a great museum.

Amelia.

What to see in…

…one day
Climb to the top of the **Torre del Moro** to get your Orvieto bearings. Pick one of the town's clutch of archaeological museums – the **Museo Claudio Faina** is rewarding – before seeking out the real Etruscan tombs, just outside the walls. The **Duomo**'s spectacular façade repays close inspection, and don't miss the equally memorable Renaissance art inside.

The rock beneath Orvieto has been carved into for centuries. **Orvieto Underground** gives you a fascinating tour, or you could descend to the bottom of the **Pozzo di San Patrizio**. Don't miss a meal at one of the excellent restaurants, or the ice cream which is some of the best around.

…a weekend or more
In a weekend you could take in the beautiful piazza, churches and Roman cisterns of **Todi**, or go to **Narni**, another hill town with spectacular underground remains. And don't miss **Carsulae** – the area's best Roman remains, on a romantically rural hillside.

Orvieto

Orvieto's tufa plateau is an obvious place for a town, and it has been inhabited since Etruscan times, when the locals started the long tradition of boring down into the rock to make wine cellars, find water, throw away rubbish and hide the bodies of the dead. The enormous Duomo dominates the town and has some fantastic frescoes. Orvieto is also the centre of Umbrian wine making and there are many good places to test the blend. A handful of good museums, a tower and several ways to explore the subterranean history of the place make it an excellent place to visit, or indeed in which to base a stay in Umbria.

Below: Orvieto panorama. Opposite page: Duomo, Orvieto.

Duomo

Piazza del Duomo, opsm.it.
Daily Apr-Sep 0730-1245, 1430-1915, Mar and Oct 0730-1245, 1430-1815, Nov-Feb 0730-1245, 1430-1715, crypt Mon-Fri 1000-1200, free. Cappella di San Brizio opens at 0900 then same hours as Duomo, €5/4 concession (includes admission to Museo dell'Opera del Duomo and Museo Emilio Greco).

Orvieto's grandest sight is its huge cathedral, towering over the town and the surrounding countryside. Inside is a mass of Gothic and Renaissance art as well as some impressive architecture. Outside are four famous panels illustrating the Creation, David and Abraham, the life of Jesus, and Heaven and Hell in exquisite – and sometimes painful – detail. At sunset the façade is at its most impressive: the tallest building in the city, the Duomo is also the last to catch the evening light.

Cappella della Madonna di San Brizio

The most richly decorated walls of Orvieto's cathedral are extraordinary expanses of colour and nightmarish activity. The frescoes of the San Brizio Chapel appear so modern that in many ways they are nearer 20th-century graphic novels than traditional Renaissance style. As flying demons send down beams of fire, naked, muscle-bound figures writhe in agony, falling outside the frames of the picture. Meanwhile, tsunamis carry away ships, the moon turns red, the undead rise from their tombs and the world ends, while angels gaze calmly down from above.

Built between 1408 and 1444, the decoration of the chapel's vaults was planned and begun by Fra Angelico in 1447, but the main panels were not painted until 1499-1504, by Luca Signorelli. They depict *The Antichrist*, *The End of the World*, *The Resurrection of the Body*, *Hell*, *The Calling of the Chosen* and *Paradise*. Memorable, but deserving of an 18 certificate, Signorelli's images may have taken their lead from Dante, as well as from the bas-reliefs on the cathedral's façade. It's hard to believe that any Orvietans have dared to sin since.

Around the region

Cappella del Corporale In the far left corner as you enter the cathedral, this chapel doesn't get the plaudits of its counterpart opposite, but perhaps deserves a little more recognition. Colourful frescoes from floor to ceiling illustrate the miracle of Bolsena in 1263 (when blood is said to have seeped from the Eucharist in the nearby town, confirming the doctrine of transubstantiation): the chapel was built to house the corporal, or linen cloth, on which the blood appeared. Lippo Memmi's *Madonna* is an especially beautiful and expressive painting. Elegant, poised and sensual, she stands looking out as angels above daintily pull back her cloak to reveal men and women below, their faces upturned in awe and hope.

Museo Claudio Faina

Piazza Faina 29, T0763-341511, museofaina.it.
Daily Apr-Sep 0930-1800, guided tours 1100 and 1600, Oct-Mar (Nov-Mar closed Mon) 1000-1700, guided tours 1100 and 1500, €4.50.

Orvieto has a confusing plethora of different museums containing archaeological finds. The best is probably this one, opposite the Duomo, named after the man who donated his family's collection. On the ground floor, the collection of the Museo Civico contains some great pieces from the nearby sacred Etruscan site of Cannicella. The stone statue of Venus, from around 530 BC, has been well worn by the passing millennia, but she retains an enigmatic smile. A huge stone warrior's head dates from the sixth century BC, and a

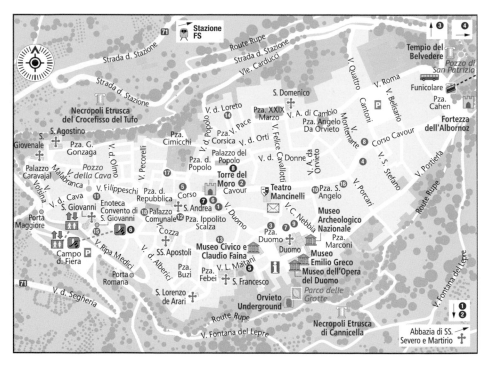

wonderfully intact, and startlingly ugly, Gorgon's head is from the fifth century BC.

Upstairs, the Faina Collection includes some stunning Greek pots, including three beautiful amphorae by Exekias, a master of the genre, from the sixth century BC. Also here are some expressive funeral urns of the second century BC, with fighting figures below and wonderfully relaxed reclining depictions of the deceased on the lids. There is an extensive coin collection, and, on the second floor, some excellent bucchero pottery with a metallic sheen, made black by using ferric oxide and dating from as far back as the seventh century BC.

Museo Archeologico Nazionale

Palazzo Papale, piazza del Duomo, T0763-341039, archeopg.arti.beniculturali.it.
Daily 0830-1930, €3, combined ticket with Necropoli del Crocifisso del Tufo €5.

Orvieto's second archeological museum has an extensive collection of Etruscan pottery, mostly organised according to the tombs in which it was found. The display is badly labelled and badly lit, but there are interesting pieces, including armour and an huge shield from the fourth century BC, and a four-headed, four-compartment pot from the same time that might have been used for condiments.

The best bits are the two recreated tombs with fourth-century-BC frescoes, fragmentary but fascinating. In one, a man plays a double flute and pomegranates form a part of the funeral feast.

Orvieto listings

Duomo, Orvieto.

Above: Part of the Orvieto Underground circuit. Opposite page: Etruscan tombs, Orvieto.

Museo dell'Opera del Duomo

Piazza del Duomo 26, T0763-343592, opsm.it.
Jan-Feb and Nov-Dec Wed-Mon 0930-1300,
1500-1700, Mar and Oct Wed-Mon 0930-1300,
1500-1800, Apr-Sep daily 0930-1900, €5/4
concession (includes admission to Cappella
San Brizio).

In effect several museums accessed with one ticket
– it includes the Chiesa di Sant'Agostino and two
picture galleries in piazza del Duomo – the Museo
dell'Opera del Duomo is a disparate collection with
some interesting highlights. The main museum,
adjoining the duomo, holds a beautiful though
strangely proportioned sculpture of the Madonna
and Child surrounded by angels (1325), which once
sat in the centre of the Duomo's façade. Attributed
to Lorenzo Maitani, it is a wonderfully poised piece.
There are several ornate Simone Martini paintings
from the early 14th century and a large, voluptuous
Santa Maria Maddalena by Luca Signorelli, painted
in 1504. What appears at first glance to be a
self-portrait of Signorelli is almost certainly a
19th-century fake – the Latin on the back of the

panel has many spelling mistakes and the wrong
materials were used. By contrast to the medieval
works, the huge 16th- to 18th-century panels in
the other rooms are bombastic and uninteresting.

The **Museo Emilio Greco** is a rather more
unlikely part of the duomo museum conglomerate.
The Sicilian sculptor finished making the new
doors of the cathedral in 1970, but this collection
centres on his interest in the female body. Sketches
and sculpture from the 1960s and 1970s are, at their
best, seductive, though some have something of
The Joy of Sex about them.

Orvieto Underground

*Piazza del Duomo 23, T0763-340688,
orvietounderground.it.*
Daily tours at 1100, 1215, 1600, 1715
(weekends only in Feb), €5.50/4.50 concession.

Built on a giant plug of volcanic stone, people
have been tunnelling down into the rock below
Orvieto for thousands of years. Guided tours
(usually at least one a day in English) show a linked
subterranean world of workplaces, secret passages

and living spaces. As you enter the underground complex a map shows some 400 of the town's excavations, but even these are only a third of the estimated total. The tour includes a 40-m deep Etruscan well, caves dug out for cement, networks of medieval dovecotes where pigeons were kept for food, and a 20th-century bomb shelter. At one time, when a tax was imposed on goods entering Orvieto, the town's underground network was even used for smuggling. The hour-long tour gives a novel and interesting insight into centuries of life here.

Torre del Moro

Corso Cavour 87, T0763-344567.
Daily May-Aug 1000-2000, Mar-Apr and Sep-Oct 1000-1900, Nov-Feb 1030-1300, 1430-1700, €2.80.

The clock is a relatively recent addition, as are the modern stairs, but the tower itself dates from the 12th century. You can take a lift to the second floor, from where it's a long climb, via the back of the clock face, to the top. The 360° views make it well worth the effort, however.

Necropoli del Crocifisso del Tufo

Just outside the city walls, T0763-343611, archeopg.arti.beniculturali.it.
Daily Apr-Oct 0830-1930, Nov-Mar 0830-1730, €3, combined ticket with Museo Archeologico Nazionale €5.

Dating from the sixth century BC, Orvieto's Etruscan necropolis is an impressive, even eerie place, where tombs constructed from massive square blocks of volcanic stone are lined up in rows at the bottom of the town's cliffs. Family names are carved on the lintels of the chambers, from where many of the finds in the town's museums were taken. You can wander freely among the dark, musty tombs, and down steps into many of them. A room at the entrance has a good display of information and a handful of finds from the necropolis.

Tip...

Consorzio per la Tutela dei Vini DOC Orvieto e Rosso Orvietano
Corso Cavour 36, T0763-343790, consorziovinidiorvieto.it.
Ask here or at tourist information for details of local vineyards open to visitors.

Enoteca Convento di San Giovanni

Via Ripa Serancia 16, T0763-341818.
Daily mid-Jun-mid-Sep, 1100-1300, 1700-1900, mid-Sep-mid-Jun, 1100-1300, 1500-1700.

In a converted convent at the western edge of the city, the *enoteca* offers tours and wine-tasting in a great setting. The original Etruscan wine cellars have been added to and built over for centuries, and wine has been stored here for 2,500 years. Exhibits in the cellars illustrate the importance of wine to Etruscan society, as well as to all societies here ever since. Above ground, the building has some fine cloisters, in the centre of which is a well built by Antonio da Sangallo, who also built the well of Pozzo di San Patrizio (see page 178). Other parts of the building, including the elegant conical tower, are being restored to allow more space for cookery and wine courses. The building is the centre of **Cittàslow**, an international organisation trying to combat the homogenizing influences of fast food with an appreciation of local produce and traditions.

Around the region

There are free tours (Mon-Fri) and wine-tasting too (2 glasses for €8). If there are enough people, you may also be able to go on a tour at the weekend. You can, of course, also buy wine here, and for the really serious, professional sommelier courses are available.

Teatro Mancinello

Corso Cavour 122, T0763-340422, teatromancinelli.it.
Daily 1000-1300, 1500-1800, €2/1 concession.

A small but grand 19th-century neoclassical theatre on the main street, ornately decorated. You can poke your head into a box, or wander up to the spacious 'foyer' where recitals are held. The theatre's season runs from October to March. Buy your tickets downstairs in the café, where you might also want to have a cup of one of their many teas.

Pozzo di San Patrizio

Viale Sangallo, off piazza Cahen, T0763-343768.
May-Aug 0900-2000, Mar-Apr and Sep-Oct 0900-1900, Nov-Jan 1000-1700, €4.50/3.50 concession.

This giant well was commissioned in 1527 by Pope Clement VII, who was worried that he might at some point have to take refuge in Orvieto. It took ten years' digging to finally hit water. The structure hasn't changed since: two independent spiral staircases, big enough for a donkey to use, twist around the 53-m-deep and 13-m-wide hole cut into the rock. Each staircase (one for up, one for down) has 248 steps. Despite the 72 windows into the shaft it's fairly dark, and cool, which may be a blessing in summer.

Pozzo della Cava

Via della Cava 28, T0763-342373, pozzodellacava.it.
Tue-Sun 0900-2000, closed second half of Jan, €3/2 concession.

An Etruscan well at the western edge of town, Pozzo della Cava would be an impressive piece of engineering of any era. A wide circular shaft drops

It's a fact...

Those who are less than generous in Italy are said to have 'pockets as deep as the pozzo di San Patrizio'.

25 m into the rock, with the water illuminated at the bottom. Unlike the Pozzo di San Patrizio, it's not possible to descend to the bottom, but it's satisfying to throw coins down – it's so far down that they start to whistle before they reach the water at the bottom. The square hole at the side is the original bore hole.

In typical Orvieto fashion, the holes in the rock here have been used for many different things over the years. For some time the well was used as a place to throw the bodies of miscreants, and there are other chutes here that were used to dispose of rubbish in medieval times. Other parts of the same complex were used as a necropolis and as a kiln, and once you've bought a ticket you'll go through an exhibition area filled with fragments of ancient ceramics found here. More recently, parts of these caves were used as air-raid shelters.

Route Rupe

Once you're in Orvieto, the tufa plateau on which it sits can easily be forgotten. But a newly-built path around the whole town threads through woods and around the base of the rock, giving great views to the west, especially at sunset. The whole circuit of the cave-threaded rock face is around 5 km. There are a few points around the edge of the city where you can join the path – see map for details.

Todi

Atop a triangular hill in the River Tiber regional park, Todi has long been singled out as one of Umbria's most picturesque spots. Legends have it that the city was founded either by Hercules, or when an eagle stole a tablecloth from a tribe colonizing the area and dropped it on the top of the hill. The settlers took this as a divine command, and both the bird and the cloth can be seen in the town's emblem. In Etruscan times the town was called Tutere, meaning 'border', and it later became Roman Tuder. In the 13th century it captured local towns Amelia and Terni and several of its most impressive buildings were constructed.

Part of Todi's urban legend is that it is 'the world's most desirable place to live'. This conclusion, reached in the 1980s, was based more on marketing than rigorous research, but it has stuck. Consequently, the streets are full of English-speaking estate agents, and property prices have sky-rocketed out of the reach of most locals. The town also gets a disproportionate number of visitors, drawn by the beautiful medieval piazza, two much-lauded Renaissance churches, a good museum and some impressive Roman remains make it well worth a visit.

Below: Sunset over southwest Umbria, looking towards Orvieto. Opposite page: Pozzo di San Patrizio.

Piazza del Popolo

With the Duomo at one end and three 13th-century palazzi around it, piazza del Popolo is a fine, well-preserved, medieval square. On the site of the ancient Roman forum, it also sits on top of the huge Roman cisterns (see below). The most striking of the piazza's buildings are the conjoined pair of Palazzo del Popolo and Palazzo del Capitano, housing the town's museum and art gallery. Palazzo del Popolo, on the corner of piazza Garibaldi, was begun in 1213, and is the older of the two. Work on its neighbour, with its grand staircase, was started 27 years later. Palazzo dei Priori, facing the Duomo, was begun in 1293. It has an unusual trapezoidal tower and a 14th-century bronze eagle.

Museo Civico e Pinacoteca

Piazza del Popolo, T075-895 6216.
Apr-Oct Tue-Sun 1000-1330, 1500-1800, Nov-Mar Tue-Sun 1030-1300, 1430-1700, €3.50.

The town's museum and picture gallery is worth a visit for its ancient pre-Roman and Roman remains and for some of its large paintings. Downstairs there are Etruscan bronze candlesticks and slingshot, and a 12th-century fragment depicting a cheerily waving Jesus with two of Todi's patron saints, Fortunato and Cassiano. A scale model of Santa Maria della Consolazione enables you to

Above: Palazzo del Popolo and Palazzo del Capitano, Todi.
Opposite page: Tempio di San Fortunato, Todi.

---

see how the building was designed, and there are relic holders, some complete with fragments of arms, teeth and so on. The Roman section has a nicely quizzical pair of doves and a bronze pig looking very well fattened.

In the picture gallery, the highlights are paintings by Lo Spagna, especially a large, colourful *Coronation of the Virgin* from 1511. Also here is a much smaller painting of *Beato Bernardino da Feltre* by the same artist from 1515.

Look out too for interesting temporary archaeological and art exhibitions in the **Sala delle Pietre**, a large room on the first floor of the palazzo.

Cisterne Romane

Via del Monte, T075-894 4148.
Apr-Oct Tue-Sun 1000-1330, 1500-1800, Nov-Mar, Sat-Sun 1030-1300, 1430-1700, €2.

An extraordinary feat of engineering in any age, Todi's dripping Roman cisterns, right below the centre of the city, are one of the region's more impressive Roman remains. Huge, atmospheric spaces, the part open to the public is merely a fraction of a complex underground network of galleries and tunnels, stretching for 5 km through the hill under Todi. This section was discovered only in 1996, during work on a shop above. The shop in question – a *tabacchi* in the piazza – has a glass floor through which you can see the remains below. Though there were local stories of a massive underground lake here, they were not widely believed until the cistern was discovered. It is 48 m long and 6.7 m high. Another cistern, on the other side of the piazza, has been known about since 1262. When full, each chamber would have held around 2,500 cu m of water. During Todi's annual arts festival, the cistern is sometimes used as an atmospheric venue for video art.

Duomo

Piazza del Popolo.
Daily 0830-1230, 1430-1830, free, crypt €1.

At the northern end of piazza del Popolo, Todi's cathedral has an impressive carved portal on a pale pink, square façade, below a large rose window. There are two smaller rose windows above the two side doors. Building commenced in the 12th century and continued for centuries thereafter. The steps at the front – a good place to sit and watch the goings-on in the piazza – were added in the 18th century. Go down the road to the right of the cathedral to see the ornate side of the building. Inside, the choir is an intricate work of carving by a father and son in the early 16th century. In the crypt various pieces from the cathedral's treasury are on display, including three 13th-century statues from the Pisano school.

Tempio di San Fortunato

Piazza Umberto I, T075-894 5311.
Campanile Apr-Oct Tue-Sun 1000-1300, 1500-1830, Nov-Mar Tue-Sun 1030-1300, 1430-1700, €1.50.

Tall and light, with elegant columns, the Church of San Fortunato overlooks the steep slope of the town's second piazza. The upper part of the façade is unfinished, though the lower half makes up for this with an ornately decorated portal with exquisitely carved leaves and figures. Inside, Masolino's *Madonna and Child*, in the fourth chapel on the left, is a beautiful painting with pretty angels on either side of the Virgin. In the apse, the statue of St Fortunato is from 1643; note the eagle with tablecloth below. Climb the 150 steps to the top of the campanile, popular with pigeons, for good views of the town and the surrounding countryside below.

In the crypt is the tomb of Jacopone da Todi (1228-1306), one of Italy's most famous medieval poets. At the age of 40, Jacopone's wife died in an accident; when he discovered that, unbeknown to him, she had been wearing a hair shirt, he gave up his comfortable existence and lived a life of penitence and poverty, wandering the countryside and writing poetry that was often acerbically critical of the church and its excesses and corruption.

Teatro Comunale

Via Mazzini, T075-895 6700.

If there's anything on at the sumptuous Teatro Comunale while you're in Todi, you may be able to wander in to this beautiful, oval, four-tiered theatre during the day to have a quick look round, or you could book seats in a box and go to see the production. The theatre was built in 1872 by Carlo Gatteschi and holds up to 500 people.

Around the region

Parco della Rocca

Apr-Oct 0630-2200, Nov-Mar 0700-1900.

At the highest point in the city, with views to the south, the Parco dell Rocca is a pleasant place for a wander among the roses and the shade of the trees. The tower known as il Mastio is all that remains of the fortifications, built here by Pope Gregory XI in 1373.

Tempio di Santa Maria della Consolazione

Wed-Mon, Apr-Oct 0900-1300, 1430-1800, Nov-Mar 1000-1230, 1430-1800, free.

A masterpiece of Renaissance architecture, the light, airy and open Santa Maria della Consolazione was probably built to a design by Donato Bramante, who also designed St Peter's in Rome. Work on the church began in 1508, and it was eventually completed 99 years later. It stands outside the city walls: you can climb down a long set of stairs from the Parco della Rocca to reach it. It has a central dome surrounded by four half-domes, as if two domes have been slid apart to allow space for another. Sixty enormous rose bosses, many with rather scary mythological creatures in their centres, line the arches.

Ab Ovo Gallery

Via del Forno 4, T075-894 5526, abovogallery.com. Mar-mid-Jan Tue-Sun 1030-1330, 1530-1930, free.

A sophisticated, high-end craft gallery, Ab Ovo was set up in Todi's medieval bakery in 2007 by an Italian/English partnership and exhibits delicate pieces of fine ceramics, jewellery, furniture and even bags, made by international artists. The pieces are carefully curated, and group shows, often loosely themed, are rotated about three times a year. Nothing here is cheap, but it may just be worth starting to save up.

Around Todi

Foresta Fossile di Dunarobba

Vocabolo Pennicchia 46, Dunarobba, Avigliano Umbro, T0744-940348, forestafossile.it. Jul-Aug Tue-Sun 1000-1300, 1630-1930, rest of summer (coinciding with the changing of the clocks) Tue-Fri 1000-1300, Sat-Sun 1000-1300, 1630-1930, winter Tue-Fri 1000-1300, Sat-Sun 1000-1300, 1400-1600, €5/3 concession. 17 km south of Todi on SP379.

Discovered in a clay quarry near the town of Avigliano Umbro in the late 1970s, the huge trees of Dunarobba are 1.5 million years old. Despite the name, these prehistoric trees are not actually fossils at all – the wood was simply preserved, mummified in clay, and it still looks like fresh timber. The trees were a type of giant sequoia and though only stumps remain, some are 5-10 m high, and 1.5 m in diameter.

Above left: Santa Maria della Consolare, Todi.
Below left: Ab Ovo Gallery, Todi.
Opposite page: Advert for Fichi Girotti, a speciality of Amelia.

Narni

At the precise geographical centre of Italy, Narni is a place strangely unaccustomed to visitors, despite being a hilltop town of some beauty and having some excellent attractions. The town's underground tour is fascinating, there are some nice Romanesque churches and a fantastic new museum and art gallery. It can require a little effort, however – some of its best sights are open only at weekends, and tourist information is decidedly unhelpful. The Umbrian town of Nequinium was renamed Narnia (after the River Nar) by the Romans when they conquered the town in 299 BC. CS Lewis quite possibly named his magical kingdom after it, but links to stone lions around the town are almost certainly fanciful.

Nearby, sleepy Amelia is a beautiful town at the centre of the Amerino area. In the other direction, Carsulae, on the via Flaminia, is one of the most complete Roman remains in Italy and sits in a stunning location under wooded hills.

Around the region

Narni Sotterranea

Via San Bernardo 12, T0744-722292,
narnisotterranea.it.
Visits by guided tour only, Apr-Oct Sat 1500 and
1800, Sun and holidays 1000, 1115, 1230, 1500,
1615, 1730, Nov-Mar Sun and holidays 1100, 1215,
1500, 1615, €5.

Narni's underground wonders were discovered in
1979 by a group of young speleologists. Despite
the fact that they had just shimmied down a rock
face on to his lettuces, an old gardener showed
them a small hole in the ground in the corner of
his plot. That hole has now been widened into a
doorway and leads into a 12th-century church,
which was used as a wine cellar by Napoleonic
troops and subsequently forgotten about.
Frescoes, also from the 12th century, show the
coronation of the Virgin and two depictions of
St Michael, to whom the church is dedicated.
Stars on a blue ceiling can be made out, as well
as some human bones buried under the floor.

The second room they discovered was a Roman
cistern, and here are some displays and recreations
of surveying tools the Romans used to build their
nearby aqueduct, which featured a tunnel that was
started from both ends and met in the middle. This
tunnel can also be visited if you book in advance.

Beyond the cistern is a room that was used by
the Inquisition as a torture chamber, complete with
some tools of the trade. Most intriguing, though,
is the cell off this room, which is covered in carved
graffiti. Most of this was done in 1759 by someone
called Giuseppe Lombardini, a guard turned prisoner
when he was suspected of helping somebody to
escape. Full of Masonic and religious symbolism,
it is a fascinating riddle as well as an insight into
the mind of someone trapped down here.

In 2008 a Byzantine mosaic was found under
the floor of the Church of San Domenico, above,
and should soon be on show to the public.

Led by one of the original speleologists, Narni
Sotterranea tours are conducted (in English as well
as Italian) with a rare enthusiasm, as well as plenty
of humour and knowledge.

Essentials

❶ **Getting around** You can park in piazza Garibaldi.

❷ **Buses** Buses run from piazza Garibaldi.

❸ **Trains** The train station, Narni-Amelia, is about 4 km
from the centre of Narni. Buses run into town.

❹ **Hospital** Via dei Cappuccini Nuovi 3, T0744-7401.

❺ **Pharmacy** Farmacia Pallotta, piazza Garibaldi
20/22, T0744-715267.

❻ **Post office** Via Vittorio Emanuele 31, T0744-763811.

❼ **Tourist information office** Pro Loco Narni, piazza
dei Priori 3, T0744-715362, Tue-Sun 0930-1230, 1700-
1900. Not Umbria's most helpful tourist office.

Narni Sottoranea.

Museo della Città di Narni

Palazzo Eroli, Via Aurelio Saffi, T0744-717117,
museoeroli.it.
Apr-Jun and Sep Tue-Sun 1030-1300, 1530-1800,
Jul-Aug Tue-Sun 1030-1300, 1630-1930, Oct-Mar
Fri-Sun 1030-1300, 1500-1730, €5/3 concession.

Narni's excellent new museum and art gallery
is a two-for-one bargain. In the Palazzo Eroli, an
ancient stone lion, purportedly used by CS Lewis
as a model for Aslan, greets visitors. Upstairs, on
the first floor, a huge pair of mammoth's tusks
precedes a collection of mainly Roman remains.
These are excellently displayed – there is no
overload of pieces and the well-chosen finds

are attractively lit, though for the moment the information is only in Italian. Audioguides in English are planned. Look out especially for the Roman carved stone sarcophagus of the family Latuedi, with three portraits of son, father and mother. There are also some good medieval pieces – an eighth- or ninth-century altar from San Martino di Taizzano has some beautiful carvings, and there are some wonderfully expressive carvings from the 12th and 13th centuries, especially two men with shields and a man with a griffin. The original 14th-century basin from the town's Piazza Garibaldi fountain is also here.

In the second-floor picture gallery, the star is without doubt Domenico Ghirlandaio's 1486 *Coronation of the Virgin*. Before you reach this there are a few beautiful pieces from the early 14th century, such as a two-sided panel depicting the Madonna: one with child, one at her coronation. Ghirlandaio's masterpiece is in its own room. Black walls make it feel a little like entering a cinema, and there is always a guide on hand to give a description of the painting, together with spotlights that cleverly isolate parts of the work. Adding to the sense of drama, Baroque music plays – only instruments found in the painting were used.

The contrast between the stylized expression of the preceding art and Ghirlandaio's detailed and dazzling, almost photographic, precision is marked. On earth below, St Francis and his associates look up to heaven above, where the Virgin is crowned, surrounded by prophets. Every face here is remarkably human, and the fabrics also show virtuoso skill. On the upper level, representing heaven, one woman stands out among the assembled men, and it has been surmised that she must have been somebody important to the artist, though her identity remains a mystery.

Gozzoli's *Annunciation* is another highlight – at the time of writing it is being restored; but it is hoped that it will be back on display in the museum soon. A café, beyond the bookshop, has great views over the valley.

Cattedrale San Giovenale

Piazza Cavour.
Daily, approximately 0900-1330, 1600-1800.

Overlooking both piazza Cavour and piazza Garibaldi, Narni's cathedral was consecrated in 1145. It has 12th-century decoration around its main door, and a portico that was added later, in the 15th century. Inside there are some ancient treasures among the strangely mixed design. The Oratorio of San Cassio, on the right-hand wall, is a small chapel built in the sixth century around the grave of the town's first bishop. The wizened remains of Beata Lucia (probably unconnected to CS Lewis's Lucy, despite many claims to the contrary) are behind glass further along the same side.

Rocca di Albornoz

Information at the museum, Palazzo Eroli, T0744-717117.
Visits by guided tour only, Apr-May Fri-Sun 1100-1300, 1500-1800, Jun-Jul Sat-Sun 1100-1300, 1500-1800, Aug-Sep daily 1100-1300, 1600-1900, Oct-Mar Sat-Sun 1100-1300, 1500-1700, €3, under 12 free.

High above Narni is one of a chain of fortresses erected by Cardinal Albornoz in Umbria to reinforce papal rule. Built between 1360 and 1378, and restored and reinforced many times since, it has a quadrilateral form with towers on its corners. To reach it follow via XX Settembre from piazza Garibaldi – it's about a 15-minute walk.

The rest of the town

Two medieval buildings, **Palazzo dei Priori and Palazzo del Podestà**, face each other across the administrative centre of town, the piazza dei Priori. The former was designed by Umbrian architect Gattapone in the 14th century. The road running north and south from here was the original *cardo maximus* of the Roman town.

Narni has several interesting churches, including the beautiful little 12th-century

Around the region

Romanesque church of **Santa Maria Impensole** (via Mazzini, just north of piazza dei Priori, daily approximately 0900-1300, 1600-1830), which has a beautiful triple-arched portico and two worn griffins guarding the door. Inside, look for the carved capitals on the columns.

Remnants of Roman Narnia in and around piazza Garibaldi include an arch and a gate in the city walls just to the west. An underground cistern (steps in the centre of Piazza Garibaldi lead down to a barred door with an easily missed light switch to the right) dates from the early Middle Ages and was fed by a Roman aqueduct.

Around Narni

Amelia

Half an hour's drive west of Narni is the sleepy hill town of Amelia, with ancient walls built around the fifth century BC. Parts have been reconstructed since, but other sections, consisting of huge blocks of stone, remain. According to Roman historian Pliny, the town may have been founded as early as 800 BC, before Rome itself.

Inside the walls is a town where not very much changes very quickly. There's the **Museo Archeologico** (piazza Augusto Vera, T0744-978120, Oct-Mar Fri-Sun 1030-1300, 1530-1800, Apr-May, Jun and Sep 1030-1300, 1600-1900, Jul-Aug 1030-1300, 1630-1930, €5) with some interesting pieces. At the top of the town, next to the cathedral, stands a 12-sided clock tower, the **Torre Civico**, which dates back to 1050 – the date is inscribed on one of the stones at the base.

Otherwise Amelia is a pretty but not overly prettified town, a place to gently wander and appreciate the light shining through old arches, cats sleeping on battered stone steps and some dusty old antique shops. It's also known for its fig-candied-orange-and-chocolate *fichi girotti*.

Carsulae

T0744-334133.
22 Mar-25 Oct 0830-1930, 26 Oct-21 Mar 0830-1730, €4.40/3.30 concession.
19 km north of Narni, off SS3bis (take turning for Fonti di San Gemini and follow signs for about 3 km).

Umbria's most complete Roman remains are in one of the region's most stunning locations, under thickly wooded hills. Not much more than a stopping post on the via Flaminia, little was written about the town in Roman times. And, in terms of spectacular architecture, Carsulae cannot compete with Pompeii or Paestum further south. Where it excels, however, is in summoning up the atmosphere of ancient times. Once you've left the ticket office and passed through the turnstiles, there's almost nothing to remind you of the 2,000 years that have passed since Carsulae was a thriving Roman town. As the via Flaminia passes through oak trees on its way to the **Arco di Traiano** (also known as the Arco di San Damiano), complete with grooves ground into the stone by ancient carriage wheels, it is easy to imagine that around the corner might be centurions returning home.

After the via Flaminia was rerouted through Interamna (Terni) and Spoletium (Spoleto) to the east, Carsulae was abandoned. Only the fourth- or fifth-century **Church of San Damiano**, in the middle of the site, was subsequently built here, using stones from the Roman ruins around it. Now restored, the church has some fragmentary 15th-century frescoes.

As well as the road itself, and the 8-m high arch (once the centre of a three-arched entrance to the town), Carsulae has both a theatre and an amphitheatre in a single entertainment complex at the edge of the site, a temple, a basilica and a forum. Pick up a map of the site at the ticket office.

Narni.

Orvieto

La Badia €€€
Località La Badia 8, T0763-301959, labadiahotel.it.
Set among peaceful olive groves south of Orvieto on the road to Bagnoregio, the 12-sided tower of this sixth-century ex-abbey can easily be seen from the edge of the town. It's a fantastic location, and there's a good restaurant too, though the rooms and suites can feel dated. The public rooms, including a slick modern bar, are pristinely contemporary, however, and there's a swimming pool in summer.

Locanda Palazzone €€€
Località Rocca Ripesena, near Sferracavallo, T0763-393614, locandapalazzone.com.
4 km northwest of Orvieto.
A handsome medieval country house, this was a resting place for 14th-century pilgrims on their way to Rome. These days it has gone upmarket a little and has elegant contemporary suites, a swimming pool and views of Orvieto. It's a wine estate, and the house is surrounded by vineyards. Staff will suggest good local walks.

Grand Hotel Reale €€
Piazza del Popolo 25, T0763-341247.
Growing old gracefully, the Grand Hotel Reale is a rare find: a stylishly antique pile that has had next to no gentrification. It may have occasional rough edges, but when you're staying in a frescoed room where King Umberto I slept in 1900, you can put up with those. There's a private chapel, some baths are solid marble, others are rolltop cast iron, and even the TVs are ancient. The stairs are wide enough to herd elephants up, and homely old leather furniture and plants decorate the place. The smallest, plainer rooms here are some of the cheapest in town.

Hotel Maitani €€
Via Lorenzo Maitani 5, T0763-342011, hotelmaitani.com.
A short distance along the street opposite the cathedral, Maitani is steadfastly old-fashioned, for those who like their hotels buttoned up. The 39 rooms have baths and early 20th-century furniture and chandeliers, and there's a bar and a big lounge. Formal and – mostly – stylish.

Palazzo Piccolomini €€
Piazza Ranieri 36, T0763-341743, hotelpiccolomini.it.
Faultlessly friendly and professional, Piccolimini is an excellent option in the heart of Orvieto. The 34 rooms and suites have sturdy wooden furniture and a good range of mod cons, such as satellite TV and minibars. The building dates back to the 15th century but the hotel feels modern, with nicely renovated rooms and big common spaces that use the original structure. Plentiful parking.

Hotel Posta €
Via Luca Signorelli 18, T0763-341909, orvietohotels.it.
Big, cool, marble-floored rooms overlook a central garden. Not all rooms are en suite – those that are have bathrooms with lots of corners. There's a new lift, but otherwise not much to show for the rather slow renovation that has been going on for a while: hopefully when it's finished it won't detract from the stylish old-fashioned nature of the place. Friendly and good value.

Il Libro d'Oro €
Località Botto, Canale, T340-948 9628, librodoro.net.
6 km south of Orvieto.
Good value apartments that can be rented on a B&B basis or used for self-catering. Rooms feature iron-framed beds, pale sofas, terracotta tiles, bare wood and views over the surrounding countryside. Shiatsu massage and meditation are available.

Locanda Rosati €
Località Buonviaggio 22,
T0763-217314, locandarosati.it.
In a rural spot a few kilometres
west of Orvieto, communal
meals are a popular aspect of a
stay at this stone country house
with a swimming pool and
verdant gardens.

Todi

For somewhere with so many
visitors, Todi has a shortage of
good accommodation in the
town centre, though there are
some good options in the
surrounding hills.

Fattoria di Vibio €€€
Località Buchella 9, Doglio,
Montecastello di Vibio, T075- 874
9607, fattoriadivibio.com.
15 km north of Todi.
A large and well-equipped
rural hotel with contemporary
touches. Rustic style
predominates –rooms are
simple, with tiles and floral
fabrics, but there's a less
expected modern edge in
the use of plate glass and steel
in the spa. Separate cottages
in the grounds (available by
the week, from €1,680 to sleep
four), packages for romantic
weekends, cookery courses and
horse-riding are all available.

Relais Todini €€€
Frazione Collevalenza,
T075-887521, relaistodini.com.
9 km south of Todi.
This handsome country house
on a hill has 12 rooms, with
frescoed walls, tapestries and
antiques. There's a spa, a good
pool and a wine cellar well
stocked with wines from the
surrounding vineyards.

Fonte Cesia €€
Via Lorenzo Leonj 3,
T075-894 3737, fontecesia.it.
A stone's throw from piazza
Umberto I, in the heart of Todi,
Fonte Cesia just about has a
monopoly over guests who
want a *centro storico* hotel.
Rooms are elegant, in a slightly
old-fashioned way, with lots
of frills and drapes, and are
well equipped, with radios,
air conditioning, satellite
television, safes and minibars.
There are 37 rooms and suites
altogether, the latter both
more spacious and more stylish.
Some also have balconies.

San Lorenzo Tre €
Via San Lorenzo 3,
T075-894 4555, sanlorenzo3.it.
San Lorenzo sets itself apart from
the average old-fashioned hotel
by making almost everything
exactly as it would have been
100 years ago. With the one
concession to modernity of
en suite bathrooms, this little
place is genuinely antique.
On the upper floor of a

17th-century house, it offers six
rooms with elegant old furniture,
19th-century fabric designs,
yellowing old pictures, and a
definite absence of telephones
and televisions. The best rooms
have views over the countryside,
and the whole place has a worn
elegance and a charmingly
homely feel.

Self-catering
Casa Menicaglie
Civitella del Lago,
T+44 (0)7687 970458,
carolyn@carolynlyons.co.uk.
**Midway between Todi and
Orvieto, 3 km from Civitella
del Lago.**
Owned by two English writers,
Casa Menicaglie is a pretty
hideaway in the hills above
Lago di Corbara in the Parco
Regionale del Tevere. Sleeping
five and available by the week
(£750), it's hard not to feel
instantly at home here. Books
line the walls and there's an
attractive open kitchen and
sitting area. Sit on the patio by
the olive grove and watch the
sun set behind Orvieto and the
wooded hills above the Tiber
Valley. At the end of the summer
there are more figs than you
could possibly eat, and probably
the only sounds will be crickets
and the occasional distant
tractor, though you may hear
the rustle of porcupines and
wild boar at night.

Eating & drinking

Hotel Minareto €€
Via dei Cappuccini Nuovi 32,
T0744-760207.
An ex-convent with great views,
the hotel has a pool and refined
rooms with metal-framed beds
and a profusion of burgundy.
There's not much evidence
left of the Capuchin monks,
however, bar some old walls and
a couple of ancient pillars in what
was once the cloister.

Torre Palombara €€
Strada della Cantinetta 3, T0744-
744617, torrepalombara.com.
6 km south of Narni.
A country villa built around
a 15th-century tower, with
views of Narni. It's a quiet,
elegant spot, with a pool
and gardens. A sympathetic
restoration, natural tones, wood
and bare stonework are used to
good effect, and cable TV and
internet access are some of the
modern comforts.

La Loggia dei Priori €
Vicolo del Comune 4, T0744-
726843, loggiadeipriori.it.
A good three-star in the centre
of Narni, dei Priori has 19 plain
rooms and suites but cosy public
spaces, with a greenery-draped
courtyard and an open fire in
winter. Some brick vaulting gives
an element of medieval styling,
and the welcome is friendly.

I Sette Consoli €€€
Piazza Sant'Angelo 1a,
T0763-343911, isetteconsoli.it.
Thu-Tue 1230-1500, 1930-2200,
closed Feb.
Orvieto's smartest restaurant,
I Sette Consoli is a barrel-vaulted
place with a garden adorned
with lots of white drapes.
There's a €45 set menu featuring
dishes such as spaghetti with
rabbit and braised veal cheek.

Antico Bucchero €€
Via de' Cartari 4, T0763-341725.
Thu-Tue 1200 onwards, 1900
onwards.
Tables outside in a beautiful little
piazza, hidden away from most
of the throng, are the biggest
draw here, though the food is
also excellent. Try the succulent
melon and ham, and the
excellent tortelloni filled with
ricotta and radicchio with
courgettes and pecorino.

Cavour 222 €€
Corso Cavour 222, T0763-393518.
Tue-Sun 1200-1600, 1900-2200.
A simple osteria halfway along
the main street, with five tables
outside under umbrellas.
There are daily specials and
good pasta with porcini.
Nothing complicated, but
a good spot for a late lunch with
a view – they serve until 1600.

Da Carlo €€
Vicolo del Popolo 9,
T0763-344406.
Tue-Sun.
On a quiet, pretty little piazza
off corso Cavour, what used to
be widely regarded as Orvieto's
best restaurant, L'Asino d'Oro,
has now been reborn under
new management as Da Carlo.
Unusually in Orvieto, it has a slick,
young feel, with baby blue and
white paintwork and bare wood.
A handwritten blackboard menu
changes regularly, but dishes
may include sausage with
grapes, pigeon with figs,
or a spicy *pollo al rabbioncino*.

La Pergola €€
Via dei Magoni 9b,
T0763-343065.
Thu-Tue 0900-1600, 1900-2400.
Popular with locals, this little
restaurant has a pretty garden
at the back and serves good,
unpretentious Umbrian food
such as beef carpaccio with
rocket and Parmesan, and
gnocchi with spinach and truffle.
The wine list also features some
interesting artisan beers.

Gelaterie

Orvieto has three great ice cream places, making it the best town in Umbria for a gelato – you should really try them all.

Dolceamaro
Corso Cavour 78, T0763-342125.
A small selection of homemade ice cream and mouth-wateringly good chocolates, plus cakes and biscuits.

Gelateria Pasqualetti
Piazza del Duomo 14,
T0763-341034.
Exquisite homemade ice cream opposite the Duomo. Try the wild strawberry or the pink grapefruit.

Gelateria La Musa
Corso Cavour 351, T0763-393861.
Fabulous homemade ice cream, including some unusual seasonal flavours, such as pears in Barolo wine.

La Volpe e l'Uva €€
Via Ripa Corsica 11, T0763-341612.
Wed-Sun 1300-1500, 2000-2230.
With small rooms under barrel-vaulted brick ceilings and white walls, this is a friendly place where the chef may well come out to chat. The back room has air conditioning and old, fading pictures. The handwritten menu is truffle-heavy, but you could also try the Lake Bolsena fish in white wine, and be sure to save some room for the excellent homemade biscuits with dessert wine.

Le Grotte del Funaro €€
Via Ripa Serancia 41, T0763-343276, grottedelfunaro.it.
Tue-Sun 1200-1500, 1900-2400.
Sit in cool, underground vaulted caves, once home to Orvieto's rope makers, or at tables outside, on the edge of the town with great views. Fish features nearly as much as meat on the menu, and there are 24 pizzas on offer too.

Trattoria dell'Orso €€
Via della Misericordia 18-20, T0763-341642.
Tue-Sat 1230-1400, 1930-2130.
One of the oldest restaurants in town, Gabriele and Ciro's place is frequented by a cross-section of Orvieto – expect to eat here next to Italian aristocrats, businessmen, market stallholders and a few in-the-know visitors. All come for the simple but expertly prepared Umbrian food with a healthy side order of friendly patter. Prices are slightly higher than in the average trattoria, and the printed menu is almost completely ignored, but the owners speak good English and if you're happy to go with their recommendations you'll be guaranteed a fabulous meal of dishes such as pancakes stuffed with spinach and ricotta, chicken with peppers, or bass with courgettes. There's plenty of character in the two rooms – one yellow and red, one yellow and green – with an eclectic and colourful art collection and a Michelangeli wooden frieze.

Zeppelin €€
Via Garibaldi 28, T0763-341447, ristorantezeppelin.it.
Tue-Sun 1230-1430, 1930-2200.
A big place with high, arched ceilings, Zeppelin has a marble bar, a garden with lemon trees and a menu with lots of exclamation marks and several set options, including a vegetarian menu and some carefully seasoned meaty choices. As well as eating, you can also cook here. One-day

courses focus on fresh pasta, poultry and game, truffles or vegetarian cuisine, or there's a half-day chocolate course.

La Palomba €
Via Cipriano Manente 16, off piazza della Repubblica, T0763-343395.
Thu-Tue 1230-1415, 1930-2200.
A local place with wood panelling and photos old and new on the walls, serving traditional Umbrian dishes with few concessions to modernity – pigeon, tripe, lamb and boar all feature. Very reasonable prices.

Pizzeria Charlie €
Corso Cavour 194, T0763-344766, pizzeriacharlieorvieto.it.
Wed-Mon 1900-2330.
Orvieto's best pizzas are served in this popular spot with small wooden tables inside and out on the main drag. There's German Paulaner beer on tap, free Wi-Fi to accompany your Margherita, and – unusually for Orvieto – it stays open late into the evening.

Cafés & bars
Barrique
Corso Cavour 111, T0763-340455.
Tue-Sun 0700-2200.
A good spot for people watching, Barrique does fantastic coffee and pretty good cakes too, and has tables outside on the street.

Cantina Foresi
Piazza del Duomo 2, T0763-341611.
Daily 1100-1930.
On the piazza, with tables facing the Duomo, this is a great spot for an *aperitivo* or a light meal – go for a standard plate of meat and cheese or a more adventurous mixed selection of wild boar or pheasant with mushrooms.

Enoteca Tozzi
Piazza del Duomo 13, T0763-344393.
Daily 0900-2000.
Two tables outside face the side of the cathedral; inside is an unexpectedly high-ceilinged place with lots of wine and decent sandwiches for €2-3.

Il Vincaffè
Via Filippeschi 39, T0763-340099, ilvincafe.it.
Wed-Fri 1230-1530, 1830-0200, Sat and Mon-Tue 1830-0200, Sun 1730-0200.
An *enoteca* that stays open late and has unusually good vegetarian options such as courgette, lemon and ricotta salad, or lentils and pepper. It's a fairly simple place, with a bar, square wooden tables and jazz playing.

Todi

Antica Osteria della Valle €€
Via Ciuffelli 17-21, T075-894 4848.
Thu-Tue 1230-1430, 1930-2200.
Seduced by Umbrian ingredients, the English chef of the Antica Osteria della Valle gave up working in restaurants in London to set up on his own here. Overcoming initial scepticism on the part of locals, it is now considered by many to be Todi's best restaurant. The seasonal menu always includes fish and a handful of signature dishes, such as ravioli with ricotta, spinach and cream of truffle. The restaurant also shows paintings from local artists, which change every few months.

Pane e Vino €€
Via Ciuffelli 33, T075-894 5448, panevinotodi.com.
Thu-Tue 1100-1530, 1830-2300.
A simple but popular little place just off the street, with a few crowded tables outside and a three-level, yellow-walled interior. Traditional Umbrian dishes predominate – the risotto with courgettes and saffron is rich and creamy, and the pasta with fresh tomatoes and lemons has a good tang to it. The mixed crostini are excellent too, and hunks of meat are enormous. Friendly service and extras such as warm homemade bread help attract both locals and visitors.

Ristorante Umbria €€
Via San Bonaventura 13,
T075-894 2737.
Wed-Mon 1230-1430,
1930-2230.
Under the arches of Palazzo del
Popolo, Umbria is a traditional
restaurant with an open fire, over
which meat is grilled, and a good
self-service buffet of vegetables.
It is best known for its terrace,
however, which has enormous
views over the surrounding
countryside. Steadfastly
Umbrian, truffles are joined
on the menu by other local
ingredients such as venison
and chestnuts. Not a place to
come if you're in a hurry, but a
great spot to linger.

Cavour €
Corso Cavour 21-23,
T075-894 2491.
Thu-Tue 1200-1600, 1900-late.
A large and good-value pizzeria,
with an equally big choice
of toppings, Cavour also has
traditional dishes, and there's
a bar with beer on tap.
The brick-vaulted interior
has slightly garish pink walls.

Cafés & bars
Enoteca Oberdan
Via Ciufelli 22, T075-894 5409.
Wed-Sun 1200-2400.
An attractive and laid-back
wine bar, Oberdan offers a good
selection of cheeses and cold
meats as well as more substantial
dishes such as spelt flour pasta
with an aubergine, pepper
and ricotta sauce. Wine is the
mainstay, however, and bottles
line the walls, around small
square wooden tables and
painted wooden chairs.

Pianegani
Corso Cavour 40, T075-894 2376.
Apr-Oct daily 0700-0100,
Nov-Mar Sun-Fri 0700-2300.
A fairly nondescript bar,
Pianegiani does unexpectedly
good ice cream, using good,
local, seasonal ingredients.

Narni

Il Gattamelata €€
Via Pozzo della Comunitá 4,
T0744-717245.
Tue-Sun around 1200 onwards,
1900 onwards.
Overlooking the piazza Garibaldi,
Gattamelata has a distinctive
portico with good views.
The menu has vegetarian
suggestions as well as traditional
local dishes such as *manfricoli*
pasta or gnocchi with almonds,
spinach and Parmesan, or you
can go for a 'thin' or 'fat' medieval
fixed menu featuring goose and
eel, by reservation only.

Il Pincio €€
Via XX Settembre 117, T0744-
722241, ristoranteilpincio.it.
Thu-Tue 1230-1500, 1930-2200.
Stylish traditional Umbrian food
with the addition of seafood on
Tuesdays, Thursdays and Fridays.
Part of the interior of the
restaurant is a cave. Themed
fixed menus through the year
for around €45 are real feasts.

La Gallina Liberata €€
Vicolo Belvedere 13,
T0744-081561.
Wed-Sun, lunch only (evenings
by reservation).
At first glance the 'liberated
chicken' is a deceptively simple
place, with three tables outside
on a sandy, slightly decrepit
stepped street. Inside it's much
smarter: barrel vaulted, with a
contemporary, flowing, painted
design suggestive of the beach
and sea. The fresh, homemade
pasta dishes are some of the
best you'll eat anywhere.
The homemade desserts are also
spectacular. A short, handwritten
menu changes monthly.

Terra & Arte €
Vicolo Belvedere 1, T0744-726385.
Daily 0800-2130.
Wine and good light meals just
off piazza Garibaldi from the
same management as Il Pincio.
Tables outside are good for
sunny days, and there are
excellent spreads of local
cured meats and cheeses.

Shopping

Books

Libreria dei Sette
Corso Cavour 85, T0763-344436.
Mon-Fri 0900-1100, Sat-Sun
1000-2000.
A good little bookshop with
lots of maps and guides.

Food & drink

Ortofrutta
Corso Cavour 236, T0763-344716.
An excellent little fruit and veg
shop selling fresh, local produce.
Also drinks and nuts.

Dai Fratelli
Via del Duomo 11, T0763-343965.
Mon-Sat 0830-1330, 1700-2000,
closed Wed afternoon.
A great selection of pecorino
as well as oozing Gorgonzola
and jars of truffles. Despite its
position in the heart of the town,
a delicatessen that always hums
with locals.

Enoteca La Rosa
*Corso Cavour 317, T0763-342957,
enotecalarosa.com.*
Thu-Tue 1200-1900.
A good modern wine shop,
they also have a range of shiny
corkscrews, should you have
left yours at home.

Marco Ubaldini
*Piazza della Repubblica 29,
T3891-551449.*
Mon-Sat 0800-1330, 1700-2000
(closed Wed afternoon).
A tiny little place packed
high with delicious things,
from bread, cheese and cured
meats to delicious Rose del
Deserto biscuits.

Gifts

Una Pagina del Libro d'Oro
*Corso Cavour 307, T340-948
9628, info@librodoro.net.*
A toy shop with a fine line in
mechanical wooden toys and
'paper animation' – interesting
things you can make that move.

Michelangeli
*Via Gualverio Michelangeli 3,
T0763-342660, michelangeli.it.*
Mon-Tue and Thu-Sat
0900-1300, 1600-2000, Wed
0900-1300.
A wander around the streets
of Orvieto will reveal wooden
friezes and 'urban furniture', on
walls, on street corners and in
restaurants. Via Michelangeli has
a particular concentration, and
the homonymous shops of this
200-year old Orvietan furniture
makers are also here, though
these days they have branched
out into toys, puppets and
rocking horses, all with a
charming Orvietan style.

Homeware

Menabò
*Vicolo del Popolo 12/14,
T0763-393900.*
Mon-Sat 0930-1400, 1600-2100.
A great collection of
Scandinavian, Italian and
international design items,
with a good line in kitchen
gadgets, lights, stationery,
cutlery and colourful crockery.

Marco Cionco Antiquario
Via Ciufelli 7, no phone.
Daily 1000-1300, 1530-1900.
An enormous selection of brass
and other metal antiques, from
bells and door knockers to lamps
and corkscrews.

Activities & tours

Cycling
Eurobici
Via Angelo Costanzi 24, Orvieto Scalo, T393-992 4469, eurobici.net.
If you fancy cycling around the Route Rupe in Orvieto, or further afield, Eurobici has bikes for rent.

Language courses
La Lingua la Vita
Via Mazzini 18, Todi, T075-894 8364, lalingualavita.com.
Courses of Italian lessons, from a week in length, start at €375 per person, including a double room.

Photography
Camera Etrusca
Corso Cavour 273, Orvieto, T0763-562005, cameraetrusca.com.
1-day courses from €200 per person, residential courses from €699 for 4 days, €1,217 per week.
Patrick Nicholas, a British photographer, has lived in Italy for 27 years and now has a gallery in Orvieto (daily in summer, 0900-2000), where he does a good trade in fine art Italian landscapes and photographic nudes in the styles of old masterpieces. He also runs guided photographic trips and photo workshops in the surrounding area. Residential courses for small groups over four days or a week include food, accommodation and, if need be, kit. It's also possible to do one-day trips. Courses focus on landscapes in southwest Umbria and parts of neighbouring Lazio and Tuscany – the so-called *civiltà del tufo*. His years of experience in the area mean Patrick knows the best places to go for great shots, and his technical know-how is put to good use too. Courses can include tuition in Adobe Photoshop and printing, and attendees are usually a good mix of experts and complete beginners.

Transport

Orvieto

Orvieto Scalo is on the main Rome to Florence line; you'll need to change to get to Perugia. With a car, it's also easy to reach Orvieto from Todi, though by public transport it's nearly impossible.

Todi

Todi is on the private Perugia to Terni FCU line (fcu.it), with about 12 trains a day from Perugia Santa Anna station (45 mins). From Orvieto buses are so infrequent as to make the journey impractical, but from Perugia there are nine buses a day, taking 1 hour 15 minutes.

Narni

There are direct trains from Spoleto to Narni-Amelia (35 mins). Buses (atcterni.it) run from Amelia (15 or so a day, around 30 mins) and there are about five a day from Orvieto (around 75 mins).

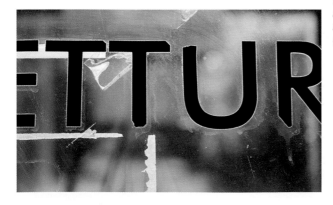

Medieval coats of arms, Gubbio.

Contents

Northern Umbria

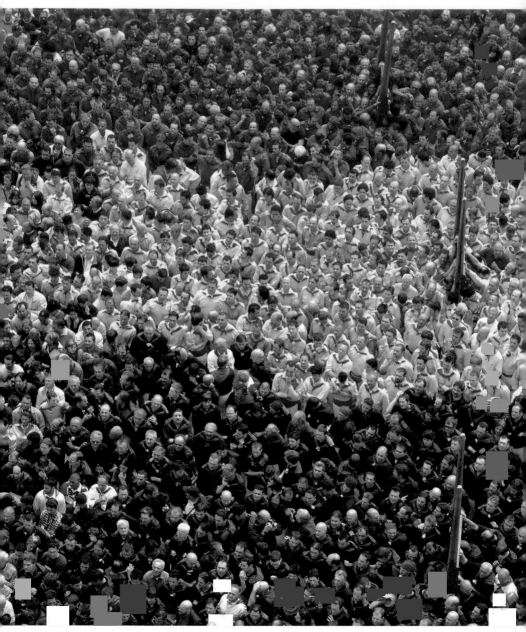

Introduction

With fewer significant towns, Umbria's north also has fewer visitors, leaving plenty of space for those who do venture this way. Gubbio, to the east, is justifiably the one exception – with remarkable architecture, some colourful local traditions and a vertiginously exhilarating cable car, the town is just about on the tourist trail. Beyond, the Parco Regionale di Monte Cucco is a favourite with hang-gliders, who often hold world championships here, drawn by the warm currents blowing up the steep mountain slopes. It also has some great walks among its high-altitude beech forests.

Up the Tiber Valley, Città di Castello is an interesting town with some world-class 20th-century art, a good chamber music festival and some fine rolling countryside, pungent with the smell of tobacco that grows here. In the vicinity, Montone is a sleepy, attractive village with good views over the hills, and there are plenty of isolated *agriturismi* in which to get away from it all.

What to see in...

...one day
Gubbio's medieval streets and hillside setting make it the jewel of Umbria's north. Start in the piazza Grande, where the **Palazzo dei Consoli** contains museums – don't miss the **Eugubian Tablets**. Higher up, the **Palazzo Ducale** has echoes of its grander Urbino namesake and the **Duomo** is worth a visit. At the bottom of the hill, ruins of a **Roman amphitheatre** can be freely explored. Get an extra injection of adrenaline from a trip in the rickety **cable car**, for great views and a glass of wine at the top.

...a weekend or more
Città di Castello can't quite match Gubbio's charm, but it's an attractive place with some good museums and excellent contemporary art. Climb the cylindrical **clock tower** and check out **Burri**'s enormous art in two sites – in the town and, memorably, in gigantic ex-tobacco drying sheds. Pretty **Montone**, in the nearby hills, makes a good side-trip. For more serious peaks, the **Monte Cucco** park has good walks as well as opportunities for hang-gliding.

The world-famous Race of the Ceri.

Gubbio

Isolated in the northeast of Umbria, at the edge of the high Apennine Mountains, traditional Gubbio retains its medieval feel, with pale grey stone arched streets and keenly held loyalties to the four ancient quarters of the city. Its central piazza is a spectacular and ambitious ensemble of Gothic architecture, and there are several worthwhile sights, including the cathedral, several churches and palazzi, and an adrenaline-inducing cable car ride to the top of Monte Ingino.

Probably the central settlement of the pre-Roman Umbri people, Gubbio is proud of its roots, and the museum houses the Eugubian Tablets, vital to the understanding of the linguistic and cultural history of Italy. The ruins of a Roman theatre sit outside the old city walls, and several enthusiastically enacted festivals and palios through the year underline the town's fascination with the past.

Even in high summer Gubbio rarely feels overrun with visitors. Contrasting with some industrial development in the plain below the town, the high hills rising to the east, which culminate in the Parco Regionale del Monte Cucco, are a cool escape into the high Umbrian wilderness.

Below: View from the Loggia Panoramica in the Palazzo dei Consoli. Opposite page: Duomo, Gubbio.

Piazza Grande

At the centre of the four quarters of the medieval town, Gubbio's 14th-century piazza was built as a unifying point, as well as to emphasize the power of the State over the Church following the construction of the Duomo, just up the hill. The building of the piazza was agreed in 1322, but it was not finished until 1483.

Despite the gigantic Palazzo dei Consoli, it is not until it is seen from below, along via Ubaldo Baldassini, that the extraordinary scale of the project becomes clear. The piazza is raised on four huge stone arches, each the size of a small house, in order to create a large flat area on the Gubbio slopes.

Facing the Palazzo dei Consoli is the **Palazzo del Podestà**, built to a similar design, but unfinished and nowadays used for temporary exhibitions.

Palazzo dei Consoli

Piazza Grande, T075-927 4298, comune.gubbio.pg.it. Apr-Oct 1000-1300, 1500-1800, Nov-Mar 1000-1300, 1400-1700, €5.

Containing the **Museo Civico** as well as the art gallery and the archaeological museum, the 60-m tall Palazzo dei Consoli towers over the town. Though the stars of the show are the famous **Tavole Iguvine** – also known as the Eugubian or Eugubine Tablets – other attractions include fantastic views from the top of the tower, some good Gothic art and even some medieval toilets.

Steps from piazza Grande rise to the main entrance and the huge, barrel-vaulted **Sala d'Arengo** (Assembly Room), which is now home to various fragments of stone from Umbri and Roman times, from gravestones to engraved signs from the ancient theatre. Downstairs, the new oriental and Risorgimento collections are generally of less interest, though there are some impressive pieces of Tibetan metalwork.

On the first floor are the Eugubian Tablets: seven large bronze plates engraved with text, five in Umbrian, two in Latin. Often compared to the

Essentials

❶ Getting around Walking is the easiest way to get around the town. There's free parking near the Teatro Romano.

❷ Buses Buses arrive at and leave from piazza Quaranta Martiri, and run from here to the cable car station and most main sites.

❸ Hospital Via San Francesco, T075-942 2111.

❹ Pharmacy Farmacia Comunale, piazza Quaranta Martiri, T07-927 2243.

❺ Post office Via Cairoli 11, T075-927 3925.

❻ Tourist information Piazza Oderisi 6, corso Garibaldi, T075-922 0693, comune.gubbio.pg.it, Mon-Fri 0830-1345, 1530-1830, Sat 0900-1300, 1530-1830, Sun 0930-1230, 1530-1830 (Oct-Mar afternoons 1500-1800).

Rosetta Stone, they describe rites and religious ceremonies, including animal sacrifices intended to protect the city from its enemies. They are important because of what they have taught scholars about pre-Roman times and language, but are also beautiful objects in their own right, with text that seems remarkably modern in both style and execution. Occasional mistakes give them an extra human angle.

There is some debate about how they were discovered, but the most common story is that in 1444 they were found by a farmer in an underground chamber near the Roman theatre, and that he sold them to the city in 1456 in return for two years' grazing rights.

Gubbio listings

❶ Sleeping

1 **Bosone Palace** *via XX Settembre 22*
2 **Relais Ducale** *via Galeotti 19*
3 **Residenza di via Piccardi** *via Piccardi 12*
4 **La Ginestra** *Valmarcola, Santa Cristina*
5 **Locanda del Gallo** *Località Santa Cristina*

❶ Eating & drinking

1 **Caffè Tre Ceri** *next to the Palazzo Ducale*
2 **Dei Consoli** *via dei Consoli 59*
3 **L'Arte Golosa** *via dei Consoli 97*
4 **La Fornace di Mastro Giorgio** *via Mastro Giorgio 2*
5 **La Madia di Giuseppe** *via Mastro Giorgio 2/6*
6 **Locanda del Cantiniere** *via Dante 30*
7 **Taverna del Lupo** *via Ansidei 21*

Look for the palazzo's *'passaggio segreto'* in order to find the medieval toilets ('Don't lift the lid,' a sign declares, ominously), complete with plumbing but without much in the way of privacy.

From here stairs rise to the **Pinacoteca**, on the top floor. The history of Gubbian art is illustrated by paintings such as a rather beautiful 16th-century *Noli me Tangere* on wood, by either Girolamo Genga or Timoteo Viti – as well as the obligatory, and unusually seductive, central Italian landscape, it incorporates a small cupboard for religious relics. Other works to look out for include a *Virgin and Child* by Guiduccio Palmerucci, with local saint Ubaldo featuring prominently. The influence of Sienese art can easily be seen here,

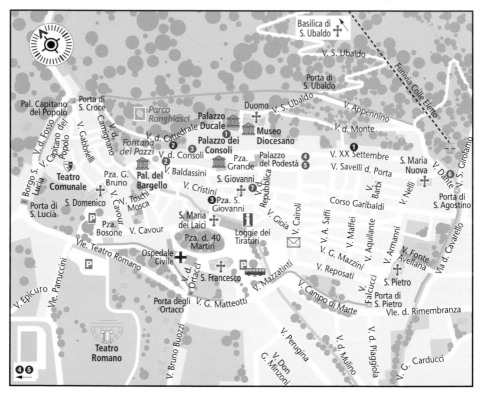

in both the profusion of gold and the tender relationship between mother and baby.

From the picture gallery, the **Loggia Panoramica** shouldn't be missed – it has great views over the town and the surrounding countryside.

In the basement, entered from the back of the palazzo, the archaeological museum (same ticket and opening hours) is, by Italian standards, not very exciting, though there are a couple of interesting pieces, including some engraved slingshot and a beautiful eighth-century stone sarcophagus.

Palazzo Ducale

Via della Cattedrale, T075-927 5872.
Tue-Sun 0830-1900, €2/free under 17.

Gubbio's Ducal Palace, opposite the cathedral, was probably designed by the same architect as the more famous palace in Urbino (see page 223), of which it is a smaller version. The seat of Duke Federico of Montefeltro when he was in town, it was built in the 1470s on the site of a Lombard building. These days the interior is fairly plain, but there is a fine porticoed Renaissance courtyard, as well as some great views across Gubbio.

Duomo

Via Cattedrale.
Daily 0900-1800, free.

Up the hill in a quiet part of town, Gubbio's cathedral has an unusual wagon-vaulted ceiling, with small side chapels off a single nave. It was probably designed by Giovanni da Gubbio, who also designed Assisi's cathedral. The building was finished around 1203.

The 1549 choir is impressively carved but inaccessible. There are fragments of original frescoes on the walls, two saints – Giovanni da Lodi and Virginia – and two other holy corpses. The many paintings around the walls include a 16th-century *Pietà* by Dono Doni. A coin machine illuminates the apse and chapel.

Museo Diocesano

Via Federico da Montefeltro,
T075-922 0904, museogubbio.org.
Summer 1000-1900,
winter 1000-1800 (may close Tue), €4.

Gubbio's diocesan museum has a good archaeological collection as well as religious paintings. Highlights include fifth- and fourth-century BC pottery and ex-votos, such as a rather surprised-looking donkey carrying two pots and some intricately painted cups. Downstairs, in Mello da Gubbio's 14th-century *Virgin and Child*, some pretty angels surround two decidedly chubby central figures. One of the most impressive objects in the museum can be seen only from the street outside – the *botte grande* is a gargantuan wine barrel from the 15th century, which once held 20,000 litres of wine.

Fontana dei Pazzi

Local myth states that three turns around this fountain, at the northern end of via dei Consoli, will make you mad. There may be a connection with stories that ancient Rome used to send people it considered mad to Gubbio.

Piazza Quaranta Martiri

This large, busy piazza at the bottom of town is the arrival point for buses. Opposite the large Church of San Francesco, the loggia, built in 1603 on top of a 14th-century portico, was once used for the stretching of wool. Nowadays fruit and veg are sold under the awnings, and there's a fully fledged market in the piazza on Tuesday mornings.

The piazza is named after the 40 townsfolk executed here by German soldiers in 1944, in retribution for partisan fighting in the hills. To its south, along via Perugina, a mausoleum commemorates those killed. Behind a flowerbed, bullet holes are still obvious in the wall.

Around the region

Chiesa di San Francesco

Piazza Quaranta Martiri.
Daily 0715-1200, 1530-1930, free.

Built in 1256, soon after St Francis's canonization, this pale stone Gothic church has three naves and an attractive cloister, the Chiostro della Pace. In the left apse, early 15th-century frescoes by Ottaviano Nelli tell the story of the *Life of the Virgin*.

Teatro Romano

Viale Teatro Romano.
Daily Apr-Sep 0830-1930, Oct-Mar 0830-1730, free.

Built some time between 55 and 27 BC, Gubbio's theatre, outside the city walls, may once have held as many as 16,000 spectators, making it one of the biggest Roman theatres. These days it's an evocative, dusty place, with grass growing up between the old stones. Some of its outer arches are still intact, and enough of the central seating survives to make it a good venue for open-air plays in summer.

An antiquarium displays pottery and other Roman remnants found in the area. Also nearby is a ruined Roman mausoleum – the original outer layer is gone, but a 6-m by 4.5-m burial chamber is intact.

Funivia & Basilica di Sant'Ubaldo

Cable car: via San Girolamo, T075-927 7507.
Mar Mon-Sat 1000-1315, 1430-1730, Sun 0930-1315, 1430-1800; Apr-May Mon-Sat 1000-1315, 1430-1830, Sun 0930-1315, 1430-1800; Jun Mon-Sat 0930-1315, 1430-1900, Sun 0900-1930; Jul-Aug 0900-2000; 1-11 Sep Mon-Sat 0930-1900, Sun 0930-1930; 12-30 Sep Mon-Sat 0930-1900, Sun 0900-1930; Oct 1000-1315, 1430-1800; Nov-Feb Thu-Tue 1000-1315, 1430-1700; €5 return.

Gubbio's biggest thrill is its eccentric cable car ride up Monte Ingino. The five-minute ride to the top, in small baskets that hold two standing passengers, gives extraordinary views of the plain below as you are whisked over the treetops. Getting in and out of the moving, creaking cages is part of the adventure – someone will tell you to

Above: Teatro Romano. Opposite page: San Giovanni Battista with its quartiere flag and Palazzo dei Consoli behind.

stand on a red spot and bundle you in; someone else drags you out at the other end. Hold tight and have your camera well strapped to your wrist.

At the top is a café, a restaurant and the Basilica di Sant'Ubaldo, patron saint of Gubbio. This church is the destination for the annual palio known as the **Corsa dei Ceri**, when the three guilds of Gubbio race against each other, with each team carrying one of the enormous *ceri* – huge wooden 'candles' each weighing around 280 kg. The *ceri* are kept here in the church for the rest of the year.

The basilica is not quite at the top of the hill – from it a path leads up to the **Rocca**, the ruins of an old castle at the summit. The scaffolding just below it is here to support the star of an enormous Christmas 'tree', made of lights, which illuminates the entire hill in December. If one trip in a basket is enough for you, from here you can continue walking north and then east, around to the summit of **Monte Anciano**, before descending via the **Monastero di San Girolamo** to Gubbio.

The Gubbio Layer

The so-called 'Gubbio Layer' was discovered at the nearby gorge, the **Gola del Bottaccione**. A 1-cm-thick sedimentary sandwich filling between rocks of the Cretaceous and Tertiary eras, it was laid down 65 million years ago at the time of the extinction of the dinosaurs. It is rich in iridium, a heavy metal rare on Earth but relatively common in comets and asteroids, giving rise to the now widely accepted theory of brothers Walter and Luis Alvarez that a massive extraterrestrial collision caused the dinosaurs to die out. The discovery of the iridium here, in 1978, changed the face of palaeontology. Subsequent finds in the Gubbio Layer of tektites – small globules of molten material formed by the extreme heat of a meteorite impact – would seem to confirm the theory.

The gorge has an extraordinary sequence of limestone strata, tilted towards the vertical so that you can walk past 100 million years of geological history. The road from Gubbio to Scheggia passes through the gorge, between Monte Ingino and Monte Foce.

Parco Regionale di Monte Cucco

East of Gubbio the Apennines rise high above the valley floor, and the beech forests on their flanks are home to wild boar, wolves, wild cats, golden eagles and porcupines. A protected area surrounds the peaks, culminating at the top of Monte Cucco, 1566 m above sea level. Below ground, the park has a huge cave system, descending over 990 m, while above is a favourite spot for paragliders and hang-gliders – the 2008 Women's Hang-gliding World Championships were held here.

There are some great walks to be done, notably to the summit of Monte Cucco but also in the **Rio Freddo Gorge** and in more remote valleys such as the **Valle delle Prigioni**. In winter, attention switches to cross-country skiing.

Monte Cucco

The easiest approach to Monte Cucco is up via del Ranco from the village of Sigillo. After several vertiginous switchbacks this forks left to **Pian di Monte** and right to the small hamlet of **Ranco**. In summer a couple of bars and restaurants open here, and many Italians set up weekend picnics on the grassy slopes beside the road.

Well-signposted paths lead from the car park below the **Albergo Ristorante Monte Cucco di Tobia** (T075-917 7194, albergomontecucco.it) out into the beech forest. Even in high summer the crowds of Val di Ranco soon disappear, and the only sounds are the breeze in the trees and a chorus of crickets in the clearings.

Park details

Park authority: **Consorzio Obbligatorio di Gestione del Parco del Monte Cucco**
Villa Anita, via Matteotti 52, Sigillo, T075-917 7326, parcomontecucco.it.

To the summit

A good, four-hour circular walk from Val di Ranco, via the summit of Monte Cucco, initially follows *sentiero 1* from the car park in front of the restaurant. Marked with red-and-white striped waymarks, as well as occasional signposts, the wide, easy path curves around through the trees before bearing right by a spring and, after about 45 minutes, climbing steeply through the **Passo del Lupo**. The forest here is especially beautiful, with sunlight filtering down through mature trees and a scattering of flowers on the forest floor. Cowbells signal the whereabouts of grazing herds. A half-hour ascent brings you out at a refuge, with good views and a large area of grass – another popular summer picnic spot.

From here a road heads north – go along it for 150 m or so, until a path (*sentiero 2*) leads off to the left. This is an especially steep climb, but well worth it for what awaits above the tree line. Turn left to follow a blessedly flat, well-constructed path along the edge of steep slopes covered with grass and orchids. The path becomes increasingly spectacular as it bends around the mountain. At the next junction, turn right on to *sentiero 14*, which leads to the summit of the mountain, with breathtaking views in all directions.

Below the summit to the south, a path back down to Pian di Monte winds east from an iron cross. You'll probably see hang-gliders and paragliders. From here you can follow the road back to Val di Ranco.

Città di Castello & Upper Tiber Valley

Little visited, Città di Castello has a surprisingly attractive *centro storico* with excellent museums, great art old and new, tasty eateries and a large selection of places to stay in the surrounding hills. The outskirts of the town are somewhat blighted by its industry – mainly tobacco processing, the crop being grown in the surrounding Upper Tiber Valley, which creates a pungent aroma as you drive along the winding roads through wooded hills.

There was an ancient Umbrian town here called Tifernum, which later became a Roman municipality. The rich Vitelli family ran the town in the 15th and 16th centuries, leaving several palaces that survive today.

Below: Tobacco fields near Città di Castello. Opposite page: Piazza Matteotti, Città di Castello.

Pinacoteca Comunale

Via della Cannoniera, T075-852 0656.
Tue-Sun Apr-Oct 1000-1300, 1430-1830,
Nov-Mar 1000-1300, 1500-1800, €6/4 concession.

Città di Castello's large picture gallery is in the
Palazzo Vitelli alla Cannoniera, built for the rich
Vitelli family around 1530. The building itself has
fine Renaissance decoration inside and out, and
houses an excellent collection of art, including
paintings by Raphael and Signorelli.

Preceded by some medieval panels of the
Madonna and Child, the collection's real strengths lie
in its Renaissance art. A late 15th-century *Coronation
of the Virgin* comes from the Florentine workshop of
Domenico Ghirlandaio, while Raphael's flaking
banner, *Gonfalon of the Holy Trinity*, would once have
been used in processions: it depicts Sts Sebastian and
Roch kneeling at the bottom of the cross, suggesting
that it was connected with an outbreak of the plague
in Città di Castello in 1499. Local artist Francesco
Tifernate's elegant 1505 *Annunciation* shows the
extent to which he was influenced by Raphael.
Nearby Cortona, in Tuscany, features as a backdrop to
Luca Signorelli's 1498 *Martyrdom of San Sebastian*. The
saint, as always, is depicted shot through with arrows;
nattily dressed archers reload their bows below, while
God looks down from above.

Cattedrale di San Florido

Piazza Gabriotti.
Daily 0900-1200, 1600-1930.

Consecrated in 1540, Città di Castello's cathedral
is an agglomeration of different eras – its strange,
unfinished façade being a prime example. Begun
in 1632, it incorporates a 14th-century Gothic
portal and 18th-century stairs.

Inside is much the same: the original dome
was destroyed in an earthquake in 1794, the ceiling
is from the 17th century, the chapel from the 18th.
While it's a welcome cool space in summer, the
cathedral is most notable for the beautiful
11th-century Romanesque bell tower, which it
mostly obscures, and its adjoining museum.

Essentials

⊙ Getting around The town is flat and easily
walkable. There's free parking outside the walls,
near porta San Giacomo and piazza Garibaldi.

⊙ Trains The station is a 10-min walk from the centre.

⊖ Buses Buses leave from piazza Garibaldi.

⊕ Hospital Largo Giovanni Muzi Betti, T075-85091.

⊕ Pharmacy Farmacia Ducci, piazza Matteotti,
T075-855 4331.

⟳ Post office Viale Gramsci 1, T075-862 8211.

⊙ Tourist information office Piazza Matteotti, T075-
855 4922, Mon-Fri 0830-1330, 1530-1830, Sat 0930-1230,
1530-1830, Sun 0930-1230.

Tip...

Most of Città di Castello's sights are closed on Mondays.

Museo del Duomo

Piazza Gabriotti 3a, T075-855 4705,
museoduomocdc.it.
Tue-Sun 1000-1300, 1500-1830, €6/3 concession
(includes entry to Campanile and discounts on
other sights).

More interesting than the average ecclesiastical
museum, pride of place here goes to some
impressive gold- and silverware and a clutch
of excellent Renaissance paintings.

In room II, on the ground floor, the **Tesoro
di Canoscio** is a sixth-century palaeo-Christian
treasure trove of 25 pieces, mostly plates and
spoons, found by a local farmer in 1935. Next door,
in room I, are two immensely beautiful pieces of
metalwork. The **Paliotto** is an altar front in
engraved and embossed silver dating from 1142
and depicting the life of Christ with extraordinarily
expressive characterization. The **Ricco di Pastorale**,
made in 1324, is a silver and gold crosier of ornate
and delicate detail, with tiny holy figures.

Upstairs is given over to paintings, a few
of which stand out. Francesco Tifernate's
Annunciation is a fine painting, the clever
positioning of the two figures drawing the
eye into the composition and emphasizing
the three-dimensionality of the space and the
landscape behind. The real stars of the show,
however, are in the large conference room beyond.
Pinturicchio's *Madonna with Child and St John* is,

despite a prematurely aging Jesus, an atmospheric
and tender piece with a misty landscape
background. And Rosso Fiorentino's *Christ in Glory*,
on the end wall, is a cinematic painting, expertly lit.

Campanile Cilindrico

Via del Modello, T075-855 4705.
Tue-Sun 1000-1300, 1500-1830, €6/3 concession
(includes entry to Museo del Duomo and
discounts on other sights). Tickets from the
museum if there is nobody at the Campanile.

Facing the cathedral, go around the right-hand side
and keep turning left to reach the bottom of the
round bell tower, which predates the current
cathedral. The lower part is Romanesque, from the
11th and 12th centuries; the upper part is Gothic,
added between 1283 and 1284. Three bells ring at
the top of the 43.5-m tower, the longevity of which
must in part be due to the 1-m thickness of its walls.

Palazzo del Comune (o dei Priori)

Piazza Gabriotti.

It's usually possible to wander in and have a poke
around Angelo da Orvieto's 1322-1338 sandstone
construction, one of the most striking town halls you
could expect to find, full of vaulted Gothic arches and
stone staircases. Next door is the 14th-century **Torre
Civica**. A tower with good views from the top, it was
closed for restoration at the time of writing.

Tipografia Grifani-Donati

Corso Cavour, T075-855 4349.
Mon-Fri 0900-1230, 1500-1900, Sat 0900-1300,
€3, or 45-minute guided tour by reservation, €10.

Since the firm's foundation in 1799, the beautifully
engineered Grifani-Donati printing presses have
been operated by eight generations of the same
family, and it is still a commercial operation today.
Artistic stone lithography is also done here: some
lithographs are on display, alongside oil paintings.
If you opt for the guided tour you also get to keep
the prints done on the way round.

Above: Duomo, Città di Castello.
Opposite page: Lithographic press, Tipografia Grifani-Donati.

Collezione Burri

Palazzo Albizzini, via Albizzini 1, and ex-Seccatoi del Tabacco, via Pierucci (west of town centre), T075-855 4649, fondazioneburri.org.
Palazzo Albizzini: Tue-Sat 0900-1230, 1430-1800, Sun 1030-1230, 1500-1800; Ex-Seccatoi del Tabacco: Mar-10 Nov Mon-Sat 0900-1230, 1430-1800, Sun 1030-1230, 1500-1800, 11 Nov-Feb Sat 0900-1230, 1430-1800, Sun 1030-1230, 1500-1800; €6/4 concession each site, or €10/6 for both.

Alberto Burri, born in Città di Castello in 1915, was one of the most important Italian artists of the 20th century. Burri himself set up this museum, on two sites, which acts as his artistic autobiography.

Trained as a doctor, he served in the Second World War. He was captured in Tunisia in 1943 and sent to a prisoner of war camp in Texas, where he started to paint. He is usually thought of as an abstract artist, but many of the paintings in the Palazzo Albizzini are, at one level, viscerally figurative. The viewer needs no special knowledge of Burri's background to realize that his early works – blood-red backgrounds glimpsed through sackcloth ripped apart and sewn up, are connected to wounds and human suffering.

These are emotional, painful works, with little or none of the abstract metaphysics often associated with 20th-century abstract art. Some of the early works have a three-dimensionality to them, as if something is trying to escape from within. This dissatisfaction with flatness is a foretaste of Burri's

Since the firm's foundation in 1799, the beautifully engineered Grifani-Donati printing presses have been operated by eight generations of the same family.

later sculpture. Burnt wood features in *Combustione Legno*, from 1957, ripped clothing in *Grande Bianco* from 1956. In the 1960s he introduced metal, and then plastic: melted, translucent, suffocating, sagging, like distorted skin. *Rosso Plastica*, from 1964, features a gaping, screaming black hole, and sexual imagery becomes increasingly prevalent as the collection moves into the 1970s.

Not all is dark, however – even the black paintings have a certain playfulness about them, and there is the sense of an increased ease with the world, though a room of brightly coloured abstract shapes still comes as a surprise.

The 11 enormous hangars of the tobacco sheds, where Burri created many of his later works, reprise his career, sometimes exactly repeating images from the Palazzo Albizzini, although on an entirely different scale. Burri was ahead of his time in choosing an ex-industrial setting for his work, and the stunningly big drying sheds, painted black at his instruction, work very well to showcase his life's work, though they lose some of the immediacy of the Palazzo Albizzini.

Montone

One of the prettiest villages northern Umbria, walled Montone, 20 km south of Città di Castello, is surrounded by wooded hills and quiet valleys. The central piazza has plenty of tables outside two cafés, and there are narrow, car-free streets and tree-lined belvederes. The **ex-Church of San Francesco** is now a museum, and contains some medieval frescoes.

There are lots of walks in the area, especially around the **Valle del Carpina**, where well-signposted routes run through the woods and open out into grassy clearings. You might see roe deer, buzzards, and even wolves.

Other good villages to explore in the area include **Morra**, where the **Oratorio di San Crescentino** is a frescoed attraction, with paintings by Luca Signorelli.

Above: Montone. Opposite page: Valle del Carpina.

Sleeping

Gubbio

Bosone Palace €€
Via XX Settembre 22, T075-922 0688, mencarelligroup.com.
Bang in the centre of town, the hotel is an ornate, antique sort of place with good views over the town from some rooms. The building is described as Renaissance, though the design is more baroque, with ceiling frescoes and gold-trimmed swirls in the smartest of the 30 rooms. Standard rooms are less decorative, but all come with satellite TV, a/c and minibars.

Locanda del Gallo €€
Località Santa Cristina, T075-922 9912, locandadelgallo.it.
23 km southwest of Gubbio on SS298 to Perugia: turn right at Mengara, signposted to Santa Cristina.
A 12th-century country house on the ridge of a hill, Locanda del Gallo has a pool and 10 rooms, with some oriental touches in its furnishings. Immersed in green, rural surroundings, it's a peaceful place, good for walks in the hills.

Relais Ducale €€
Via Galeotti 19, T075-922 0157, mencarelligroup.com.
In three buildings near the top of town, the Relais Ducale is a smart, American-Italian family-run place with 30 antiques-filled rooms. Some good contemporary touches, such as modern prints, balance out the occasionally old-fashioned feel of the place. Other big pros include fantastic gardens filled with wisteria and fruit-trees, great views, and – best of all – a secret passage dug for the Dukes of Montefeltro through the shale into the hillside. Suites and junior suites (€€€) come with added extras such as massage chairs, Jacuzzis and geranium-fringed private balconies overlooking the town.

La Ginestra €
Valmarcola, Santa Cristina, T075-920088, agriturismolaginestra.com.
23 km from Gubbio on SS298 to Perugia, turn right at Mengara, signposted for Santa Cristina.
An isolated 30-ha organic farm along nearly 4 km of dirt road between Gubbio and Perugia. Six separate apartments in three buildings include a converted tower, and there is table tennis, a gym, a hot tub, a library and a good pool.

Residenza di via Piccardi €
Via Piccardi 12, T075-927 6108, agriturismocolledelsole.it.
On a quiet street in the centre of town, the residence offers simple but spotlessly clean rooms and a nice garden for breakfast. For a slightly higher price, apartments with small kitchens are also available. Bathrooms are tiled and pristine and, although the fabrics may clash, the friendly reception makes this even better value for money.

Città di Castello

Hotel Tiferno €€
Piazza Rafaello Sanzio 13, T075-855 0331, hoteltiferno.it.
A hotel since 1895, Tiferno has a few great pieces of antique furniture mixed in with its pale, 20th-century style. The junior suite has a double bed on a mezzanine, and all rooms have spotless, white-tiled modern bathrooms. There's a fitness area on the ground floor.

Il Cucciolo €
Vocabolo Figlino 31, Petrelle, T075-850 4138, aziendailcucciolo.it.
19 km south of Città di Castello. From being a famous dog trainer in New York to running an *agriturismo* in deepest rural Umbria may not be the most obvious career switch, but it's one that Breon O'Farrell has carried off with some success. He and his Italian wife run this farm near the Umbria-Tuscany border with laid-back charm, though if you're not a fan of dogs this is probably not the place for you. The organic farm is in an isolated, peaceful spot, with views of two nearby castles, and there's a good 12-m swimming pool. Apartments are generously sized, with wood fires, and there are solar panels for hot water. In the *limonaia*, a communal space, board games are piled high, and there are also swings and slides for kids.

Eating & drinking

Monterosello €
Frazione San Maiano, località Seripole, vocabolo Monterosello, T075-857 7031, monterosello.it.
8 km southeast of Città di Castello.

High in the hills above San Maiano, Monterosello is a large, working, organic farm, almost entirely self-sufficient in energy and with a wild area, a swimming pool and a boating lake.
The range of courses run here includes Umbrian cooking and yoga, and there are great views in all directions across the hills and valleys of northern Umbria. Simple but solidly built rooms are in two buildings, 1 km apart. The only downside might be that when full (capacity is 60 people) it could feel a little impersonal.

Self-catering
Residenza Antica Canonica
Via San Florido 23, T075-852 3298, umbriaholidays.net.
Right beside the cathedral in a medieval building, these attractively furnished and well-equipped apartments have kitchens and Wi-Fi, wooden beams and tiled floors. A family apartment for four can be rented from €400 per week.

Montone

Torre di Moravola €€€
Moravola, T075-946 0965, moravola.com.
10 mins from Montone, south of road to Pietralunga.

So well hidden away that the owners usually meet guests in Montone, stylish Torre di Moravola is a hilltop 10th-century fortified tower, converted in a stunning fashion by a British architect and a designer into an exclusive hotel with five tower suites. It's a sleek mix of the traditional and the modern, combining state-of-the-art minimalism with ancient Umbria. The food is all organic, and mainly home grown, and the swimming pool is a striking black mirror of water. Massages and treatments are available, and great views abound in every direction.

La Locanda del Capitano €€
Via Roma 5/7, Montone, T075-930 6521, ilcapitano.com.
In the centre of Montone, the Locanda del Capitano is a friendly, welcoming place, with comfortable rooms done up in an old-fashioned, if slightly generic, style. The two best rooms have balconies overlooking the village roofs to the hills beyond. In the 14th and 15th centuries the building was home to Braccio Fontebraccio, a mercenary after whom the town's piazza is named. Downstairs is a posh restaurant offering dishes such as foie gras with caramelized onions and brioche. The same owners have a villa for rent outside Montone (casellina.com).

Gubbio

La Fornace di Mastro Giorgio €€€
Via Mastro Giorgio 2, T075-922 1836.
Wed-Mon 1200-1430,1930-2230.
On steps leading down from via XX Settembre, this quality restaurant is in the 14th-century factory of ceramicist Giorgio Andreoli. Despite its aspirations, it's a friendly, unstuffy place. The food is Umbrian with a touch of high-end imagination; expect meats such as pigeon, veal and venison, expertly seasoned with herbs and spices.

Taverna del Lupo €€€
Via Ansidei 21, T075-927 4368, mencarelligroup.com.
Tue-Sun 1215-1500, 1900-2400.
Gubbio's smartest eatery is named after St Francis's wolf, which apparently used to come to this spot for food. It's a formal and expensive place, with thick tablecloths and dark wood furniture, and service can be slow, but they serve good traditional truffle-based dishes.

La Madia di Giuseppe €€
Via Mastro Giorgio 2/6, T075-922 1836.
Wed-Sun 0930-2230.
Attached to Gubbio's top restaurant, La Fornace di Mastro Giorgio, the next-door *enoteca* advertises itself as a wine bar with snacks and light bites, but it's more than that and makes a

great place for lunch. In a handsome barrel-vaulted stone cellar, La Madia is decorated with a wine press, giant barrels, wine boxes and lots of bottles. The lentil soup may be the tastiest you'll eat anywhere in Umbria, and the plates of meats and cheeses are also excellent.

Locanda del Cantiniere €€
Via Dante 30, T075-927 5999.
Wed-Sun 1200-1430, 1900-2230.
A cosy place with good pasta dishes and a rare vegetarian set menu (€15, including water and wine). Carnivores are also well catered for, with dishes such as sausage and *rapini* and Chianina beef with truffles. Open brickwork and neutral tones add to the relaxed atmosphere.

Ristorante dei Consoli €
Via dei Consoli 59, T075-927 3335.
Sun-Fri 1200-1500, 1900-late.
A smart but fairly plain, family-run place on the main street without too many pretensions. There's an €18, three-course lunch menu, which might feature *umbricelli* with porcini and pork with mushroom sauce followed by *tozzetti* and Vin Santo.

Cafés & bars
Caffè Tre Ceri
T075-929 1210.
Daily 0900-1730.
Next to the Palazzo Ducale, this café has tables in the Giardini Pensili overlooking the town.

L'Arte Golosa
Via dei Consoli 97.
Mon-Sat 1200-2400,
Sun 1330-2400.
Fight your way through the crowds of locals for Gubbio's best homemade ice cream, from the bargain price of €1.50 for two luscious flavours.

Città di Castello

L'Osteria €€
Via Borgo di Sotto 1,
T075-855 6995.
Mon-Sat 1230-1430, 1930-2230.
Popular with locals and visitors alike, l'Osteria is in a pretty, quiet piazza just off piazza Matteotti. The printed menu lists mainly pizzas, which are good value but served only in the evenings. Look instead for the *menu del giorno*, chalked up on the wall, which may include dishes such as steak with porcini mushrooms or carpaccio of swordfish with rocket. There are tables outside under cover, or you can head through the trailing plants to rooms inside.

Trattoria Lea €€
Via San Florido 38, T075-852 1678.
Tue-Sun 1230-1430, 1930-2200.
One of the most popular restaurants in Città di Castello, Lea offers good traditional local fare, such as pasta and chickpeas, and sausage with lentils. There are tables outside on the street or inside in vaulted rooms. If you're in town for the summer

festa, you'll find waiting staff dressed in medieval garb.

Vineria del Vasaio €€
Piazzetta del Vasaio,
T075-852 3281.
Mon-Sat 1900-0200.
A cosy, barrel-vaulted wine bar that also serves good food, such as gnocchi with pesto or tuna cooked in Chianti wine with cannellini beans. The large round tables, the piano and the late closing might be conducive to making some local friends.

Cafés & bars
Caffè Latino
Piazza Matteotti, T075-852 2641.
Tue-Sun 0700-0200.
A hip spot right on the main piazza, Caffè Latino calls itself an American bar, but is as Italian as they come. There are ancient frescoes on the vaulted ceiling and slick contemporary design everywhere else. Comfy wicker sofas mean you can sit outside in the piazza, and tasty free bar snacks accompany your *aperitivo* at lunchtime as well as in the evening.

Montone

Erba Luna €€
Parco della Rimembranze 16, via San Albertino, T075-930 6405, erbalunaristorante.com.
Wed-Mon (daily Jun-Sep), breakfast and *aperitivo* from 1100, lunch from 1200, *aperitivo* from 1830, supper from 1900.

In a fabulous, high-ceilinged, brick-vaulted space built right into Montone's walls, and with tables outside under trees, Erba Luna is a stylish place. Huge lamps, entwined wire candlesticks and chilled jazzy music create a great atmosphere, though the reception can be frosty. The food is the real strength though, with dishes such as leek soufflé, warm porcini salad and ravioli with ricotta and radicchio, and there's a good wine list too.

L'Antica Osteria €
Piazza Fortebraccio 5,
T075-930 6271.
With plenty of tables on Montone's main square, this café is run by the same management as the nearby **Taverna del Verziere** (via dell'Ospedale 25) and is usually open when the taverna is not. Good cakes and a €15 lunch menu.

Entertainment

Festival delle Nazioni
Aug-Sep, various locations in and around Città di Castello, festivalnazioni.com.
Excellent festival of chamber music and dance (see page 48).

Umbria Film Festival
Montone, umbriafilmfestival.com.
A small festival for alternative films, shown in Montone's piazza in July (see page 48).

Shopping

Gubbio

Mastri Librai Eugubini
Via della Repubblica 18,
T075-927 7425.
Apr-Dec daily 0900-1730.
A great selection of handmade leather-bound notebooks and albums, as well as some elegant pens and inkwells.

Tipici Prodotti
Via dei Consoli 99, T075-922 0888.
Daily 0930-1300, 1530-1900.
One of several shops in Gubbio selling a profusion of salami, cheese and pasta. They will happily make up sandwiches on request. Look for the two wild boars' heads outside.

Città di Castello

House
Corso Vittorio Emanuele 20,
T075-855 4854.
Tue-Sun 1000-1300, 1700-2000, Mon 1700-2000.
High quality products for the Italian (or wannabe Italian) home, from cushions to well-made Italian coffee pots.

La Perugina
Corso Cavour 2a.
Wed-Mon 0900-1300, 1700-1930.
A great fresh pasta shop. Giulietti, next door, has good local cheeses and meats to go with it.

Transport

Gubbio

Not on the train line, Gubbio is served by regular buses from Perugia (40 km). The nearest station is 19 km away at Fossato di Vico on the Rome-Ancona line. It's a 30-minute bus journey into Gubbio.

Città di Castello

Città di Castello is on the private Ferrovia Centrale Umbria line (fcu.it): trains run north from Perugia (1 hr) and Todi (around 2 hrs). Mainline trains from Rome or Florence stop at Arezzo, from where there are regular SITA buses to Città di Castello (around 90 mins).

Contents

Northern Marche

Beach huts, Pesaro seafront.

Introduction

I n Urbino, northern Marche has one of the Italian Renaissance's most celebrated towns, full of the art and architecture that made the area such a centre of culture in the middle of the last millennium. From here it is an easy hop to the sea, where both Pesaro and Fano have good beaches and old centres with a style that belies their beach resort status.

Further inland, to the north, geology thrusts the Montefeltro upwards into eccentric shapes, notably at San Leo and Gradara, where famous castles lord it over their surroundings. It is an area of poets and artisans too, of beer and cheese, as well as traditional arts, and the place to come if you're looking for open-air sculpture or antique varieties of fruit. Under the ground there's plenty more to see: Europe's biggest cavern is just the beginning of the huge cave network at Frasassi. In the surrounding regional park there are opportunities to walk through gorges and wooded valleys to ancient abbeys and old hermitages.

What to see in...

...one day
If you only have time to see one place in northern Marche, **Urbino** is it. The Renaissance **Palazzo Ducale** dominates the town and takes a good half-day to see. The house where Raphael was born is more interesting for its history than anything you can actually see, so it might be better to pass by en route to the richly frescoed **Oratorio di San Giovanni**. Also don't miss the views from the **Albornoz castle**. Less than half an hour's drive away, the **Gola del Furlo** makes a fascinating side trip, where you can walk up to a giant **profile of Mussolini** on the hill.

...a weekend or more
An extra day or two opens up opportunities to explore the hills and fortresses of the interior, where Renaissance castles and the forgotten fruit of **San Leo** and the rugged Montefeltro are both draws. Alternatively, hit the beaches on the coastline at **Fano** or **Pesaro**, both of which have attractive old centres, and explore another romantic castle, **Gradara**, nearby.

Cigarette break, Urbino.

Urbino &
Gola del Furlo

Hill-town Urbino, birthplace of Raphael and home to spectacular Renaissance architecture and the National Gallery of the Palazzo Ducale, is perhaps the Marche's most obvious tourist attraction. It has been a centre of learning and culture since the Renaissance: its university was founded in 1507, and Pope Clement XI was born here in 1700. Today, students outnumber other inhabitants in a town where many of the symbols of Urbino's apogee of influence and power in the 15th century remain in place.

To the south, the narrow Gola del Furlo squeezes the river Candigliano and squirts it out towards the Adriatic, below a semi-derelict profile of Mussolini on the cliffs above.

Palazzo Ducale.

Palazzo Ducale

*Piazza Duca Federico, T0722-322625,
galleriaborghese.it.*
Mon 0830-1400, Tue-Sun 0830-1915, €4/2
concession, free EU citizens under 18 and over 65.

The huge palace built by Federico da Montefelcro
and his wife Battista Sforza dominates the town.
Work on it started in 1465, at a time when the
court was a reference point for the Italian
Renaissance. Architect Luciano Laurana took
charge of the project, though Piero della Francesca
was also involved and Battista Sforza herself was
instrumental in incorporating Renaissance theories
about the links between culture and design into
the structure. When she died in 1472, at the age of
26, Laurana left, and the nature of the construction
changed, with Renaissance thought taking a less
prominent role. As a result, the later rooms are less
vibrant, their purpose often less clear.

The entrance to the palace takes you
straight into the **Cortile d'Onore**, a large, elegant,
porticoed courtyard. Brick and stone are used
to create patterns, and engraved lettering along
the cornice reads: "Federico, Duke of Urbino,
Count of Montefeltro and Casteldurante, Knight
of the Holy Roman Church and Commander of
the Italic Confederation built this house, raised
from its foundations to celebrate his glory and
that of posterity," before going on to detail his
military successes.

Just off the courtyard, in a position of unusual
prominence, the Duke's library is these days bereft
of books, though a colourful projection scrolling
on to the walls effectively demonstrates the
ornateness of the manuscripts that once lined the
room. The books themselves are now held in the
Vatican Library.

Downstairs, to the right of the entrance, is the
area that once held the practical workings of the
palace – the kitchens and washrooms, wine cellars
and ice-rooms. The intelligent design of the building
can also be seen here, with pipes that carried hot
water and ventilation as well as drainage.

Essentials

Getting around From the main car park at piazza
Mercatale, steep steps or a lift take you up into the
centro storico.

Trains Urbino isn't accessible by train: the nearest
stations are Pesaro or Fano.

Buses The bus station is in piazza Mercatale
(T0722-2196): buses run from here into the centre.

Hospital Viale Comandino 70, T0722-301272.

Pharmacy Farmacia la Medica, piazza della
Repubblica, T0722-329829.

Post office Via Donato Bramante 28, T0722-377917,
Mon-Sat 0830-1830.

Tourist information office Via Puccinotti 33,
T0722-320437, urbinoeilmontefeltro.it.

Tip...

For €10, the *biglietto unico* admits you to all of
Urbino's main sights.

Galleria Nazionale delle Marche The palace's
most obvious attractions are upstairs, however,
where the paintings of the National Gallery of the
Marche are exhibited. Highlights include Piero della
Francesca's poised *Madonna di Senigallia* and his
Flagellation of Christ; a famous, but unattributed,
painting of the *Ideal City*, from around 1470, which
demonstrates great skill in the use of perspective;
Giovanni Bellini's *Sacra Conversazione*; and, best of
all, Raphael's *La Muta*, or *Portrait of a Gentlewoman*,
an enigmatic and intriguing portrait. Other notable
works include Paolo Uccello's *Miracle of the
Desecrated Host* (1465-1469) – a six-panel
storyboard, painted for the predella of an
altarpiece, illustrating the story of a Parisian Jew
burned at the stake for having profaned the host.

Also on this floor is the apartment of the duke
himself, including the spectacular alcove bedstead
– a sort of wooden box, painted and with lots of
wood embossing – in which he slept. The room
still referred to in some places as the *Sala degli*

Urbino listings

● Sleeping

1 Ca' Andreana
   via Ca' Andreana 2
2 Ca' Vernaccia
   via Paroramica 10, Pallino
3 Raffaello *Vicolino Santa*
   Margherita 38/40
4 San Domenico
   piazza Rinascimento 3
5 San Giovanni
   via Barocci 13

● Eating & drinking

1 Al Girarrosto
   piazza San Francesco 3
2 Al Cantuccio
   via Budassi 62
3 Antico Furlo *via Furlo 60*
4 Caffè del Sole
   via Mazzini 34
5 I Dolci di Battista
   via Raffaello Sanzio 19
6 L'Angolo Divino
   via Sant'Andrea 14
7 La Ballestra *via Valerio 16*
8 Le Tre Piante
   via Voltaccia della Vecchia 1
9 Trattoria del Leone
   via Cesare Battisti 5
10 Vecchia Urbino
   via dei Vasari 3/5

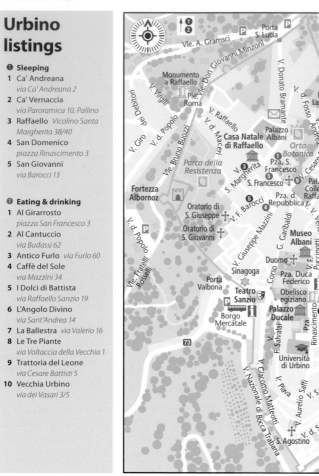

Uomini d'Arme ('room of the men-at-arms') has now been renamed the **Sala delle Nozze di Federico**, after a restoration uncovered fragments of murals that include Battista Sforza's coat of arms (a lion and a quince tree) showing that the room was probably decorated for the marriage of Federico and Battista.

Don't miss Federico's **studiolo**, a small room panelled with extraordinary works of intarsia (inlaid wood), illustrating symbols of learning –

mathematics, music, astronomy and the fine arts – with exceptional three-dimensionality.

The third floor of the palace opens only for 20 minutes every hour, on the hour, which is probably enough. Compared to the masterpieces on the second floor, much of the art here seems hackneyed and there is an excess of soft-focus, rosy-cheeked 17th-century ephemera, though there are some notable exceptions, such as Sassoferrato's three-panelled *Annunciation*,

Adoration and Circumcision, which stands out for its use of colour and well-observed detail, and an exquisite 16th-century ebony chest, inlaid with ivory.

Back on the ground floor, the archaeological section of ancient inscriptions in stone is only of passing interest, but there's a café and a shop, should you be in need of retail or caffeine therapy.

Duomo

Piazza Duca Federico.
Daily 0730-1300, 1400-2000, free.

In 1781 an earthquake damaged Urbino's cathedral, and after eight years of restoration the entire dome collapsed down into the cathedral below. Subsequent reconstruction has left a building that is more impressive in size than in beauty, though two chapels, at either side of the apse, survive from earlier times and are worth a look for their ornate detailing. The right-hand **Cappella della Concezione** has a fragment of 14th-century fresco of the Madonna and Child over the altar.

Casa Natale di Raffaello

Via Raffaello 57, T0722-320105, accademiaraffaello.it.
Mar-Oct Mon-Sat 0900-1300 and 1500-1900, Sun 1000-1300, Nov-Feb Mon-Sat 0900-1400, Sun 1000-1300, €3.

Raffaello Sanzio was born in Urbino on 28 March 1483, and his house, just up the hill from the piazza, can be visited. He was the son of a well-known painter, Giovanni Santi, who died when Raphael was 11; his mother died soon after he was born. The one original painting here by Raphael is an early fresco, originally thought to be by his father.

Oratorio di San Giovanni & Oratorio di San Giuseppe

Via Barocci, T347-671 1181 (mobile).
Mon-Sat 1000-1230, 1500-1730, Sun 1000-1230, €2.50 and €2 respectively.

These two small neighbouring churches both have artistic claims to fame. The Oratorio di San Giovanni

is especially spectacular, the interior being richly decorated with mostly intact frescoes illustrating the life of St John the Baptist. Look for the small dog present in many of the images. Painted by brothers Jacopo and Lorenzo Salimbeni in 1416, the images are great examples of a style known as 'flamboyant Gothic'.

On the right-hand wall as you face the altar, nine panels cover St John's birth, his meeting with Mary, his baptism of Jesus and his preaching to the masses. On the wall behind the altar is an extraordinarily complex and inventive Crucifixion, while on the left wall John appears twice with no head. The figure in the black cloak here is Pietro Spagnolo, a much-respected Urbino hermit whose body now lies below the altar.

The Oratorio di San Giuseppe is less remarkable, though it contains Federico Brandani's lugubrious life-sized Nativity scene in a specially built grotto. The main room, a high-ceilinged vaulted space, is also worth a look for its floor-to-ceiling decoration.

Fortezza Albornoz

Park: daily 0900-1900, free.

Though you can't enter the fortress itself, Urbino's castle grounds are a popular spot for the view they give back over the town, especially at sunset, when you'll probably find pairs of lovers lolling under every apple tree.

Orto Botanico

Via Donato Bramante 28, T0722-303774.
Mon-Wed and Fri, 0800-1230, 1500-1730, free.

A peaceful and serious garden, Urbino University's collection of plants is a shady place, where occasional dappled beams of sunshine make it down through the trees to the flowers and plants below. An information board explains the relationship of the areas of the garden to parts of the body, but most visitors are happy just to wander in and out of the walled rows of plants, all hand labelled in Latin.

Museo della Città

Palazzo Odasi, Via Valerio 1, T0722-309270, museodelmetauro.it.
Wed-Mon 1000-1300, 1500-1800, free.

Closed for restoration at the time of writing, Urbino's town museum, in the Palazzo Odasi, is designed to "contain ideas rather than objects" and is part contemporary art, part conventional museum.

Urbino's golden age

The settlement of Urvinum Mataurense became a Roman municipality in the third century BC. For hundreds of years it held an important strategic position, though its golden age was not until the 15th century, by which time it had been under the control of the Montefeltro family for two centuries. When Oddantonio da Montefeltro became Duke of Urbino in 1443, aged just 16, he was more interested in owning fast horses than looking after his territories, and after a year of misrule he was thrown to his death from a window of his palace by an angry mob. Federico, his illegitimate half-brother, took over and began to build bridges.

By the time he married his second wife, the 14-year-old Battista Sforza, in 1460, Federico had already gained a reputation as a wise ruler. Over the 12 years of their marriage, Urbino became a focal point for the Renaissance, and Piero della Francesca was among those who came to work at the ducal court.

After the death of Federico's son and heir in 1508, the influence and importance of Urbino began slowly to ebb away. In 1523 the court moved to Pesaro, and in 1631 the last duke died. The estate passed to the papacy, and the Palazzo Ducale was emptied of many of its treasures. At the same time, a generous dowry for the marriage of Vittoria della Rovere into the Florentine Medici family, reputedly to compensate for her 'awkwardness', meant that the city lost even more of its artistic patrimony.

In 1700, Urbino-born Giovanni Albani became Pope Clement XI and reversed some of the city's decline, but, though it continued to be one of Italy's most important centres of learning, its days at the centre of Italian influence were long gone.

Gola del Furlo

A 20-minute drive southwest of Urbino, the Furlo Gorge is a spectacular ravine cut precipitously through the Apennine Mountains by the green, meandering river Candigliano. This east-west route was the narrowest pass of the via Flaminia – one of ancient Rome's most important roads.

The gorge was also a favourite spot of Mussolini, and he had an enormous profile of his face built at the top of the towering cliff on the gorge's northern side. Best seen from the village of Furlo itself, Il Duce's face is still recognizable, despite having being blown up by partisans.

On the wooded slopes above the gorge there are good walks, and the chance to stop and picnic on Mussolini's broken nose. The easiest approach is a 90-minute walk from Pagino, a tiny hamlet northwest of Furlo, where there is parking next to a church. From here, follow the track between fields, branching left at a shrine, which becomes a stony path after about 15 minutes. Keep right at a fork in the path by a tall tree after another 10 minutes and climb for another 45 minutes or so through pine and cedar trees until you reach a dog-leg left just before a red and white barrier. Ten minutes along this grassier path brings you out to a clearing at the top of the hill. Turn left here on to a path that shortly emerges on to the rocky upturned face of the fascist dictator, with stunning views east to the Adriatic, west to the Apennines and vertiginously down to the green waters swirling through the gorge far, far below.

San Leo & Montefeltro

Tucked into the northern corner of Marche, Montefeltro is a strange, half-forgotten landscape of rocky outcrops, sheer cliffs and rolling green hills – a sort of central Italian Middle-earth. San Leo is the area's most obvious attraction – a town with a Renaissance castle that towers over it on the sheer cliff above, with views to the tiny republic of San Marino. There are other highlights though, such as the little-known Parco Naturale Sasso Simone e Simoncello, and a big landscape full of little treats such as the Garden of Forgotten Fruit and Pietrarubbia, an isolated hamlet in the hills, rich in art and museums.

Below: Pennabilli. Opposite page: Looking down from Mussolini's broken nose to the Gola di Furlo.

Around the region

La Fortezza

Mar-Oct daily 0900-1900, winter hours to be decided, €8 or €10 combined ticket with Torre Campanaria and Museo d'Arte Sacra.

San Leo's castle is the epitome of imposing, built as an extension of a precipitous rock face jutting out of the Marecchia Valley. It is an obvious place for a fortress, and indeed there has been one here since the sixth century, and perhaps as far back as Roman times. From the 17th to the early 20th century it was used as a prison and, despite its elegance, it remains a formidable building, with little of the fairytale castle romance of nearby Gradara. Much of the design seen today is the work of Renaissance architect Francesco di Giorgio Martini, who reinforced and enhanced the existing structure for Federico da Montefeltro in the 15th century. Having captured the castle in 1441, Federico's enhancements strengthened it against cannon fire and made it more or less impenetrable. The castle contains a small museum of weapons and armour, a torture chamber and various cells where unfortunate prisoners spent their last days.

The Fortezza is a five-minute walk uphill through woods from the village below, or there's a car park just outside the walls.

Essentials

❶ Getting around San Leo is tiny, but if you don't fancy a bit of a climb you might want to catch the bus or a taxi up the hill to the castle.

❷ Buses Direct from Rimini twice a day or change at Pietracuta.

⊕ Hospital Ospedale Sacra Famiglia, Novafeltria, T0541-919399.

✚ Pharmacy Farmacia Rurale, piazza Dante Alighieri, T0541-916160.

✎ Post office Piazza Dante Alighieri 2, T0541-916274, Mon-Sat 0830-1830.

❶ Tourist information office Palazzo Mediceo, piazza Dante Alighieri 14, T0541-916306, san-leo.it, 0900-1900.

Palazzo Mediceo e Museo d'Arte Sacra

Daily 0900-1900, though hours may vary, €8 or €10 combined ticket with Fortezza and Torre Campanaria.

In the centre of San Leo, the Palazzo Mediceo houses the tourist information office as well as a small museum of sacred art. Luca Frosino's Botticelli-esque *Madonna and Child* (1487-1493) shows the Virgin flanked by local saints Leo and Marino.

Duomo di San Leone

Daily 1000-1900, free.

Construction of San Leo's cathedral, a fine Romanesque building, was completed in 1173. The raised presbytery is a handsome feature, as are the high Romanesque arches. Built from pale sandstone, it has a well-worn but dignified feel. Look for Roman columns and carved capitals used in the building.

Behind the duomo is the **Torre Campanaria** (daily 1000-1200, 1500-1900), also 12th century: a square bell tower built straight on to a rocky outcrop.

Pieve di Santa Maria Assunta

Daily 1000-1900, free.

A bare stone building with plenty of atmosphere, this ancient church was probably first erected in the eighth century and rebuilt in the 11th, though the crypt downstairs may be an even earlier chapel where the fourth-century St Leo used to pray. Ancient Roman elements, such as capitals at the top of columns, were used in the church's construction. The elegant stone canopy over the altar is from the ninth century.

Parco Naturale Sasso Simone e Simoncello

parcosimone.it.

The hills of this little-known regional park have rocky plateaux and woods of oak and beech trees, maple and hornbeam. Owls, buzzards, kestrels and peregrine falcons patrol the skies, while down below deer, porcupines and wolves roam. The park

Duomo, San Leo.

covers nearly 5,000 ha and rises to 1,415 m at the summit of Monte Carpegna, the watershed between the Foglia and Marecchia Valleys. There is a visitor centre near Pietrarubbia at **Ponte Cappuccini** (via Montefeltresca, T0722-75350, Mon-Fri 0900-1300, Sat 1000-1200, Sun 0900-1200), and local tourist information offices can also provide maps of walking and cycling routes.

Castello di Pietrarubbia

T0722-750031, comune.pietrarubbia.pu.it.

Until recently a ruined hamlet, complete with its own little castle on top of the hill, Pietrarubbia has some of the best views in central Italy, across a wide expanse of rolling countryside to the high hills of the Parco Naturale Sasso Simone e Simoncello, as well as to San Leo and San Marino.

The entire place has now been taken over by an association and is run with enormous enthusiasm as a restaurant, hotel (see page 237), museums, art complex and open-air gallery. The **sculpture museum** (variable hours – ask at the hotel or restaurant if it's closed), in a great space overlooking the hills, exhibits some interesting

work from the art school that is based here. Other, larger pieces are scattered around the village, some of them by Italian sculptor Arnaldo Pomodoro, turning the whole place into a contemporary sculpture park. There's also an interesting museum of ceramics that were found during the restoration of the village.

A path leads up between wild roses from the far end of the village to a restored lookout tower at the top of the hill, from where the views are fantastic.

L'Orto dei Frutti Dimenticati

Pennabilli, montefeltro.net/pennabilli.
Daily 0900-1900, free, guided tours on request from the tourist office (T0541-928659).

One of seven open-air museums in and around Pennabilli, grouped together as **I Luoghi dell'Anima**, the Garden of Forgotten Fruit is both a serious attempt to preserve ancient species of fruit trees and a sculpture garden with a view. It's also a good reason to call in on the pleasant hill town of **Pennabilli**, home to Italian poet and screenwriter Tonino Guerra, many of whose projects enliven the cultural life of the area.

Yoga & fucking it

The Hill that Breathes

Hidden away along a winding road among thick woods near Urbino, arriving at The Hill that Breathes is a special experience. First, it's a beautiful place: two old farmhouses have been carefully and lovingly restored; there's a geodesic dome, which looks a bit like a spaceship that has landed in the forest; and winding paths through the trees lead to a swimming pool with a view.

But it's the atmosphere here that really works. In other hands, a holistic centre specializing in yoga weeks might well be a holier-than-thou kind of place, with having a good time a long way down the list of priorities. But John and Gaia, having left the rat race of advertising in London, have infused this place with infectious, laid-back fun. Their literature never takes itself too seriously, and even around the site there are, quite literally, signs of their sense of humour – note the signposts for 'left' and 'right'. The tongue-in-cheek endorsement on their website is "'I visited once and will certainly be back' – Jesus Christ".

The food also strikes just the right balance – it's vegetarian, but that doesn't mean it's always too healthy. Ulisse, the Italian chef, cooks fantastically tasty dishes, such as gnocchi with Gorgonzola, and runs two cookery classes a week to boot. Plus, if you want to spy on his kitchen secrets, he's usually happy to have guests help him out. There are also some good local wines, available using an honesty box system.

Rooms are decorated in cool, earthy colours, with polished cement, some open brickwork and splashes of colour such as the flowery red bedspreads. Upstairs rooms have well-designed mezzanines and sleep three. There are also double and single rooms.

Most people spend most of their time outside, lazing by the pool or in hammocks, going for woodland walks down to the river, or playing table football. At the top of the hill, a yoga platform offers an alternative to the dome, which is a visually (and aurally) breathtaking space but can get warm. Classes run for two hours in the morning and two in the afternoon; they're not obligatory, and some people choose to skip afternoon classes for trips out to local sights.

As well as yoga weeks, there are martial arts courses, family weeks, and in 2008 the Barefoot Doctor ran a week's course. The increasingly popular Fuck It weeks, dedicated to letting go, to "finding real freedom by realizing that things don't matter so much (if at all)", are run by John himself and have spawned a new book.

Treatments such as reflexology and massage are available in tipis, there's a camp fire and a 'Shhh' zone, but if that's a bit too right-on for you, there is also a cinema projection screen, and lots of board games. There's even a 'shop', which consists of a box in the office containing local organic honey, truffles and raku ceramics.

Whether you're a keen ashtanga yoga enthusiast, or just fancy getting away from it all in a relaxing environment, it would be hard to have anything other than a fantastic time here. Guests talk in glowing terms about how much they love it, and most plan to come back. As a result you may need to book ahead. Week-long courses run from Thursday to Thursday to take advantage of cheaper flights.

Via Ca' Loreto 3, Località Girfalco, Urbino, T+44 (0)870-609 2690 (UK), thehillthatbreathes.com. £595-695 per person per week.

Pesaro & the coast

With a smattering of art nouveau architecture and the birthplace of composer Rossini among its sights, Pesaro is a Marche seaside resort with an attractive *centro storico*, some good high-end shopping, a rather dated seafront and a good beach. The Romans founded the town as Pisaurum, in the territory of the Piceni, in 184 BC. On the via Flaminia, it was an important trading post. Pesaro's heyday was in the 16th century, when the della Rovere family moved their court here from Urbino.

To the immediate north of town, the natural park of Monte San Bartolo rises out of the sea. Beyond is the romantic walled town and castle of Gradara, at Marche's most northerly point. To the south of Pesaro, Fano is a smaller beach resort with a fishing fleet, good restaurants and more Roman remains.

Fano beach huts.

Piazza del Popolo

The arched building on the western side of Pesaro's main piazza is the 15th-century **Palazzo Ducale**. If you ask the gateman he will probably let you in to look at the courtyard. The fountain in the middle of the piazza was built in 1593.

Musei Civici

Piazza Toschi Mosca 29, T0721-387541, museicivicipesaro.it.
Jul-Aug Wed and Fri-Sun 0930-1230, 1600-1900, Tue and Thu 0930-1230, 1600-2230, Sep-Jun Tue-Wed 0930-1230, Thu-Sun 0930-1230, 1600-1900, €4/2 concession, or €7/3 combined ticket with Casa Rossini, free under 14.

Comprising Pesaro's art gallery and ceramics museums, the Palazzo Toschi Mosca contains a large maiolica collection, together with some colourful and mildly interesting pieces from the 16th-century Duchy of Urbino – the duke and his wife can be seen in unforgiving profile in stone at the top of the stairs. Highlights of the art gallery are a little thin on the ground, though Giovanni Bellini's Renaissance altarpiece of the *Coronation of the Virgin* is an impressive work. On the stairs, garnering many second glances, Francesco Nonni's 1939 life-sized ceramic *Salome*, severed head in hand, is depicted as a sleek nude.

Casa Rossini

Via Rossini 34, T0721-387357.
Jul-Aug Wed and Fri-Sun 0930-1230, 1600-1900, Tue and Thu 0930-1230, 1600-2230, Sep-Jun Tue-Wed 0930-1230, Thu-Sun 0930-1230, 1600-1900, €4/2 concession, free under 14.

Gioacchino Rossini, composer of *The Barber of Seville* and many other operas, was born here in 1792. The house was declared a national monument in 1904 and these days contains a collection of prints of Rossini and his contemporaries. In the cellar, Rossini operas play on a constant loop, though the sound quality is poor. Beyond the historical curiosity there's little to detain visitors for very long.

Cattedrale

Via Rossini, T0721-30043.

The most interesting parts of the cathedral are the mosaics found underneath the floor. On two levels, they were uncovered in the 19th century and date from the sixth and fourth centuries respectively. Glass panels allow visitors to look down on fragments of the 600 sq m of what was probably the floor of an early Christian basilica. The Romanesque façade of the cathedral survived a 19th-century renovation that left little else of beauty.

Opposite, the **Museo Diocesano** (T0721-371219, Tue and Sat-Sun 1600-2000, Wed-Fri 1700-2230, €3) has archaeological and art sections.

Biblioteca & Museo Oliveriano

Palazzo Almerici, Via Mazza 97, T0721-33344.
Library Mon-Fri 0830-1330, 1430-1845; museum Jul-Aug 1600-1900, Sep-Jun 0900-1200, free. Outside of Jul-Aug, ask upstairs at the library, and somebody will open the museum for you.

Superior Pesaro's more obvious sights are the library and museum in the Palazzo Almerici. The archaeological museum has finds from the Picene necropolis at Novilara, south of Pesaro – oil lamps and coins among its collection – while upstairs the working library has some beautiful illuminated manuscripts, including a Neapolitan book of hours from 1625 and a 1767 encyclopaedia of science that explains in meticulous detail how to make cannon balls. Ask to see the **Sala Manoscritti**, which has a fascinating map from 1508-1510 showing the first sketchy concept of the Americas.

Around the rest of town

On the eastern edge of the old town, in piazza Matteotti, there is a covered excavation of a **Roman villa**. Just north of here, the **Rocca Costanza** (not usually open to the public) is a hulking 15th-century fort that was used as a prison up to 1989.

To the south of piazza del Popolo, the well-preserved 14th-century front of the **Chiesa di San Domenico** is now no more than a façade, though you can go through the main door to get money from a Post Office cash machine. The **Chiesa di Sant'Agostino**, on corso XI Settembre, has an even more ornate façade, dating back as far as 1398. The **Santuario della Madonna delle Grazie**, on via San Francesco, has another beautiful portal, this time from 1356-1373.

Towards the sea, a huge metal **globe** sculpture by Arnaldo Pomodoro dominates piazzale della Libertà. Just near here is Pesaro's best Liberty-style building: the **Villino Ruggeri**, built between 1902 and 1907 for pharmacist Oreste Ruggeri: it is not open to visitors but can be viewed from viale Trieste.

Around Pesaro

Parco Naturale del Monte San Bartolo

parks.it/parco.monte.san.bartolo.

A little like the better-known Parco del Conero further south, San Bartolo is a rare stretch of the Adriatic coast where hills reach to the sea, preventing the development that has blighted much of the coastline. And while it is hardly a wilderness, its rural nature means it is a relatively peaceful area, and a good place for walking – ask for a map at the tourist information office in Pesaro or Fano. The website has information on places to stay in the park.

Gradara

Tourist information office: *Via delle Mura 4, T0541-964673, gradarainnova.com*
Jun-Aug daily 0900-1300, 1500-2300, Sep-May Mon-Sat 0900-1300, 1400-1800, Sun 1000-1300, 1400-1800.

Construction started around 1150 on this impressive castle and walled town, one of the most intact medieval structures in Italy. Lucrezia Borgia lived here for a while and it was the setting for one of Italy's most famous love stories: the tragedy of Francesca and Paolo (see opposite).

From the entrance to the medieval town at the **Torre del Orologio** it's possible to walk a good stretch of the walls along the **Camminamenti di Ronda** (Jun-Aug 1000-1300 and 1400-2300, Sep-May 0900-1300, 1430-1830, €2), and also climb to the top of one of the town's 17 towers.

The **Rocca** itself (castellodigradara.com, Mon 0830-1315, Tue-Sun 0830-1830, also evenings in Jul-Aug, €4/2 concession), lovingly restored in the 20th century, is an atmospheric place – the epitome of most castle fantasies, it has red-draped four-poster beds, frescoed walls, beautiful heavy furniture and long dining rooms. There are a few worthwhile paintings, such as a *Madonna Enthroned* by Giovanni Santi, father of Raphael. Don't miss the barrel-vaulted chapel on the ground floor, with an altarpiece by Andrea della Robbia.

Gradara.

Francesca & Paolo

The story of Francesca and Paolo has been immortalized in verse by Dante in the *Divine Comedy* and in stone by Rodin with *The Kiss*, put to music by Rachmaninov and painted by Ingres.

The beautiful Francesca da Rimini, daughter of the Lord of Ravenna, was married off by her father to Gianciotto, son of the Lord of Gradara, around 1275. It was a marriage designed to seal the peace between the two families, who had previously been at war. Paolo, the younger and, by all accounts, more attractive brother of Gianciotto, was sent to marry Francesca by proxy. Apparently it was not until the day after the wedding that Francesca realized whom she had really married.

Gianciotto spent much of his time in Pesaro, leaving his wife alone in Gradara castle. Paolo took to visiting Francesca and the two read together, including the story of Lancelot and Guinevere. They became lovers but were caught by Gianciotto, who killed them both with his sword. Dante, their contemporary, placed the pair in the Circle of Lust in his *Inferno*.

Fano

Just down the coast from Pesaro, Fano is a smaller resort that doubles as a fishing town, with a Roman arch leading to a compact *centro storico*. The town has an unexpectedly young vibe, with bookshops and clothes shops as well as pensioners on bikes. There are two good beaches: the smaller, sandy **Spiaggia Lido** and the longer, pebbly, **Spiaggia Sassonia**. Between the two is the fishing port, adding some industrial grit to the town, as well as some excellent fish restaurants.

Piazza XX Settembre

On Fano's central piazza, the **Palazzo del Podestà**, next to the tower, dates from 1299 and was the seat of power in the area. It was first used as a theatre in the 17th century and now houses the 19th-century **Teatro della Fortuna**.

The tower was rebuilt after being destroyed in the Second World War. In the centre of the piazza is a 16th-century fountain, the **Fontana della Fortuna**.

Museo Archeologico e Pinacoteca

Palazzo Malatestiano.
Tue, Thu and Sat 0930-1230, 1500-1800, Wed and Fri 0830-1330, Sun 1000-1300, 1600-1900, €3.50.

Fano's town museum and art gallery, entered through a Renaissance arch off the main piazza, has an *Annunciation* by Guido Reni and works by Giovanni Santi and Guercino. Archaeological remains among its collection include a Roman mosaic of a man riding a leopard. Summer concerts are held outside in the handsome courtyard.

The ornately sculpted 14th- and 15th-century tombs of members of the Malatesta family, who once lived here, can be seen in the ex-**Church of San Francesco**, a block to the east.

Cattedrale dell'Assunta

Piazza Clemente VIII.

Rebuilt in 1124 after a fire, Fano's cathedral has been much changed since, though the Romanesque portal survives, and the interior has a remarkable stone pulpit held up by the backs of four lions, one of which is in the process of nibbling off someone's head. The pulpit was put together in the 20th century from various ancient pieces, some of which may predate the church.

Roman Fano

The most impressive Roman monument in Fano is the huge **Arco d'Augusto**, the main gate into the old town, built in 9 AD by Emperor Augustus. The upper part was partially destroyed in a siege in 1463. What may be the remains of the Roman **forum** are visible under the Church of Sant'Agostino. Remains of a Roman **amphitheatre** can be visited by guided tour on Tuesday evenings in summer (corso Matteotti, 2130), and other Roman remains will be opened to the public once the restoration of the Luigi Rossi school off corso Matteotti is completed.

Sleeping

San Domenico €€€
*Piazza Rinascimento 3,
T0722-2626, viphotels.it.*
Once a convent for the church
that it abuts, a stay at the smart
San Domenico allows you to
breakfast in the porticoes of the
ex-cloister and sleep in the
convent's rooms upstairs, though
presumably the holy order did
without air conditioning and
minibars. Comfortable, well-sized
rooms have shiny wooden floors
and a mix of generic modern
furniture and early 20th-century
pieces. New rooms, due to open
at the end of 2008, have views
across the piazza Rinascimento
to the Palazzo Ducale. Private
parking and a great central
location. The owners have
another hotel, the Bonconte,
just outside the city walls.

Ca' Andreana €€
*Via Ca' Andreana 2, near
Gadana, T0722-327845,
caandreana.it.*
Fifteen minutes' drive to
the northwest of Urbino,
Ca' Andreana is a pretty and
secluded house set among
rolling hills. There's a great
swimming pool with views over
the surrounding countryside and
a good restaurant, also open to
non-guests, which uses organic
ingredients produced on the
farm for dishes such as tagliatelle
with saffron, or roast pork with
green pepper and porcini

mushroom sauce. The six
rooms are done up in country
farmhouse style, with prints and
botanical drawings on the walls;
there's a friendly dog, an outdoor
table tennis table, and guests
can rent mountain bikes or cook
for themselves on the wood-
fired barbecue.

Hotel Raffaello €€
*Vicolino Santa Margherita 38/40,
T0722-4896,
albergoraffaello.com.*
In an 18th-century building
with a friendly welcome and an
excess of marble, Hotel Raffaello
has some of Urbino's best views
– across the rooftops of the town
towards the Palazzo Ducale.
Make sure you get one of the
five rooms with a view, though:
those without are comfortable
but fairly plain.

Ca' Vernaccia €
*Via Panoramica 10, Pallino,
T0722-329824,
locandaurbino.com.*
About 5 km from the centre
of Urbino, Ca' Vernaccia (also
signposted, a little confusingly,
as La Tartufara) opened in 2004,
having been rebuilt from the
ruins of a local farm. There are
good views along the ridges of
the hills to Urbino, and there's
a restaurant specializing in
truffles. Rooms and apartments
are simple, and some are on the
small side, but nicely done out
with wooden beams and
spotlessly shiny bathrooms. It's

good value too – cheaper than all
but the simplest hotels in Urbino
itself – though there's no pool.

San Giovanni €
Via Barocci 13, T0722-329055.
On a winding street near the
centre of town, rooms upstairs
with views are especially good
value. Bathrooms are tiled and
immaculately shiny, though the
bedrooms themselves can feel
dated; if possible, avoid the
ground floor rooms, which are
on the dark side of dim.

Locanda San Leone €€
*Strada Sant'Antimo 102,
T0541-912194,
locandasanleone.it.*
Down the hill a few kilometres
from San Leo, this peaceful,
wizened *agriturismo* is set in a
verdant garden through which
a stream flows into a lake. Rustic
rooms have bare wood, art and
colourfully painted walls. There's
a restaurant too.

Borgo Storico Cisterna €
Santa Lucia Cisterna 12,
Macerata Feltria, T335-8335976,
lacisterna.net.
This fantastically isolated ancient farm is 1 km from Macerata Feltria, east of Pietrarubbia. Buildings have been added around a 12th-century tower in a careful and very high quality restoration, with skilful stonework. The interiors, too, have had lots of care – the antique furniture is all from Marche, and the original stone drains have been retained in the ground floor rooms – under one of these are grain silos from Roman times. There's a restaurant, open also to non-guests, and work is continuing to restore and extend a farm that was once important enough to warrant fortifications.

Il Castello €
Piazza Dante Alighieri 11/12,
T0541-916214, hotelristorante
castellosanleo.com.
Right on the main San Leo piazza, which the best rooms here overlook; those at the back, with views over the valley, are quieter. Go for one of the

good-value antiques-filled rooms, which have much more character than the modern ones. Tiled bathrooms are sparkling, and downstairs there's a café, restaurant and bar, with good options for light lunches including *piadine* (flat bread sandwiches).

Locanda il Vicariato €
Pietrarubbia, T0722-750031,
ilvicariato.it.
In a restored hamlet (see page 229) at the edge of the Parco del Sasso Simone e Simoncello, il Vicariato is an *albergo diffuso*, so your room could be in one of several buildings scattered around the place. Rooms, though not large, are good value and have plenty of character, with wooden beams, open stonework and splashes of colour. Bathrooms are newly tiled and everything is spotlessly clean.

Pesaro

There are no hotels in Pesaro's *centro storico*.

Hotel Vittoria €€€
Piazzale della Libertà 2,
T0721-34344, viphotels.it.
One of a small group of hotels in Urbino and Pesaro, Vittoria, in an ex-casino, is smaller and more personal than its big brother the Savoy, nearby. It's faultlessly formal: padded leather and polished wood abounds and

there are bellboys, fully kitted-out maids and sea views. Rooms are comfortably old fashioned, bathrooms more modern.

Villa Cattani Stuart €€
Via Trebbiantico 67,
T0721-55782, villacattani.it.
Go for one of the rooms in the 17th-century villa, rather than the rather soulless 'business' rooms in the modern wing of this hotel about 10 minutes' drive south of Pesaro. A spectacular swimming pool and formal gardens are the highlights. The business orientation means that rooms come equipped with all mod cons and there's Wi-Fi and highly professional service.

Villa Serena €€
Strada di San Nicola 3, T0721-
55211, villa-serena.it.
In a house built as an Italian aristocratic summer retreat, guests are looked after by the current Count Pinto and his family. The hotel and restaurant, 10 minutes' drive south of Pesaro, are elegant but unstuffy, and there are well-tended gardens and a swimming pool. All of the generous nine rooms are different, with old furniture and abundant character. Huge fireplaces, a banqueting room and an interesting art collection add to the enormous charm of the place.

Eating & drinking

Badia €
Strada della Torraccia 20,
T0721-405730,
badiagriturismo.it.
A horse-breeding farm inland from Pesaro, Badia does bed and breakfast with eight simple, smart, new rooms. Guests can sometimes help out in the stables or around the farm with the organic crops.

Hotel des Bains €
Viale Trieste 221, T0721-34957,
innitalia.com.
One of the few hotels near the seafront that doesn't look like a concrete tower block. And while it's not quite stylish, it does retain occasional touches from its heyday in the early 20th century. Rooms are generous and comfortable, with minibars, TV, large gilt-framed mirrors and dated wooden furniture.

Fano

Relais Villa Giulia €€€
Via di Villa Giulia 40, Località San Biagio, T0721-823159,
relaisvillagiulia.com.
If you can afford it, this is by far the best choice in and around Fano. Set among peaceful vines and olive trees to the north of town, sun streams through old windows into a building originally constructed for the nephew of Napoleon. Nowadays it is an elegant, antique country pile, complete with labrador, swimming pool, lots of books

and magazines and old wooden toys. There's a restaurant too, just for guests.

Astoria €
Viale Cairoli 86, T0721-800077,
hotelastoriafano.it.
The pick of the rather ugly seafront hotels, Astoria is well placed at the edge of the sandy Spiaggia Lido. The common spaces are unexpectedly contemporary, with wicker furniture and black and white photos, though the rooms are rather dated.

Casa Masetti €
Via Montevecchio 104,
T328-230 5099, bbcasamasetti.it.
Fano's only accommodation in the old centre is this lemon yellow, 18th-century townhouse one block away from the piazza. There are just three simple, comfortable rooms, all with private bathrooms, and a shared reading room.

Urbino

There is a good range of eateries in Urbino, from cheap pizzerias catering to poor students to expensive restaurants.
Look out for *cresce sfogliate* – an unleavened bread typical of the town.

Vecchia Urbino €€€
Via dei Vasari 3/5, T0722-4447,
vecchiaurbino.it.
Wed-Sun 1100-1600, 1900-0100.
A smart place on a quiet side street just inside the city walls, Vecchia Urbino has an oil sommelier and a front door plastered in stickers advertising its inclusion in Italian foodie guides. There's an interesting tasting menu, including dishes such as ricotta with honey, a vegetarian menu and some unusual pasta choices, such as *garganelli* with orange and julienne of prosciutto. The meat options are more standard.

Al Girarrosto €€
Piazza San Francesco 3,
T0722-4445.
Daily 1230-1445, 2000-2300, closed Mon in winter.
The prime attraction of this place is its position (and outdoor tables in summer) on the elegant piazza behind San Francesco. The traditional Urbino unleavened bread, *cresce sfogliate*, can be tried as a starter and there are some good risotto

options for a minimum of two people. After that, grilled meat is the mainstay of the menu.

L'Angolo Divino €€
Via Sant'Andrea 14, T0722-327559, angolodivino.com.
Tue-Sat 1200-1430, 1915-2230, Sun 1200-1430.
Enter by the kitchen and then go downstairs to reach this brick-walled cellar restaurant below street level. The heavily marketed specialities of the house are *pasta nel sacco* – pasta parcels with porcini mushrooms and truffles – and *salami matto* – rather unexciting meat slices in a cheese sauce. There are some other, better, pasta options though, and the meaty second courses (such as rabbit, or lamb with wild sage) are good too. Service can be slow.

La Ballestra €€
Via Valerio 16, T0722-2942.
Wed-Mon 1200-1500, 1900-2400.
Good food at good prices and a great outdoor seating area under umbrellas on one of Urbino's quiet back streets. There are 42 types of pizza, which also come in 'giant' size, but also plenty of meaty second courses such as lamb or roast pork. Inside there are wooden floors and big lampshades, but most people choose to sit outside if they can. The only downside might be the sometimes eccentrically uninterested service.

Le Tre Piante €€
Via Voltaccia della Vecchia 1, T0722-4863.
Tue-Sun 1200-1500, 1900-2330.
At the edge of town, with a pretty little wooden patio outside overlooking the nearby hills, this is a friendly spot with good portions of excellent Urbino home cooking, served without pretension. There's a pizza menu too, alongside tasty choices such as spaghetti with crab and mushroom and steak with parmesan and peppercorns.

Trattoria del Leone €€
Via Cesare Battisti 5, T0722-329894, latrattoriadelleone.it.
Daily 1830-2330, also Sat-Sun 1230-1430.
There are some good vegetarian choices among the more traditional menu options in this little restaurant in 15th-century rooms underneath the Church of San Francesco. There's also a tasting menu of various small dishes that includes La Cotta

beer, made nearby in the hills of the Montefeltro. Original collograph prints line the walls, though they sit a little strangely with an ugly water feature. It's popular, so book ahead at busy times of year.

Al Cantuccio €
Via Budassi 62, T0722-2521.
Wed-Mon 1200-1500, 1900-2330.
Friendly and informal, Cantuccio is popular with local Italians for its succulent, wood-fired pizzas, also served at lunchtime. There's no outdoor seating, and, when it's full, not much space inside either, but that's all part of the charm. There is a traditional Italian menu, but the pizzas are the thing to come for.

Cafés & bars
Caffè del Sole
Via Mazzini 34, T0722-2619.
Daily 0700-0200.
Down the hill from piazza della Repubblica, this is a

multifunctional place, almost always open, either as a bar, café or both. There are several German, British and Irish beers on tap, and light meals, including sausage with roast potatoes, are available. Tables on the street make a great spot to sit and watch Urbino's comings and goings.

I Dolci di Battista
Via Raffaello Sanzio 19, T0722-4409.
A few doors down, on the corner of the main piazza, is a popular but rather industrial gelateria. You'd do much better to come up the hill to this place, where everything, including the pastries and the ice cream, is homemade. There are some tables out on the square opposite, and your evening *aperitivo* comes with bar snacks.

Gola del Furlo

Antico Furlo €€€
Via Furlo 60, Furlo, T0721-700096, anticofurlo.it.
Daily 1200-1430, 1930 till late. 23 km southeast of Urbino, at the end of the Furlo Gorge.
Mussolini stayed in room 3 of the hotel attached to this restaurant, perhaps to get the best view of his profile on the mountain above. The food here is simple but expertly prepared and presented with an aesthete's eye. Dishes such as poached egg with white truffle, and pasta with pecorino and pepper are

elevated above their usual level, and a €25 three-course menu *del giorno* is good value. There's an elegant interior with an open wood fire in season, or an outdoor terrace across the road. There are also seven rooms, should you want to stay.

San Leo & Montefeltro

Il Vicariato €€
Via Castello 10, Pietrarubbia, T0722-75390.
Daily 1200-1500, 1930-2300.
Another part of the Pietrarubbia project (see page 229), the Vicariato restaurant is a stylish place, with candles, an open fireplace, interesting art on the walls and a tasty menu featuring local ingredients such as Montefeltro wines and cheeses, as well as wild boar, lamb and rabbit. Try the excellent cherry wine.

La Cotta €
Via Vecellio, Località Cà Corsuccio, Mercatale di Sassocorvado, T334-252 0471, lacotta.it.
12 km east of Pietrarubbia.
Mon-Wed and Fri-Sat 1900-2330.

Transformed from a tumbledown farmhouse into a swish microbrewery complete with a restaurant, La Cotta is a popular destination up a steep road from the valley floor. A new wood-fired pizza oven will provide accompaniments to three types of artisan, organic beer: *chiara* (clear – a light ale), *ambrata* (amber – a cool, malty beer) and *rossa* (dark ale – a smooth, warm-toned bitter).

Osteria la Corte di Berengario II €
Via Michele Rosa 74, San Leo, T0541-916145.
Wed-Mon 1215-2400.
This cosy little place just off the main piazza has a good local menu featuring dishes such as pasta with chickpeas, and rabbit with wild fennel. Next door there's a gelateria, and beyond that a *liquorificio*, selling all sorts of homemade concoctions, so you don't need to go far to make a real night of it.

Felici e Contenti €€
Via Cattaneo 37, T0721-32060,
feliciecontenti.com.
Wed-Mon 1200-1415, 1900-
2300, pizzas till 2330
Pizzas and traditional Marche
dishes in a comfortable setting
in two rooms just off piazza
Esedra, deep in the *centro storico*.
The walls are adorned with
contemporary black and white
photographs and there are also
seats outside in the piazza.

Osteria di Pinocchio €€
Piazza Antaldi 12, T0721-34771,
osteriadipinocchio.com.
Mon-Sat 1230-1500, 1930-2400,
Sun 1930-2330.
An appropriately long room,
with sponged blue ceilings,
and Pinocchio puppets and
dolls decorating the yellow walls
alongside past and present family
photos. Simple dishes such as
pasta with beans are popular
with locals, who also come
for the excellent homemade
desserts. Homemade pasta
and large tasty salads make
it a good spot for lunch.

C'Era Una Volta €
Via Cattaneo 26/28, T0721-30911,
ceraunavolta-ps.com.
Tue-Sun 1200-1430, 1900-2430.
Pesaro's best pizzas are served
in the heart of the old centre,
in a slightly bizarre restaurant,
where wooden tennis racquets,
palmistry posters and a fake shed

roof decorate the place, and
staff wear t-shirts bearing the
enigmatic slogan, "Danger –
don't drink water...but don't drink
life." The pizzas, however, are
exquisite – huge, crispy, chewy
things that are simultaneously
substantial yet melt in your
mouth – and it buzzes with
people from early until late.

La Guercia €
Via Baviera 33, T0721-33463,
osterialaguercia.it.
Mon-Sat 1200-1600, 1745-2230.
Ask to see the large Roman
mosaic recently discovered
under the floor of the cellar in
this intimate little trattoria hidden
away under an arch, just off piazza
del Popolo. The mid 20th-century
murals of barrels and rural scenes
are much more modern, though
also more scratched. Unusually for
restaurants in this seaside town,
the menu concentrates on the
fare of the land: beans and pasta,
mozzarella and rocket. Locals fill
the benches and wooden chairs,
creating a good atmosphere.
Homemade desserts are on
display under the hanging
bunches of plastic grapes.

Pizzeria La Boa €
Viale Trieste 295, T0721-31993.
Daily 1100 onwards.
A bar, café and pizzeria, Boa is
a convenient spot for a quick
bite between games of volleyball
on the beach. Good pizza is
available by the slice, or you can
get a giant one to take away.

Inside and out there is plenty of
smart modern furniture to sit at
and watch the world go by

Cafés & bars
Caffè Ducale
Piazza del Popolo 21,
T0721-34279.
Red and black tables and chairs
outside on Pesaro's central
piazza give this place a decadent
air. A good place for an *aperitivo*,
with a generous buffet of snacks
from 1900, and great people-
watching, especially as dusk falls
on the piazza, though it tends to
clear out soon after.

Enoteca 075
Palazzo Gradari, Via Rossini 24,
T0721-64916,
zerosettantacinque.com.
Mon-Sat 0800-2200,
though hours may vary.
Pesaro's best setting for a tipple
or a bite to eat: light meals and
good wine are served at designer
white wicker seats in the arched
courtyard of Palazzo Gradari. It's a
laid-back place, with jazz playing
and eye-catchingly hip orange
walls inside.

Gelateria Gianfranco
Piazza le Lazzarini 10,
T0721-64179.
Tue-Sun 1300-2200.
Pesaro's best ice creams and a
great wide choice of flavours.
Try one of several varieties of
chocolate, pine nut, or *zuppa*
inglese (trifle) flavour containing
real pieces of cake.

Listings

Around Pesaro

Osteria della Luna €€
Via Umberto I 6, Gradara,
T0541-969838,
osteriadellaluna.com.
Tue-Sun 1030-1530, 1830-2330.
One of several decent eateries in the medieval walled town of Gradara, greenery-covered Luna has tables outside and serves good homemade *piadine* as well as pasta dishes such as *caramelle* pasta filled with ricotta, walnuts and porcini mushrooms. Other places to try in the town are the popular **La Botte**, just inside the gate, and **Il Bacio**, on via Roma, with good views up the hill to the castle.

Fano

Da Maria €€
Via IV Novembre 86,
T0721-808962.
Tue-Sun 1200-around 2300, but closed when sea is too rough to fish.
A popular little trattoria, with a rather wonderful homely old-fashioned style, serving fresh fish. Traditional dishes vary depending on what has been caught.

Osteria al 26 €€
26 Via Giorgio, T0721-820677.
Wed-Mon 1930-2330.
A hip place with a handful of tables outside in the small, quiet street, where little candle lamps swing from the walls. In the barrel-vaulted interior, big modern art decorates the walls and the cuisine has fusion touches – try the carpaccio or the vegetarian ravioli with radicchio, walnuts and ricotta.

Il Cantinone €
Via Arco d'Augusto 62,
T0721-825922, ilcantinone.net.
Tue-Sun 1200-1500, 1900-2330, pizzas in evenings only.
Il Cantinone offers a seafood menu or wood-fired pizzas in the evening, either outside under canvas or in the cosy interior, where there are occasional live Portuguese Fado performances.

Trattoria Quinta €
Viale Adriatico 42, T0721-808043.
Mon-Sat 1215-1430, 1915-2200.
There is a palpable sense of urgency at the Quinta, which always seems busy, even out of season, as waiters rush around serving enormous plates of tagliatelle with *frutti di mare* or gnocchi with prawns and courgette, followed by *calamari fritti*, or a mixed fish grill. There are no frills here, just remarkably good and excellently fresh good value seafood. There are tables outside, under cover or not. A quarter of wine is only €1.20, and don't miss out on local speciality *moretta* – a mix of coffee, aniseed liqueur and lemon peel.

Entertainment

Urbino

Annual events in Urbino include the **Festival di Musica Antica**, with lots of Baroque and early music in July; the **Festa del Duca** in August, a historical celebration and recreation of the reign of Duke Federico, involving lots of colourful costumes; and the **Festa dell'Aquilone**, a kite festival in September.

Pesaro

Teatro Rossini
Piazza Lazzarini, T0721-387620.
Built in 1637, Pesaro's grand theatre changed its name to Rossini in 1855 and now hosts operas during the annual Rossini opera festival (T0721-38001, rossinioperafestival.it) in August.

Cinema-teatro Sperimentale
Via Rossini, T0721-387543.
Plays and some interesting cinematic events, such as the **Mostra Internazionale del Nuovo Cinema** (International Exhibition of New Cinema), happen in this 500-seater theatre in the centre of town.

Centro Arti Visive Pescheria
Corso XI Settembre 184,
T0721-387651.
Look out for exhibitions and shows at Pesaro's contemporary visual arts centre in the spectacular ex-fish market.

Shopping

As a university town, Urbino has several good bookshops as well as some good fashion boutiques, some selling designer label clothes at knockdown prices.

Raffaello Degusteria
Via Donato Bramante 6/8/10, T0722-329546, raffaellodegusteria.it.
Mon-Sat 0900-1300, 1600-2000.
An upmarket deli, Raffaello sells wine and organic meat and cheese but also posh biscuits, high quality cookware, jars of all sorts of delicacies and three types of the local La Cotta beer.

Zona-Vì
Via Donato Bramante 69, T0722-327661.
Mon-Sat 0930-1300, 1600-1930.
One of the hippest of the town's clothes shops, selling street label shoes and tops as well as occasional one-off pieces by the owner's fashion designer daughter.

Pesaro

Pesaro has good shopping, with a number of designer fashion outlet shops, lots of smart home and kitchenware shops and a good few delicatessens where you can put together picnics for the beach.

Brendhouse
Via Rossini 60, T0721-639121, brendhouse.com.
Tue-Sun 0900-1300, 1600-2000, Mon 1600-2000.
One of Pesaro's best designer home shops, Brendhouse does a good line in candles and candlesticks, storage boxes and crockery, as well as selling fresh flowers.

Gioachino Gusteria
Via Morselli 12/14, T0721-370460, gioachinogusteria.it.
A smart contemporary deli selling homemade chocolates, fancy cakes, artisan beer, pasta and honey.

Transport

Urbino

Inland from the coastal train line that runs through Pesaro and Fano, Urbino is accessible by car or bus only. Seven buses daily arrive from Pesaro (90 mins).

San Leo

In summer (Jun-Sep) there are two direct buses a day from Rimini to San Leo; at other times it's necessary to change at Pietracuta. There's no public transport on Sundays. For the rest of the area a car is pretty much essential.

Pesaro & the coast

Pesaro is on the Rimini-Rome train line, with frequent trains in both directions. Fano's train station is also on the main coastal line. Autolinee Bucci (autolineebucci.com) run buses every half an hour from Fano to Pesaro, and less frequently to Urbino.

Contents

Fruit and veg market in the cloister
of San Francesco, Ascoli Piceno.

Central & southern Marche

Introduction

Ancona, a busy Adriatic port, is the region's biggest city, and budget flights mean that many now arrive and depart here. A couple of great restaurants, a Roman arch and an under-appreciated old centre are reasons to hang around.

Just to the south is Marche's most attractive stretch of coast, protected by the Conero regional park. Green hills come right down to the sea and there are some excellent beaches. Further inland, the Frasassi park hides some of the world's most spectacular caves, and to the south, Macerata is a little-visited university town with a fantastic contemporary art museum and some good nightlife, as well as an al fresco summer opera season in its distinctive elongated theatre. The surrounding area is rich in Roman remains, most obviously at Urbisaglia, which has a Roman theatre and an atmospheric amphitheatre.

Ascoli Piceno is the highlight of the south, a proud town with a spectacular stage set of a piazza sitting between the mountains and the sea. There's good contemporary art as well as a Roman bridge and a handful of medieval towers.

In few of these places will you come across more than a handful of foreign tourists – a blessing most of the time, this can also be a curse outside the brief summer season, when many sights close down.

…one day
Ascoli Piceno is a lively and rewarding town for a visit. The **piazza del Popolo** is the big draw, with the **Church of San Francesco** at one end and plenty of opportunities to linger over coffee among its porticoes. Don't miss the fruit and vegetable market in the **cloisters**. The excellent Renaissance art in the **Pinacoteca** is a good prelude to more contemporary works in the **Galleria d'Arte Contemporanea**. A wander around the back streets should include the **Roman bridge** and a few survivors of what was once a thriving population of medieval towers.

…a weekend or more
If Ascoli's 20th-century art has whetted your appetite for more, **Macerata** has some of central Italy's best contemporary painting. Otherwise, choose from **Urbs Salvia** for Roman remains, **Frasassi** for some of Europe's biggest caves and **Conero** for walking and beautiful, wild coastline and beaches. If you are passing through **Ancona**, stop for long enough to see the town's beautiful **cathedral**.

Stacked boats, Portonovo.

Ancona

The name 'Ancona' comes from the Dorians, who colonized the place in the fourth century BC and named it 'Ankon', which means 'elbow'. It was an important Roman port; later it was destroyed by the Saracens in 839 and heavily attacked in both World Wars. Today it is one of the major departure points for ferries to Croatia, Greece and even Turkey.

The small, quiet old centre has enough to keep you busy for a day or two if you're flying or sailing in or out, though the train station and port areas are markedly less attractive. The cathedral is a distinctive building on top of the hill, while below is the Roman arch of Trajan. The archaeological museum has lots of ancient finds, and there are a couple of picture galleries too. To the east, at the far end of viale della Vittoria, is il Passetto, with a strange-looking lift down to a small beach below. Accommodation is not Ancona's strong point, but there are some fantastic restaurants to make up for that, especially if you like seafood. The town also makes a good base for exploring the Conero Peninsula just to the south, a regional park that includes some of Italy's best Adriatic beaches.

Below: A Roman wall in the port. Opposite page: Cattedrale di San Ciriaco.

Cattedrale di San Ciriaco & Museo Diocesano

Piazzale del Duomo, T071-200391.
Cathedral: Winter 0800-1200, 1500-1800;
summer 0800-1200, 1500-1900. Museum:
May-Sep Sat 1000-1200, Sun 1700-1900,
Oct-Apr Sat 1000-1200, Sun 1600-1800; free.

At Ancona's highest point, on the summit of
Guasco Hill, the duomo combines Romanesque,
Gothic and Byzantine elements. It is dedicated to
the second-century Judas Cyriacus, patron saint of
the city. The church was consecrated in 1128,
though the crypt has the remains of an older,
sixth-century basilica, with mosaics and frescoes,
and there was probably an earlier temple to Venus
on the same site. The beautiful five-arched portal,
in white and pink stone, dates from around 1228.
Inside, the cathedral is built in the form of a Greek
cross, with a ribbed dodecagonal dome.

The museum, round to the left as you face
the duomo, has a collection of 400 paintings,
sculptures and ancient manuscripts.

Nearby are the remnants of the 97-m diameter
Roman amphitheatre. Being restored at the time
of writing, it once held 7,000-8,000 spectators.

Museo Archeologico Nazionale delle Marche

Palazzo Ferretti, Via Gabriele Ferretti 6,
T071-202602, archeomarche.it.
Tue-Sun 0830-1930, €4/2 concession,
free under 18 and over 65.

Marche's archaeology museum is rich in Roman
remains, and would be worth a visit just for the
elaborately three-dimensional ceilings of the
palace in which the collection is exhibited.
Diagrams of excavated tombs show in great
detail how and where pottery and other remains
were found, though there is little information
in English. Some of the most impressive pieces
are the beautiful metal garlands in room 22, one
of which was found on the skull of an excavated
Roman body. Upstairs, an otherwise dull prehistoric
section has the skeleton of a bear, which, it is
believed, died young due to a bad back.

Essentials

❶ Getting around Most of the old centre is walkable,
though a bus or taxi saves the long walk to the beach
at Il Passetto.

🚉 Trains The main station, at piazza Nello e Carlo
Rosselli, is in the modern part of town to the south:
buses run from here to the port and old town centre.

🚌 Buses Conerobus (T071-280 2092, conerobus.it).
Tickets for local buses cost €1 (€1.50 on board) and last
60 minutes.

🏥 Hospital Ospedale Umberto I, largo Lorenzo
Cappelli 1, T071-202095.

✚ Pharmacy Farmacia Centrale, corso Mazzini 1,
T071-202746.

🔖 Post office Largo XXIV Maggio 2, T071-501 2260.

❶ Tourist information office Via Thaon de Revel 4,
T071-358991.

Ancona listings

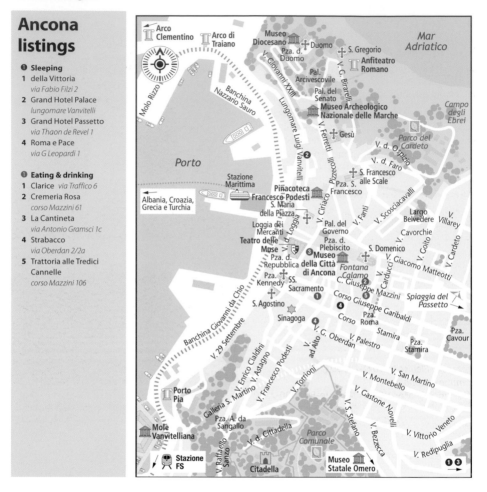

Pinacoteca Francesco Podesti & Galleria di Arte Moderna

Palazzo Bosdari, via Pizzecolli 17, T071-222 5041, comune.ancona.it.
Tue-Sat 0900-1900, Sun 1000-1300, 1600-1900, mid-Jun-Sep also Mon 0900-1900, €4.60.

Seven well-lit rooms make up Ancona's picture gallery. Highlights include Andrea del Sarto's *Madonna with Child and St John*, Sebastiano del Piombo's three-quarter *Portrait of Francesco Arsilli*, and – very much the star of the show – Titian's *Pala Gozzi*, his first dated work, from 1520. It depicts the Madonna and Child with St Francis, St Blaise and Luigi Gozzi, who commissioned the work. Recently restored, the painting is on a raised platform with steps at the back – climb these to see Titian's rough sketches on the back. Look too for the *Pala di San*

Agostino, most interesting for its depiction of 16th-century Ancona. Upstairs is the city's rather patchy contemporary art collection.

Chiesa di Santa Maria della Piazza

Piazza Santa Maria.

A 13th-century church, Santa Maria della Piazza has a beautifully ornate three-part façade, rich in figures and animals, which is being restored at the time of writing. Inside, early Christian mosaics can be seen through glass in the floor.

Piazza del Plebiscito & piazza Roma

A huge statue of Pope Clement XII, from 1738, dominates the city's central piazza. Behind, in the **Chiesa di San Domenico**, is a 1558 Crucifixion by Titian. To the south, the city's second main axis, piazza Roma, has bars, cafés and market stalls; on corso Garibaldi, crossing it, is the beautiful 16th-century **Fontana Calamo**, commonly known as the tredici cannelle, or '13 taps', a row of masked heads spouting water into a trough.

Museo della Città di Ancona

Piazza del Plebiscito, T071-222 5037, comune.ancona.it.
Mid-Jun-Sep, Mon 0930-1200, Tue-Fri 1800-2200, Sat-Sun 1000-1300, 1800-2200, Oct-mid-Jun, Tue-Wed 1000-1300, Thu-Sun 1000-1300, 1600-1930, €3.

Ancona's well-designed museum gives a good historical context to the city and the region. Most information is in Italian, but there is enough to keep non-Italian speakers interested, including a large wooden model of the city from 1844 and a video and slideshow in the basement.

Arco di Traiano

By the port, Trajan's arch was erected in AD 115 in honour of the Roman emperor who had built the northern quay, increasing the importance of the city. What is left today is only the middle section

Above: Arco di Traiano.
Below: Le Tredici Cannelle.

of what was originally a bigger arch. Pope Clement XII, having further extended the quay, built himself a neighbouring arch in 1738.

Il Campo degli Ebrei

Parco del Cardeto, via del Cardeto, T071-222 4099, parcodelcardeto.it.
Apr-Sep 0830-2030, Oct-Mar 0800-1730, free.

At one time the Jewish population of Ancona numbered over 3,000, and the restored Jewish cemetery, on a hill above the city centre, is an unexpectedly evocative and moving place. It was in use from 1428 to 1863, when part of it was requisitioned by the military, and a new cemetery was opened elsewhere. During the restoration

Around the region

1,058 stones were found, and while some have been moved and lined up, others have been left scattered around the grassy area. Around the rest of the park are walks with views out over the sea.

Conero

South of Ancona's busy sprawl is a different world altogether: the **Parco del Conero** (parcodelconero.eu), a peaceful, largely rural, protected area, where the hills meet the sea. Portonovo is as bustling as it gets, with a beach backed by cafés and restaurants; to the south, Sirolo is a prettier village, and Numana is a fishing town. There are easy strolls along marked paths through woods to relatively unfrequented beaches, or more serious hikes across the hills. The seafood is excellent, and if you want more in the way of action, it's possible to windsurf or hire bikes or boats.

Portonovo

Less a village than a loose collection of buildings behind the beach and up the hill, Portonovo is the northern centre of the Conero regional park. There are a couple of small shops and the bus stops here. Information boards point out walking routes – an easy 90-minute walk goes around the natural saltwater lake of **Lago Grande**. If you walk along the seafront you will eventually come to the **Church of Santa Maria di Portonovo** (T071-56307, daily 1700-1900), in a spectacular and somewhat precipitous position, shored up against the sea.

Sirolo

A beautiful town perched high above the sea in the middle of the Conero park, Sirolo has streets of pastel-painted terraced houses and a path down to a beautiful beach of fine shells and pebbles. Sheltered by a breakwater, the water is clean and clear and excellent for swimming.

Numana

A fishing village at the southern edge of the park, Numana lacks some of the charm of Portonovo and Sirolo, but it does have an archaeological museum, **Numana Antiquarium Statale** (daily 0830-1930, €2), with fascinating exhibits taken from the many Picene tombs discovered in the area. Most impressive are the finds from the tomb of the so-called 'Queen of Numana', actually found near Sirolo, with a chariot and two horses. The metal wheel rims of the chariot are arranged in a case in their original positions, alongside some fabulously ornate pottery as old as the seventh century BC.

Loreto

South of Conero, nearby Loreto is the second most popular pilgrimage site in Europe, after Lourdes. The town centres (indeed grew up) around the extravagant **Basilica della Santa Casa** (Apr-Sep 0630-1230, 1430-2000, Oct-Mar 0645-1230, 1430-1900, free), which, in turn, is built around the simple house of Mary and Joseph, brought from Nazareth in the 1290s on the wings of angels, or by crusaders, depending on which version of the story you read. Inside the Santa Casa, the statue of the black Loreto Virgin is a 1922 copy of the original, which was destroyed in a fire. The **Piazza della Madonna** is an extraordinary, theatrical space and the basilica a grand building, though non-believers may find the wailing and praying uncomfortably hysterical.

Left: Conero Park from Sirolo.
Opposite page: Frasassi caves.

Frasassi

Above some of Europe's biggest and most spectacular caves, the Frasassi natural park has tall, steep wooded hills, sharply cut through by the Frasassi and Gola Gorges. The attractive hill village of Genga is the centre of this isolated, rural Apennine region, but it is so sleepy as to render it more or less comatose for most of the year. The caves themselves are a popular tourist attraction, but in most of the rest of the park you'll meet few people, and even fewer visitors.

Grotte di Frasassi

Genga, T0732-90090, frasassi.com.
Guided tours in English Jun-Sep daily at 0945, 1115, 1245, 1445, 1615, 1745, other times possible if booked in advance; tours in Italian at other times (check website for details), closed 10-30 Jan, €15/13 concession, €10 children 6-14, free under 6, price includes museum admission.

Some of the world's most spectacular caves, the Grotte di Frasassi are 1,400,000 years old, though they were discovered by humans only in 1971. A combination of sulphur and water eroded the rock to create the cave system – the paths of the original sulphurous streams are illuminated in blue. The water here, rich in minerals, is quick to create stalagmites and stalactites, which grow at a rate of one or two millimetres a year. So far, 30 km of caves have been explored, and a walkway has been constructed through five caverns – the biggest of these may be the largest single cavern in Europe.

The most spectacular part of the cave complex is the gargantuan Grotta Grande del Vento, 200 m high, 165 m long and 110 m wide. The place is so immense, and so bereft of context that one's eyes play tricks. Only when it is pointed out that a stalagmite on the wall is 3 m tall and further away than the length of a football pitch do the massive dimensions begin to sink in. It was here that the cave network was discovered: the moment when someone dropped a stone over the edge into the darkness and heard it eventually hit rock over 150 m below must have been every speleologist's dream.

From here the walkway rises and falls between 20-m stalagmites, and below a stalactite hanging way above that is 7 m long and estimated to weigh 6-7 tonnes, before opening out into wider spaces, richly furnished with extraordinary white filigree – it's like being in an enormous melting wax cathedral.

There are more intimate treasures here too – small pools of water sparkling with jewel-like crystals and curtains, and 'organ pipes' of minerals formed by millions of years of drips. There is even

Tip...

The ticket office for the caves is next to the car park and train station in Genga; from here a bus shuttles visitors to the entrance – allow plenty of time for queues and transfers. Tours can be booked in advance online or by phone: you should arrive at the ticket office half an hour before the booked time. Speleological visits must be booked at least a week in advance (blue trail 2 hrs 30 mins, €35, red trail 4 hrs, €45).

a species of blind lizard that lives in the caves, though you'll be lucky to see one. As you go through the caves, you will have various features pointed out – both geological and fantastical. One of the giant stalagmites supposedly looks like Dante. Easier to discern among the weird and wonderful mineral shapes are the camels and the shepherd, as well as a rather sad polar bear. These characterizations had a practical use for the cavers who discovered the network, orientating them in relation to landmarks in the dark.

The temperature in the caves is a constant 14°C. A guided tour – a round trip of about 1.5 km into the mountain – takes about an hour. From the caves back to the car park it's possible to walk alongside a stream for about 1.5 km.

More serious 'adventure' tours, of two levels, are available if you book in advance. Equipment is provided, and the two trails leave the tourist paths and pass through narrow passages to reach two more caverns.

L'Abbazia di San Vittore & Museo Speleo Paleontologico ed Archeologico

San Vittore, T0732 90241.
Museum Mon-Sat 1000-1300, 1430-1830, Sun and Aug daily 0830-1930, €4/2 concession, free with cave ticket.

San Vittore's museum complements a cave visit with the geological background: there's a good 3D model of a mountain cut through the middle and the fossil of a 3.5-m ichthyosaur, a sea predator similar to a large shark.

The museum is attached to the Abbey of San Vittore, a beautiful Romanesque building, stocky on the outside, slim and elegant within. Founded in 1007, it reached the height of its power in the 13th century, when it was in charge of more than 40 local churches and castles.

Parco Naturale Regionale Gola della Rossa e di Frasassi

parcogolarossa.it.

Good walks in the park include a 6 km trail through the **Scappuccia Valley**, north of Genga, taking in a gorge and a wooded valley. You might even meet a rare spectacled salamander. The park has a summer-only information office at the Frasassi caves ticket office and an infrequently open office in Genga. A better bet might be to buy a decent map and print out some of the route information on frasassi.com.

Tempietto del Valadier & Santa Maria Infra Saxa

In the Frasassi Gorge, 1.5 km west of the entrance to the caves, two buildings sit in a cave above the stream. The smaller Santa Maria Infra Saxa (St Mary in the Rocks), from which Frasassi gets its name, was formerly a hermitage and dates back to the 11th century. Inside is a well-tended shrine; the uneven floor is the surface of the rocks below. The second building, the octagonal Temple of Valadier, was built in the early 19th century on the orders of Pope Leo XII, who was born in nearby Genga. It fits remarkably snugly inside the cave, from where there are good views down to the gorge.

Right: Tempietto del Valadier.
Opposite page: Gola di Frasassi.

Macerata

A university town with a pale brick centre, mostly built between the 15th and 18th centuries and enclosed by 16th-century walls, Macerata has a summer opera festival in its distinctive Sferisterio outdoor theatre and one of the region's best contemporary art museums. The student population makes sure that the bars are lively and the surrounding hills have some interesting Roman remains and ancient towns to explore.

The nearby ruins of the Roman Helvia Ricina were plundered to build the medieval town, which was declared a city in 1320. The university was founded in 1290.

Below: Il Pozzo, Macerata. Opposite page: Loggia dei Mercanti, Macerata.

Piazza della Libertà

The town's central piazza has at its corner the **Loggia dei Mercanti**. Built in 1504-1505, and an elegant example of Renaissance architecture, it contrasts with the more solid building style that dominates Macerata. These days you can have a coffee or an *aperitivo* on comfy wicker seats under its arches – a prime spot for watching the world go by.

The **Palazzo dei Priori** along the northern side of the piazza is a rather brutal building. Opposite, it is possible to climb the 64-m **Torre Civica**, adjacent to the **Teatro Rossi** (tours at 1100 and 1600, ask at the information office on piazza Mazzini), for views of the surrounding countryside stretching from the Sibillini Mountains to the sea. The original clock was built in 1570 by the Ranieri brothers, who also made the famous clock of St Mark's in Venice – some of the workings can be seen inside the tower and the original may soon be restored and replaced.

Duomo

Piazza Strambi.

With more than its fair share of Baroque grandiosity, chandeliers and portentousness, construction of Macerata's Duomo was started in the 15th century; the façade was never finished. At opposite sides of the apse are two interesting versions of the same subject: *The Madonna Enthroned with Saints*. Allegretto Nuzi da Fabriano's 1369 triptych has Mary between Sts Julian and Anthony Abbot. In the 16th-century version, attributed to Giovanni de Carolis, Julian makes another appearance, this time with Anthony of Padua, and Mary's 'throne' is this time a cloud, on which she and Jesus perch rather precariously.

Basilica della Madonna della Misericordia

Piazza Strambi.

Across the piazza from the duomo, Macerata's basilica, built in 1736, is the smallest in the world (the status of basilica is conferred by the pope).

Essentials

❶ Getting around The town centre is small and walkable. If you're driving, try to find parking outside the narrow one-way systems in the centre.

Ⓒ Trains The station is just to the south of the centre.

❸ Buses There are frequent buses to nearby Urbisaglia and the Abbazia di Fiastra.

⊕ Hospital Via Santa Lucia 2, T0733-2571.

✛ Pharmacy Eredi Cappelletti, Corso Matteotti 23, T0733-230871.

⤳ Post office Via Corridoni Filippo 21, T0733-276111.

❶ Tourist information office Piazza Mazzini 10, T0733-230735, summer Tue-Sun 1000-1300, 1600-1900, winter 1000-1300, 1500-1800.

Its overwrought interior, an oval design by Luigi Vanvitelli, is extraordinarily decorated with paintings and plasterwork, and the dim, fake-candle lighting creates an eerie feel.

Museo Palazzo Ricci

Via Ricci 1, T0733-261487, fondazionemacerata.it. Jul-Aug, daily 1000-1300, 1600-2000, Mar-Jun and Sep-Dec Sat-Sun 1000-1300, 1600-2000, free.

Macerata's excellent contemporary art museum is the best in the region – an intelligently collected and carefully curated selection of Italian 20th-century art. The collection originally belonged

Around the region

to a bank, and the bank manager clearly had an eye for much more than just investment.

Three floors take you through all the important movements of contemporary Italian art, including Futurism, Surrealism and Abstraction. There is some good sculpture too, but it's the paintings that are really exceptional. Almost everyone is represented, from Severini through De Chirico to Morandi and Scipione, who was born in Macerata in 1904. Expertly and lovingly curated, the paintings are well laid out to give a sense of the progression of themes and styles. There's a beautiful 1932 Crucianelli nude, *Nudo su divano*, staring confidently out of the canvas wearing only her shoes, and Carlo Carrà's *Madre e figlio* demonstrates an exceptional use of colour as well as an interesting twist on more usual depictions of motherhood. There are lush landscapes, acutely perceived portraits, Futurist trains and beautiful still lifes. The ground floor also has interesting temporary summer exhibitions.

Pinacoteca & Museo Civico

Closed at the time of writing, Macerata's museum and gallery should open in 2009 in new premises in the **Palazzo Buonacorsi**, on via Don Minzoni, between the duomo and piazza della Libertà. Highlights of the town's art collection include paintings by Carlo Crivelli and Sassoferrato. A part of the museum is given over to antique carriages, for which the town is famous.

Sferisterio

sferisterio.it.
Jun-Sep 1200 and 1700, Oct-May 1200 and 1600, €2 entry plus €2 optional guided tour, book in advance at Macerata Incoming tourist information office, piazza Mazzini, T0733-234333, maceratincoming.it.

Used for the summer opera festival, as well as other musical events from mid-June to mid-September,

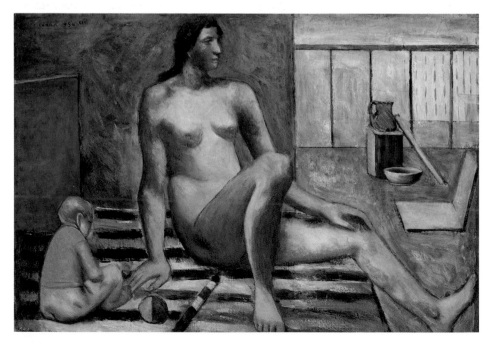

Above: Piazza Alta, Sarnano.
Opposite page: Carrà's *Madre e Figlio.*

Macerata's distinctive theatre was originally built between 1819 and 1829 as a sports stadium. The game of *palla al bracciale*, which required a long wall down one side of the arena, was once the most popular sport in Italy, and its stars were some of the best-paid sportsmen in the world in the 19th century. In its day the Sferisterio held around 8,000 people – these days capacity is a mere 2,800. Built into the medieval city walls, it has a semi-elliptical shape and excellent acoustics that permit opera to be performed here unamplified, though they do stop the traffic outside.

Around Macerata

To the east, attractive hill towns such as **Montelupo** punctuate the route to the over-developed coast. To the south and west, the mountains of the Sibillini

begin to dominate. The road to **Sarnano**, itself a handsome town with a particularly striking central piazza at the top of a low hill, is an especially good one. The detour to **San Ginesio** is worth it for the wide-angle panoramic views alone.

Abbazia di Fiastra

abbadiafiastra.net.
Jul-mid-Sep daily 1000-1230, 1500-1830, mid-Sep-Jun, Sat-Sun only, €4/2.50 concession.

Founded by Cistercian monks in 1142, this abbey south of Macerata has been developed as a visitor attraction, complete with café, pizzeria and car park. There's a nature reserve too, with 100 ha of woodland where you may see roe deer and badgers. Material from the nearby Roman remains at Urbs Salvia was used in the construction of the abbey, and occasional pieces of Roman capitals can be seen. Downstairs, under the 15th-century cloister, is an archaeological museum and some spooky cellars.

Urbs Salvia

T0733-506566.
Jul-mid-Sep daily 1000-1300, 1500-1900, mid-Sep-Oct and mid-Mar to mid-Jun Sat-Sun 1000-1300, 1500-1800, Nov-Feb Sat-Sun 1000-1300, 1500-1630, €6/5 concession.

To the south of Abbazia Fiastra, the remains of the Roman town of Urbs Salvia, just outside modern-day Urbisaglia, have benefited from EU investment: a new network of paths and a beautiful but rather pointless bridge connect the sites, the most impressive of which is the amphitheatre, just off the SS78.

Previously in Picene territory, Urbs Salvia may have been built around the second century BC; it became a Roman colony under Emperor Augustus. It was completely destroyed by King Alaric, the Visigoth famous for the sack of Rome, in the early fifth century. Dante mentions it as a desolate place.

Ringed with tall oak trees, the remains are evocative, especially with the Sibillini Mountains behind them. When the site is closed, there is little to stop visitors climbing the gate to have a look around.

Macerata to Ascoli Piceno

This drive takes in ancient abbeys, a Roman amphitheatre and lots of great views of the Sibillini Mountains.

From Macerata, head southwest on the SP77. If you have plenty of time, you could make a detour along the SS77 to the west to visit **Tolentino**, where the Basilica di San Nicola has a nice cloister and some fine frescoes. Otherwise, push on south for around 20 minutes to reach the Romanesque **Abbazia di Fiastra** (see page 259), an abbey set in a nature reserve with some good walks.

Another 6 km southwest along the same road brings you to Urbisaglia and the Roman remains of **Urbs Salvia**, including an impressive amphitheatre (see page 259). Another 15 minutes further south, branch right off the road towards **San Ginesio**,

Above: Amphitheatre, Urbs Salvia. Opposite page: The crypt of the duomo, Ascoli Piceno.

along a stunning ridge road with views to the north and south. San Ginesio has an unusual church, the **Collegiata della Annunziata**, with a beautiful Gothic façade (being restored at the time of writing). Even more striking is the wide-angle vista from the park at the western end of the town, over the Monti Sibillini and Marche countryside all the way to Monte Conero.

Head back on to the SS78: the road bends south as it skirts the eastern edge of the Sibillini National Park. If you have time, you could branch west into the park here, up the Fiastrone Valley towards Fiastra. Further south, **Sarnano** is a pretty, small town with more views and a spiral of medieval streets leading up to the showpiece **piazza Alta** at the summit of its hill, where the 13th-century **Santa Maria di Piazza** has frescoes and a statue of Jesus whose beard is reputed to grow if it's about to rain. There's a *pinacoteca* too, with a Carlo Crivelli *Madonna*.

From **Amandola** (where there is another *pinacoteca* and a couple of museums), another 15-20 minutes south, a road leads to **Montefortino** (with yet another *pinacoteca*) and then west into the **Gola Infernaccio** – Hell's Gorge. Here you can walk alongside the river Tenna and through the narrow gorge, before climbing through beech woods to the **Eremo di San Leonardo**, a hermitage built in the 20th century by a single monk. Just beyond here is a waterfall.

Return to Montefortino and continue east to rejoin the SS78, driving south along winding roads between wooded hills until it eventually joins the SS4. If you have time, turn right here to find the **Castel di Luco**, near Aquasanta Terme. Otherwise, turn left and follow the road to the beautiful town of **Ascoli Piceno**.

Ascoli Piceno

At the southern edge of Marche, equidistant between the mountains and the sea, Ascoli Piceno has a stunning piazza and two excellent art galleries.

A regional centre, it is a place that is proud of its ancient Picene history: it was the capital of these pre-Roman people. In the Middle Ages it had around 200 towers, a handful of which survive today, as does a Roman bridge. Its centre is these days an attractive and lively place, and one that doesn't close down outside July and August, unlike some of its neighbours. There are many old churches and some good shopping streets, which fill up with locals in the evenings. They celebrate Mardi Gras here in a big way, and the Quintana, a medieval celebration in July and August, sees jousting and lots of dressing up.

Evening *passegiata* in piazza del Popolo.

Piazza del Popolo

The shadows and reflections of passing figures cast on the shiny stones add to the beauty of Ascoli Piceno's showcase piazza. To see it at its best, come in the evening, when the piazza fills with the people of Ascoli wandering, drinking at cafés and chatting.

At one end, the **Chiesa di San Francesco** has an attached Renaissance portico, the **Loggia dei Mercanti**. Look for the plaque in the wall used to check on the sizes of bricks that were once sold here. The church itself was built, rather slowly, between the 12th and 15th centuries, leaving a Romanesque-Gothic hybrid building. Behind it, in the cloister, is what must be one of Italy's most photogenic fruit and vegetable markets. Off the main cloister you may be able to peer through the gate into another smaller one.

On the west of the piazza, the **Palazzo dei Capitani**, built in the 13th century on top of an ancient Roman structure, had a Renaissance portico and loggia added to its courtyard in the 16th century. Next door is the famous *stile Liberty* **Caffè Meletti** (see page 270). The low porticoed buildings around the edge of the piazza were built in the 16th century.

Piazza Arringo

Ascoli's second piazza, the elongated piazza Arringo is a more staid place, with fountains, a couple of cafés, the duomo, the archaeological museum, and the offices of the *comune*, which also contain the *pinacoteca*, the town's excellent art museum.

Pinacoteca

Piazza Arringo, T0736-248663, ascolimusei.it.
10 Jul-20 Aug Tue-Sun 1000-2300,
16 Mar-9 Jul and 21 Aug-Sep Tue-Sun 1000-1900,
Oct-15 Mar Tue-Fri and Sun 1030-1700,
Sat 1000-1900, combined ticket for all 3 civic museums €8/5 concession.

Ascoli's art gallery is one of the region's best, and its grand setting in the Palazzo del Comune adds to the experience. Carlo Crivelli's triptych of the *Madonna*

and Child (contemplating an apple) sees the pair joined by Sts Lucy, Anthony Abbot and Sebastian, and there are some other good examples of pre-Renaissance art, including several by Crivelli's follower Pietro Alemanno. The anonymous seven-panel story of the *Life of Mary* from the first half of the 14th century is an expressive work despite its primitive proportionality.

Aristocratic rooms are impressively replete with antique furniture and chandeliers, though the lighting isn't great for viewing the paintings. Titian's large depiction of *St Francis Receiving the Stigmata* is especially badly lit. Other works to look out for include Guido Reni's *Annunciation* of 1628-1629 and Tiberio Titti's grandly costumed unnamed woman, painted at the turn of the 17th century.

Several 16th- and 17th-century works depict Ascoli complete with many of its old towers. Romolo del Gobbo's 1905 bronze statue of a flying Paolo and Francesca (see box, page 235) is gravity-defying, and *Fior di Vita*, Cesare Reduzzi's late 19th-century marble nude, is remarkably passionate for someone made of stone.

Galleria d'Arte Contemporanea

Corso Mazzini 90, T0736-248663, ascolimusei.it.
10 Jul-20 Aug Tue-Sun 1000-2300, 16 Mar-9 Jul
and 21 Aug-Sep 1000-1900, Oct-15 Mar Tue-Fri
and Sun 1030-1700, Sat 1000-1900, combined
ticket for all 3 civic museums €8/5 concession.

Ascoli Piceno has a rich history of 20th-century
art, and an unusually good contemporary art
gallery, in a fine, high-ceilinged space. Rotating
temporary exhibitions concentrate on local artists,
and the permanent collection also has excellent
works, including paintings and sculpture by the
likes of Severini, Morandi and Trubbiani. Osvaldo
Licini, an artist from Ascoli, is represented by his
excellent, incisive and characterful portraits, and
the exquisite *Paesaggio con l'Uomo* from 1925.
His later, abstract work is also well featured in
the collection.

Cattedrale di Sant'Emidio

Piazza Arringo.
Daily 0700-1200, 1530-1830, free.

With an elaborately decorated interior, Ascoli's
Duomo is an over-the-top mix of starry blue
ceilings and chandeliers. Carlo Crivelli's 10-
panelled polyptych from 1473 in the **Cappella del
Sacramento**, to the right of the nave, also has its
fair share of gold in its ornate Gothic frame, but the
painting itself is the artist's masterpiece, full of woe
and compassion, especially in the central panel.

Downstairs, the atmospheric crypt is a forest
of pillars, and you can peer through a barred door
into the town's 15th-century underground
ex-cemetery. Next door to the cathedral, the
octagonal **Baptistery** (open rather infrequently
and usually only at weekends) was built in the
12th century on the site of a previous chapel.

Above: Chiesa dei Santi Vincenzo e Anastasio. Opposite page: The market in the cloister of San Francesco.

Chiesa dei Santi Vincenzo e Anastasio

Piazza Ventidio Basso.

Built in the 11th century, the Romanesque church of Sts Vincent and Anastasius has an interesting façade with 64 stone frames that may once have held paintings. Over the door, the eponymous saints stand either side of the Madonna. In the crypt are some sixth-century frescoes.

Via dei Soderini

At the medieval heart of Ascoli, via dei Soderini has most of the town's surviving towers – they once numbered over 100. One has been turned into a youth hostel. Near here is the **ponte Augusteo**, a Roman bridge across the river Tronto, which has a single span of 21 m and a passageway underneath the road surface, which it is sometimes possible to visit.

Around Ascoli Piceno

Acquasanta Terme

16 km southwest of Ascoli.

Love of the water here goes back to Roman times, and people still come for the thermal baths, which are rich in minerals. The small town has two Roman bridges: Ponte di Quintodecimo and ponte Romano, which were once crossings on the via Salaria. The highlight, however, is a beautiful round medieval castle, **Castel di Luco**, built in the 11th century, which sits on a large lump of rock above the town.

Museo Archeologico

Piazza Arringo, T0736-253562.
Tue-Sat 0830-1900, €2.

The wealth of ancient finds in the area are collected here, and among the usual fragments of engraved Roman stones are some interesting pieces and a couple of impressive mosaics, notably a large and ornate design featuring an optical illusion – the central head can be seen as two different faces, depending on which way up it is viewed.

Ancona

Grand Hotel Palace €€
Lungomare Vanvitelli, T071-201813, hotelancona.it.
Next to Ancona's port, the Grand Hotel Palace is a stylishly old-fashioned place, with 40 rooms and eight apartments. The lounge is big, and rooms have slippers, air-conditioning and views over the sea. Bathrooms are done in teal tiles with stainless steel fittings, and the breakfast room on the top floor has great views over the port's comings and goings.

Grand Hotel Passetto €€
Via Thaon de Revel 1, T071-31307, hotelpassetto.it.
Ancona's best hotel is the epitome of early 20th-century Italian resort cool. Art Deco design elements such as leopard-skin chairs and big mirrors dot the spacious lounge, alongside plants and fresh flowers. There is art on the corridor walls and rooms have balconies, views and satellite TV. There's a swimming pool too.

Hotel della Vittoria €
Via Fabio Filzi 2, T071-55764, hoteldellavittoria.it.
Halfway up viale della Vittoria, the hotel of the same name makes a convenient stopover, with 18 light, modern rooms with tiled bathrooms and wooden floors but not a lot of character. There's a restaurant, closed on Fridays, and parking is available.

Roma e Pace €
Via Giacomo Leopardi 1, T071-202007, hotelromaepace.it.
A grand old place with an antique feel. Rooms are on the small side but have air-con and Jacuzzis, as well as writing bureaux. Breakfast is on the paltry side of generous, but the hotel has a certain degree of retro style.

Conero

Hotel Emilia €€
Collina di Portonovo 149a, T07l-801117, hotelemilia.com.
One of the few stylish contemporary hotels around, Emilia, a couple of kilometres inland, has a minimalist, almost Bauhaus feel, and an attitude which is much more laid back than the more buttoned-up Fortino down the hill. Black and white jazz photos decorate the walls, there's an excellent contemporary art collection, books and pianos. The bar has colourful stools and outside there is a good pool, plenty of grass and great views. Rooms are elegant and predominantly white. A shuttle bus runs down the hill to the beach.

Hotel Fortino Napoleonico €€
Portonovo, T071-801450, hotelfortino.it.
A converted Napoleonic fort in prime position on Portonovo beach, Fortino Napoleonico is a smart place with plenty of character to go with its luxuries. There's a bar and a restaurant, and the grand piano gets played every night. You can watch the sun set from a terrace overlooking the sea, and a garden has its own beach access. Rooms attempt Napoleonic style, and even the man who cleans out the minibars wears a bow tie.

Locanda Rocco €€
Via Torrione 1, Sirolo, T071-933 0558, locandarocco.it.
Seven pale rooms, with light, elegant fabrics, contemporary lighting and bare stone walls create a sophisticated, minimalist feel to this classy small hotel on the edge of Sirolo, built right into the walls at the gate going south out of town. Downstairs there's a restaurant specializing in seafood, with a pleasant outdoor terrace.

Frasassi

Locanda Palazzo €
Palazzo 206, T0731-981372, locandapalazzo.com.
About 25 km north of the Frasassi caves, a 19th-century manor house with generous and homely rooms decked out with antiques in the midst of beautiful countryside. There are three suites, and booking is for a minimum of three days, or a week at the height of summer.

Macerata

Le Case €€
*Locale Mozzavinci 16/17,
T0733-231897, ristorantelecase.it.*
Fifteen minutes west of Villa
Potenza, Le Case is a sprawling
place in extensive grounds. The
hotel has 13 rooms and a suite, all
in a country-house antique style.
There's a brick-arched restaurant
with a vaguely medieval feel and
a fêted and cosy *enoteca* with
terracotta walls and an open fire,
known for its excellent food. Use
of the wellness centre, with a
large indoor pool, is included in
the price.

Agriturismo Coroncina €
*Contrada Fossa 16, Belforte del
Chienti, T0733-906227,
agriturismocoroncina.it.*
Accommodation on an organic
farm, with woods, a stream and
a 'beauty farm', complete with
hydro-massage and sauna.
The vegetarian restaurant
has yellow walls and a terrace,
and a 10-course tasting menu.

Albergo Arena €
*Vicolo Sferisterio 16,
T0733-230931.*
Tucked in behind the Sferisterio,
the Arena has comfortable rooms
without much spare space but
with all mod cons, including
minibar, TV and Wi-Fi. The best
rooms have small balconies with
flowers, there's some private
parking and the breakfast buffet
is uncommonly good.

Ascoli Piceno

Borgo Storico Seghetti Panichi €€€
*Via San Pancrazio 1, T0736-
812552, seghettipanichi.it.*
In the Tronto Valley, with views
to the Sibillini Mountains, the
hamlet hotel of Seghetti Panichi
is owned by a bona fide princess
and consists of a villa, a fortress,
a cottage and an oratory
decorated with frescoes.
It's a friendly place, with gardens
and sumptuously decorated
suites, rich in colour and filled
with antiques. Those in the
cottage come complete with
small kitchens, and there's a
restaurant, pool and sauna.

Palazzo Guiderocchi €€
*Via Cesare Battisti 3, T0736-
244 011, palazzoguiderocchi.com.*
Courteous and smart,
Guiderocchi is in an old
converted townhouse, with
an arcaded courtyard and nice
touches such as bowls of apples
by the lift. Large rooms have
botanical art and flat screen TVs;
the suite has a mezzanine and a
high ceiling with sloping
wooden beams.

Villa Cicchi €€
*Via Salaria Superiore 137,
Abbazia di Rosara, T0736-
252272, villacicchi.it.*
3 km south of Ascoli Piceno.
Villa Cicchi describes itself as an
'agriturismo de charme', and it's a
description that fits, without the

usual frilliness. A country
villa built in the 1600s, it is part
Country Life elegance, part rustic
farmer's cottage. Four of the six
rooms have ornately frescoed
ceilings, and the rest of the place
is wonderful, with open fires, and
old agricultural equipment in the
huge cellars. Mass is still held in
the little family chapel, *vino cotto*
is still made here, and, despite
the pool and the Wi-Fi, the
whole place has a genuine feel of
antique Marche countryside to it.

Aurora €
*Contrada Ciafone 98, Santa
Maria in Carro, Offida, T0736-
810007, viniaurora.it.*
Half an hour's drive northeast
of Ascoli, Aurora is an organic
vineyard in the hills where you
can stay in one of six well-
equipped apartments. There's
a two-night minimum stay.

Language and Art B&B €
*Via dei Soderini 16, T347-531
2280, languageandart.com.*
In the heart of the most ancient
part of Ascoli, this friendly and
unusually stylish B&B has views
over the Roman bridge and the
medieval towers. Antiques and
piles of books fill the 16th-
century house and the
'help-yourself' breakfast comes
complete with a freshly made
cake every day. Rooms are
comfortable and homely, with
wooden floors, rugs, and lots
of art and ceramics.

Eating & drinking

Strabacco €€€
Via Oberdan 2/2a, T071-56748, osteriastrabacco.it.
Tue-Sun 1215-1500, 1915-0300.
One of Ancona's great restaurants, Strabacco has a wine list as thick as a telephone directory and a friendly, jovial atmosphere that can't all be put down to the amount of wine consumed. The food is a draw too – try the sea bass with olives, tomatoes and potatoes; the chocolate tart is also good. You'll get four types of homemade bread and, should you find the wine list a little overwhelming, good-natured recommendations. Ageing wooden seating, fairy lights, theatrical nostalgia and an antique dresser all add to the appeal.

La Cantineta €€
Via Antonio Gramsci 1/c, T071-201107, cantineta.it.
Tue-Sun 1200-1440, 1930-2400, Mon 1200-1440.
A traditional and down-to-earth place with red and white checked tablecloths and a fantastically eclectic selection of paintings on the walls, from Jesus and Modigliani to a naked bather. Glazed tiles, wood cladding and aproned waiters add to the atmosphere and there's fantastic seafood at good prices. Try the squid salad or the spaghetti alle vongole. Popular, loud and atmospheric, it fills up with Italian families,

especially on Sunday lunchtimes, when the rest of Ancona seems to shut down.

Trattoria alle Tredici Cannelle €€
Corso Mazzini 108, T071-206012.
Mon-Sat 1215-1430, 2000-2230.
A long narrow room with wooden beams, yellow and white tablecloths, a bar and ceiling fans, this is a rustic place that specializes in salt cod, though you might also try the prosciutto with figs.

Clarice €
Via Traffico 6, T071-202926.
Mon-Fri 1230 onwards and 1945 onwards, Sat 1230 onwards.
With fake bricks, young Italians and a wide range of art, most of it sea-related, Clarice is a simple trattoria with no pretensions but plenty of charm. The menu includes local specialities (salt cod, squid with peas) as well as Italian classics (ravioli with tomato, basil and mozzarella), and the atmosphere is friendly and informal. The house wine, at a remarkably cheap €1.03 a quarter, is surprisingly drinkable. Large lamps, a ceiling fan, and tables outside in the quiet side street.

Cafés & bars
Cremeria Rosa
Corso Mazzini 61, T071-203408.
Great ice creams in the heart of town.

Note di Vino
Corso Mazzini 106, T393-059 9972.
Daily 1800 till late.
Jazz, brown striped tablecloths, candles and a good wine list, all available by the glass. Also light meals – plates of cheese and ham or seafood.

Capanina €€
Portonovo, T071-801121.
Daily 1230-1430, 2000-2230, bar 0830-2430.
Palm shades and deck chairs outside a pale yellow restaurant on the beach. *Tagliatelle nere* and lots of other fish dishes feature on the menu, and they also do proper pizzas.

Clandestino €€
Baia di Portonovo, T071-801422, morenocedroni.it/clandestino.
Easter-20 Sep Thu-Sun aperitivo from 1630, 1930-2400, Sat-Sun also 1200-1500, Jul-Aug open daily.
A cool, beach-shack vibe in a place that claims to have invented 'Italian *susci*'. International beers and English crisps are on offer alongside some excellent local wines. The tuna carpaccio is excellent, as is the swordfish salad, and don't miss the chocolate mousse, served with salted breadsticks and clementine oil. Lilies, apple-flavoured olive oil, blue painted wood, a bamboo ceiling and groovy laid-back

tunes all add to the hip quotient. Staff float around dressed in white linen, warm bread is served in a paper bag, and the cutlery is as long as your arm.

La Lanterna €€
Piazza Vittorio Veneto, Sirolo, T071-933 1382.
Tue-Sat 1200-1430, 1900-2230.
A stylish enoteca in an ancient building in the centre of Sirolo, with food such as *strozzapreti* pasta with clams and cherry tomatoes, cuttlefish salad and tuna steak. The walls are lined with wine bottles and there is a good selection to drink by the glass.

Pesci Fuor d'Acqua €
Portonovo, T071-213 9019.
Tue-Sun 0900-2200, Fri-Sat evenings only in winter.
A café-cum-pizzeria with a big wood-burning oven. You can eat in or take your pizza away to munch on the beach; they also do excellent *cornetti* for breakfast.

Frasassi

Da Maria €
Pierosara, T0732-90014.
Fri-Wed 1200-1500, 1900-2230.
If you have a car, or fancy a 2-km walk up the hill from the caves, Da Maria is the best eating option around. Steadfastly Italian, it is a wonderfully bizarre mix of bad taste, from the plaster cupids holding up the candlesticks to the brass butterflies on the wall.

Traditional central Italian food doesn't get much better than this, and it's immensely popular with locals, who flock here for Sunday lunch and keep the place buzzing, as do the homemade grappas and bitters. If you want something nearer to the caves, **La Cantina**, favoured by cave guides, is the best option in San Vittore.

Macerata

La Volpe e l'Uva €€
Via Berardi 39, T0733-237879.
Mon-Sat 1800-0200.
A traditional, brick-vaulted osteria, on a quiet side street, that sells wine long into the night. Dishes include penne with sausage and pecorino cheese and lots of local veal.

Osteria dei Fiori €€
Via Lauro Rossi 61, T0733-260142, osteriadeifiori.it.
Mon-Sat 1200-1500, 1900-2300.
Run by three siblings since 1980, this proponent of slow food offers a friendly atmosphere and home cooking with a sprinkling of invention. Antipasti include walnut bread with oranges, olives and ham, and the pasta, including *vincisgrassi* (the local version of lasagne, with many thin layers of pasta), is excellent. Service is quick and efficient and, though the internal decoration is nothing to write home about, there is also some outdoor seating.

Il Pozzo €
Via Costa 5, T0733-232360.
Wed-Mon 1230-1430, 1800-0300 (kitchen from 2000), daily in summer.
Businessmen, ageing locals and hip students all frequent this vaulted bar-cum-pub at lunchtime for its excellent buffet. For €10 you can have as many servings as you like of a selection of local dishes, and a generously sized glass of wine is thrown in too. Not only is it a bargain, it's an excellent way to try Marche cuisine without necessarily knowing what everything's called. In the evenings there's an à la carte menu and the bar keeps it buzzing until the early hours. There is sometimes live music, and photos of past concerts decorate the walls.

Cafés & bars
Faber Café
Vicolo Ferrari 10/12, T0733-262950, fabercafe.it.
Tue-Sun 1900-0200.
In the middle of Macerata, a slick bar that does something different – its Italian owner is a fan of beer, and since 2007 has been trying to educate his fellow Maceratans. There are five excellent beers on tap, and plenty more in bottles. Ask for a special beer cocktail or chat about real ale in a setting that feels like the most metropolitan of cocktail bars. English and Scottish beers predominate, but there are also good Italian ales.

Ascoli Piceno

Trattoria dell'Arengo €€
Via Tornasacco 5, T333-471 3333.
Tue-Sun
Just off piazza Arringo, this is a popular, good value, traditional place with art on the walls under arches. There are red fairy lights and golden tablecloths, and the menu is dominated by pasta and grilled meat.

Trattoria Laliva €€
Piazza della Viola 13, T0736-259358, trattorialaliva.it.
Thu-Mon 1900-2330,
Sat-Mon also 1200-1500.
A bright place, with walls painted in shades of green, relaxed Laliva has set menus (try the 'menu for the curious' for €30) and a good mix of the inventive (they specialize in candied olives) and the traditional. Try the superb lentil soup or the roast pork in *vino cotto* sauce but save some room for the excellent homemade desserts.

Da Middio €
Via delle Canterine 53, T0736-250867.
Tue-Thu 0830-1630, Fri-Sat 0830-1630, 1830-2400.
Bright lights, paper tablecloths and no written menus: Da Middio offers up great local food with little fuss for very little money. A €16 fixed-price menu gets you wine and three of four courses. Fish features strongly and there are some excellent pasta dishes. Turn up early for a seat, especially in the evening, or be prepared to wait at the bar with some boisterous locals.

Cafés & bars
Caffè Meletti
Piazza del Popolo, T0736-259626, caffestoricomeletti.it.
Daily, early till late.
A destination in its own right, Meletti is a Liberty-style café that makes its own *amaro* to a traditional local recipe, featuring aniseed. It's also a fine spot for a coffee, on the town's central piazza, with large gilt-framed mirrors and elegant furniture.

Il Tannino Orgoglioso
Piazza Ventidio Basso, T320-698 0070.
Daily 1130-1400, 1930-0200.
A lively wine bar with a cross-vaulted ceiling, stone walls, wooden tables and loud music. Snacks are available to accompany the wine, which flows late into the night.

Yoghi
Piazza Arringo 39, T0736-257414.
Mon-Sat 0730-2400, Sun 0830-1400, 1615-2400.
Nominally a yoghurt bar, Yoghi has a good selection of fruit that you can mix as you wish, but there's also a chocolate theme for the less healthy – the great biscuits, hot chocolate thick enough to stand a spoon up in and bars of handmade chocolate all give this brick-vaulted café on piazza Arringo a decadent feel.

Ancona

Ancona Jazz
T071-207 4239, anconajazz.com.
The main focus for the city's music festival is a fortnight or so at the end of July and beginning of August, but other events are scattered through the year. Free concerts take place in piazzas, while ticketed events happen in the Teatro delle Muse and other locations around town. Recent artists have included Pat Metheny and Brad Mehldau.

Lascensore
Piazza IV Novembre, T071-358 0388, lascensore.biz.
A club next to Il Passetto where you can eat and drink as well as listen to live jazz, which starts at around 2230. The interior is an interesting mix of chintz and industrial, with large air ducts, metal chairs and floral curtains and cushions.

Macerata

Sferisterio Opera Festival
T0733-230735, sferisterio.it.
The summer opera season is short but sweet. There are usually three or four performances of three different operas, from mid-July to mid-August, and an enlightened ticket policy means that while front-row seats go for €150, there are unreserved standing tickets for just €15. Also look out for other gigs and events at the Sferisterio during summer.

Shopping

The narrow via degli Orefici has some small boutique shops, including **Papier**, selling books and art.

Books
Feltrinelli
Corso Garibaldi 35,
T071-207 3943.
A good selection of books and one of the few shops in Ancona open on Sundays.

Gulliver
Corso Mazzini 27, T071-53215.
A decent selection of guidebooks.

Food
Bonità delle Marche
Corso Mazzini 96/98,
T071-53985.
A delicatessen with lots of choice for putting together a good picnic.

Activities & tours

Boat trips
Traghettatori del Conero
T071-933 1795,
traghettatoridelconero.lt.
Daily 0930 and 1030 from Numana, €20/10 concession, 1030 from Sirolo, €15/10.
Trips around the coast last about three and a half hours: ring to check timetable.

Cycling
Conerobike
Via Peschiera 30/a, Sirolo,
T071-933 0066, conerobike.com.
The organization promotes mountain biking in the Parco del Conero – they have a map of the park that you should be able to get from tourist information offices, and they also rent bikes, by the hour, or from €14 per day.

Watersports
PWB
Portonovo, T333-526 8997.
Along the beach from Portonovo, PWB rent out windsurfing boards and also offer tuition – a course of four lessons costs €150 plus €30 insurance. They have surfboards too, but these get little use as the waves are seldom good enough.

Transport

Ancona is on the main Adriatic coast train line and there are also direct trains to Rome, via Foligno, where you can change for Perugia. For transport to and from the airport see page 274. Bus 94 from piazza Cavour in Ancona (conerobus.it) does the 20-minute journey to Portonovo nine times a day but not always at the most convenient times – check the timetable before you set out.

Frasassi

There is a train station, San Vittore Terme, opposite the ticket office for the Frasassi caves, though to reach it you will probably have to change at Genga, on the Rome-Ancona line. The caves are well signposted, and easily reached by car, off the SS76.

Macerata

For trains from Ancona (1 hr 10 mins), or from the south, to Macerata, you'll need to change at Civitanova Marche.

Ascoli Piceno

For the two-hour train journey from Ancona you'll need to change at San Benedetto del Tronto. Pescara, which also has international flights, is slightly nearer (about 90 mins).

Contents

Practicalities

Getting there

Air

From UK and Ireland
Flights to Milan or Rome depart from UK and Irish destinations frequently. Alternatively, fly right to the heart of Umbria with **Ryanair** (ryanair.com), which flies from London Stansted to Perugia three times a week in winter, five times a week in summer, and to Ancona four times a week in winter and daily in summer. Other central Italian regional airports such as Bologna, Pisa and Rimini are also possible arrival points for travel to the region. Overland travel via train and coach or car is viable, especially as it's a prerequisite from major airports anyway, but from London it will take a leisurely 18 hours driving to reach Italy's green heart.

From North America
No direct flights. Flying to Rome or Milan and then onwards travel is the route into Umbria. **Continental**, **American Airlines** and **Delta** fly direct from New York to Rome Fiumicino and Milan. **Delta** also flies to both cities from Toronto via NY.

From rest of Europe
Aside from the London Stansted flights, there are also two daily Alitalia flights to Milan Malpensa and three flights a week to Girona in Spain with Ryanair. Airports in Rome and Milan are well connected to every major European city. Rail travel to Umbria's capital, Perugia, takes between 2½ to 5 hours (from Rome and Milan respectively). **Motorail** (autoslaaptrein.nl) services run from the Netherlands to Livorno or Bologna, allowing you to drive on and drive off.

Airport information

Perugia and Ancona airports are the easiest arrival points into the region, though it's central enough to mean that airports outside the area are also possible. Rimini or Bologna (especially for northern Marche), Pisa (especially for northern Umbria) and Rome (especially for southern Umbria) are all a couple of hours or less by train.

Both Perugia and Ancona are small airports with very few flights – for transatlantic flights, or from the rest of Europe, it's easiest to change in London or fly to Rome. There are also connecting flights to Perugia from Milan, and to Ancona from Milan and Rome.

Perugia Sant'Egidio
T075-592141, airport.umbria.it.
Even by the standards of small provincial Italian airports, Perugia is tiny. And while retrieving your luggage with a planeload of other people in what feels like a cupboard can be a struggle, it does make arriving and departing a generally quick and easy process. The airport is on the plain about 20 minutes' drive from both Perugia and Assisi, and there are taxis (about €30 to either) and **Sulga** buses (T800-099661, sulga.it), which meet Ryanair flights and go to piazza Italia in the centre of Perugia for €3.50. There are also car rental companies, including Avis, Hertz and Maggiore, and a small information desk.

Ancona Falconara
T071-28271, aeroportomarche.com.
Another small provincial airport, Ancona Falconara is connected to the train station in the town centre by hourly bus J (**Conerobus**, T071-283 7411, conerobus.it), which takes around 35 minutes and costs €1.70 – buy tickets from the news stand in the departures hall. There is also a train station at the airport, but services are infrequent. Taxis to the centre of Ancona (T071-918221) cost around €35 and take 30 minutes. Car rental offices include Avis, Hertz, Europcar, Maggiore and Sixt.

Rail

Rail journeys involve a **Eurostar** to Paris, then onwards overnight sleepers to the most convenient Italian rail hubs: Milan (5 hrs from Perugia), Rome (2 ½ hrs) or Bologna (3 hrs). For international tickets and information, try **raileurope.com** (T0870-584 8848). For Italian train information search **Trenitalia** (T06-6847 5475, trenitalia.it) and for Umbrian regional transport, **Umbria Rail** (fcu.it).

Road

The 1,050 km journey from London to Perugia will take 18 hours' driving time. The A1 *autostrade* (motorway) that splices Italy vertically provides a fairly direct route to Perugia (a 4 ½ hr drive from Milan). Exit at Valdichiana, approximately 100 km after Florence, and follow signs for Perugia.

Going green

With somewhat limited flight options, Umbria and the Marche demand an extended stay – this in itself is a key to greener travelling. Taking public transport through the rolling hills and vineyards of the region allows you to sit back and enjoy the view. Most rewardingly, the extra effort required to access the region leaves it relatively unmobbed by tourist crowds.

Bus/coach

Eurolines (T0870-580 8080, nationalexpress.co.uk) operate three services per week from London Victoria to Milan, taking around 28 hours. Prices start at £95 return. From there, a **Sulga** (sulga.it) coach service travels from Milan to Perugia's piazza Italia twice a week (7 hrs, €25.30 one way). Sulga also run numerous bus and coach services throughout Umbria and also several to Rome.

Getting around

The major towns in the region are mostly connected by train, with the notable exceptions of Gubbio and Urbino. Train stations are often at the peripheries of towns, however, meaning that a bus journey or taxi ride is necessary to reach the town centre. Buses also run to most places, though they are often infrequent, and just about non-existent on Sundays. For the freedom to go to more out-of-the-way places, when you want, a car is invaluable, especially if you plan to stay in an *agriturismo* in the countryside.

Touring Club Italiano produce good general maps of the area – a free version of the Umbria half of their *Umbria e Marche* map is often available in tourist offices. For more detail, **Kompass** do a series of walking and cycling maps that cover some of the region's most popular areas. For real detail of local areas, maps produced by the **Club Alpino Italiano** are hard to beat, but equally hard to get hold of, though they can usually be found in towns on the edges of national and regional parks.

Rail

Three main lines serve the region: the **Rome to Ancona** line, via Spoleto and Foligno; the **Rome to Florence** line up the Tiber Valley, via Orvieto, and the **Adriatic coastline**. Fast Eurostar trains run along all of these routes, as well as ordinary (and cheaper) regional trains. There is also a branch from Foligno to Terontola via Perugia, Assisi and Spello, connecting both of the major Umbrian lines, and some Eurostar trains use this route, though it's often necessary to change at Foligno or Terontola.

To complicate matters further, there is a private train line (Ferrovia Centrale Umbra, fcu.it) running from Terni in the south via Todi and Perugia to Città di Castello in the north, and then on to Sansepolcro, in Tuscany. In Perugia this uses a different station to the mainline trains – Sant'Anna.

Tickets are cheap, though the price is approximately double for the faster, more

comfortable Eurostar trains: ferroviedellostato.it has timetables and prices. Some examples of journey times and single, second-class fares are: Perugia to Assisi, 20 minutes, €2.05; Perugia to Spello, 30 minutes, €2.65; Ancona to Spoleto, 2 hours 15 minutes, €8.20; Ancona to Ascoli Piceno, 1 hour 40 minutes, €6.15.

Tickets (except for journeys on the Ferrovia Centrale Umbra) can be booked at trenitalia.com, where the type of train is indicated with the initials ES (Eurostar), IC (Intercity) or REG (Regional). Amica fares are cheaper advance tickets (if you can find one), flexi fare costs more but is – you guessed it – flexible, and standard fare is just that. In general, it's cheaper and more convenient to book online or at ticket machines for the journeys you need to take than it is to buy a pass. When using a service such as Eurostar Italia or InterCity, booking is advised and a surcharge in addition to a pass will often be required; passes therefore lose their thrift factor for tourists. On many Italian trains it's possible to travel 'ticketless', meaning you get on the train and quote your booking reference when the conductor comes round.

Booking and buying tickets at the counter or via machines in train stations is convenient if you can't access the internet. Remember, you must validate train tickets at the yellow stamping machines before boarding.

Road

Car
EU nationals taking their own car need to have an International Insurance Certificate (also known as a *Carte Verde*). Those holding a non-EU licence also need to take an International Driving Permit with them. Unleaded petrol is *benzina*, diesel is *gasolio*.

Italy has strict laws on drink driving: steer clear of alcohol to be safe. The use of mobile telephones while driving is illegal. Other nuances of Italian road law include children under 1.5m required to be in the back of the car and that a reflective jacket must be worn if your car breaks down on the carriageway in poor visibility. Make sure you've got one. Since July 2007, on-the-spot fines for minor traffic offences have been in operation – typically they range between €150-250. Always get a receipt if you incur one.

Speed limits are 130 kph (motorway) 110 kph (dual carriageway) and 50 kph (town). Limits are 20 kph lower on motorways and dual carriageways when the road is wet. *Autostrade* (motorways) are toll roads, so keep cash in the car as a backup even though you can use credit cards on the blue 'viacard' gates. **Autostrade** (T055-420 3200, autostrade.it) provides information on motorways in Italy and **Automobile Club d'Italia** (T06-49981, aci.it) provides general driving information. ACI offers roadside assistance with English-speaking operators on T116.

Be aware that there are restrictions on driving in historic city centres, indicated by signs with black letters ZTL (*zona a traffico limitato*) on a yellow background. If you pass these signs, your registration number may be caught and a fine will be winging its way to you. If your hotel is in the centre of town, you may be entitled to an official pass – contact your hotel or car hire company. However, this pass is not universal and allows access to the hotel only.

Car hire

Car hire is available at all of Italy's international airports and many domestic airports. You will probably wish to book the car before you arrive in the country, and it's best to do so for popular destinations and at busy times of year. Check in advance the opening times of the car hire office.

Car hire comparison websites and agents are a good place to start a search for the best deals. Try holidayautos.co.uk, easycar.com, carrentals.co.uk.

Check what each hire company requires from you. Some companies will ask for an International Driving Licence, alongside your normal driving

licence, if the language of your licence is different to that of the country you're renting the car in. Others are content with an EU licence. You'll need to produce a credit card for most companies. If you book ahead, make sure that the named credit card holder is the same as the person renting and driving the car to avoid any problems. Most companies have a lower age limit of 21 years and require that you've held your licence for at least a year. Many have a young driver surcharge for those under 25. Confirm insurance and any damage waiver charges and keep all your documents with you when you drive.

Bicycle

A mountain bike is a good way of seeing some of the region's countryside, but mostly the towns are too hilly and cobbled for bikes to be much use for getting around. Towns are also generally small enough for you to be able to walk anywhere fairly quickly. Outside of the towns, Italians are keen weekend lycra wearers, but it hasn't done anything to make cycling on the roads any safer.

If you want to cycle for pleasure, Lake Trasimeno (see page 114) and Orvieto (see page 195) are good places.

Bus/coach

Sulga (sulga.it) run buses between Perugia and Rome, Naples, Milan and Florence. **Sena** (sena.it) is a low-cost bus service to Siena and Milan, also from Perugia. **Spoletina** buses (spoletina.com) cover Spoleto, Trevi, Montefalco and Spello. **APM** (apmperugia.it) run services in Perugia and Assisi, as well as longer (*extraurbani*) services to Todi, Castiglione del Lago and Gubbio. To reach Urbino, **Adriabus** (amibus.it) operates a service every hour or so from Pesaro station, taking about 45 minutes (€3). Buses mainly run from outside, or at least near, train stations.

Directory

Customs and immigration

UK and EU citizens do not need a visa, but will need a valid passport to enter Italy. A standard tourist visa for those outside the EU is valid for up to 90 days.

Disabled travellers

Italy is a bit behind when it comes to catering for disabled travellers, where access is sometimes very difficult or ill thought out. Contact an agency before departure for more details such as **Accessible Italy** (aacessibleitaly.com) or **Society for Accessible Travel and Hospitality** (sath.org).

Emergency numbers

Ambulance T118; **Fire** T115; **Police** T113 (with English-speaking operators), T112 (*carabinieri*); **Roadside assistance** T116.

Etiquette

Bella figura – projecting a good image – is important to Italians. Take note of public notices about conduct: sitting on steps or eating and drinking in certain historic areas is not allowed. You need to cover your arms and legs for admission to some churches – in rare cases even shorts are not permitted. Punctuality is apparently not mandatory in Italy, so be prepared to wait on occasion.

Families

Whether you're on a traditional beach break or popping into a city gelateria, families are well accommodated in Italy. Children are well treated, and there's plenty to do besides endless museum visits. The family is highly regarded in Italy and *bambini* are indulged. Note that lone parents or adults accompanying children of a different surname may sometimes need to produce evidence of guardianship before taking children in and out of the country. Contact your Italian embassy for current details (Italian embassy in London, T020-7312 2200).

Health

Comprehensive travel and medical insurance is strongly recommended for all travel. EU citizens should apply for a free European Health Insurance Card (ehic.org), which has replaced the E111 form and offers free or reduced-cost medical treatment.

Late-night pharmacies are identified by a large green cross outside: T1100 for addresses of the three nearest open pharmacies. The accident and emergency department of a hospital is the *pronto soccorso*. The main hospital in Perugia is the Azienda Ospedaliera di Perugia, via Enrico dal Pozzo, T075-578 2861.

Insurance

Comprehensive travel and medical insurance is strongly recommended for all travel – the EHIC is not a replacement for insurance. You should check any exclusions, and that your policy covers you for all the activities you want to undertake. Keep your insurance documents separately; emailing all the details to yourself is a good way to keep the information safe and accessible. Ensure you have full insurance if hiring a car; you may need an international insurance certificate if you are taking your own car (contact your current insurers).

Money

The Italian currency is the Euro. There are ATMs (*bancomat*) throughout Italy that accept major credit and debit cards. To change cash or travellers' cheques throughout Umbria and Marche, look for a *cambio*. Many restaurants, shops, museums and art galleries will take major credit cards. Paying directly with debit cards such as Cirrus is less easy in many places, so withdrawing from an ATM and paying in cash may be the better option. Keep some cash for toll roads if you're driving.

Practicalities

Police

There are five different police forces in Italy. The *carabinieri* are a branch of the army and wear military-style uniforms with a red stripe on their trousers and white sashes. They handle general crime, drug-related crime and public order offences. The *polizia statale* are the national police force and are dressed in blue with a thin purple stripe on their trousers. They are responsible for security on the railways and at airports. The *polizia stradale* handle crime and traffic offences on the motorways and drive blue cars with a white stripe. The *vigili urbani* are local police who wear dark blue (in summer) or black (in winter) uniforms with white hats; they direct traffic and issue parking fines in the cities. The *guardia di finanza* wear grey uniforms with grey flat hats or green berets (depending on rank). They are charged with combating counterfeiting, tax evasion and fraud.

In the case of an emergency requiring police attention, dial 113, approach any member of the police or visit a police station.

Post

Italian post has a not entirely undeserved reputation for being unreliable, particularly in the handling of postcards. Overseas post will require *posta prioritaria* (priority mail) and a postcard stamp will cost from €0.60. Buy stamps (*francobolli*) from *tabacchi* (look for T signs) to avoid the huge queues in post offices.

Safety

The crime rate in Italy is generally low, though rates of petty crime are higher. Umbria and Marche are generally very safe. Take general care when travelling: don't flaunt your valuables; take only what money you need and split it; don't take risks you wouldn't at home. Beware of scams and con-artists, and don't expect things to go smoothly if you partake in fake goods. Car break-ins are common, so always remove valuables. Take care on public transport, where pickpockets or bag-cutters operate: do not make it clear which stop you're getting off at – it gives potential thieves a timeframe to work in. Racism and sexism exist, but are usually born of ignorance rather than aggression. Earthquakes are a possibility – if you experience one, stay in the open if possible or, if not, shelter in a doorway.

Telephone

You need to use local codes, even when dialling from within the city or region. The prefix for Italy is +39. You no longer need to drop the initial '0' from area codes when calling from abroad. For directory enquiries call T12.

Time difference

Italy uses Central European Time, GMT+1.

Tipping

Only in the more expensive restaurants will staff necessarily expect a tip, although everyone will be grateful for one; 10-15% is the norm, and it's increasingly common for service to be included in your bill on top of the cover charge. When you're ordering at the bar a few spare coins may speed service up. Taxis may add on extra costs for luggage, but an additional tip is always appreciated. Rounding up prices always goes down well, especially if it means avoiding giving change – not a favourite Italian habit.

Voltage

Italy functions on a 220V mains supply.
Plugs are the standard European two-pin variety.

Language

In hotels and bigger restaurants, you'll usually find English is spoken. The further you go from the tourist centres, however, the more trouble you may have, unless you have at least a smattering of Italian.

Italians from the rest of the country often consider modern-day Umbrii and Marchigiani to speak with a rather slow, rural Italian, and though such attitudes are exaggerated, you may be able to detect a country lilt to some spoken language in the region. That said, it's seldom hard to understand.

Umbrian as an ancient language was one of the prime influences of Latin, but it died out nearly 2,000 years ago and few if any of its linguistic traces survive. Umbro and Marchigiano dialects still exist, especially in rural areas, and sometimes in the names of traditional local dishes. Closely connected to each other, they are also close to standard Italian, though you may notice the occasional dropping of the last syllable, and substitution of 'u' for a final 'o'.

Vowels

- **a** like 'a' in cat
- **e** like 'e' in vet, or slightly more open, like the 'ai' in air (except after c or g, see consonants below)
- **i** like 'i' in sip (except after c or g, see below)
- **o** like 'o' in fox
- **u** like 'ou' in soup

Consonants

Generally consonants sound the same as in English, though 'e' and 'i' after 'c' or 'g' make them soft (a 'ch' or a 'j' sound) and are silent themselves, whereas 'h' makes them hard (a 'k' or 'g' sound), the opposite to English. So *ciao* is pronounced 'chaow', but *chiesa* (church) is pronounced 'kee-ay-sa'.

The combination 'gli' is pronounced like the 'lli' in million, and 'gn' like 'ny' in Tanya.

Basics

thank you   *grazie*
hi/goodbye   *ciao*
good day (until after lunch/ mid-afternoon)   *buongiorno*
good evening (after lunch)   *buonasera*
goodnight   *buonanotte*
goodbye   *arrivederci*
please   *per favore*
I'm sorry   *mi dispiace*
excuse me   *permesso*
yes   *si*
no   *no*

Gestures

Italians are famously theatrical and animated in dialogue and use a variety of gestures.

Side of left palm on side of right wrist as right wrist is flicked up   Go away

Hunched shoulders and arms lifted with palms of hands outwards   What am I supposed to do?

Thumb, index and middle finger of hand together, wrist upturned and shaking
What are you doing/what's going on?

Both palms together and moved up and down in front of stomach   Same as above

All fingers of hand squeezed together   To signify a place is packed full of people

Front orside of hand to chin   'Nothing', as in 'I don't understand' or 'I've had enough'

Flicking back of right ear   To signify someone is gay

Index finger in cheek   To signify good food

Numbers

one	*uno*	17	*diciassette*
two	*due*	18	*diciotto*
three	*tre*	19	*diciannove*
four	*quattro*	20	*venti*
five	*cinque*	21	*ventuno*
six	*sei*	22	*ventidue*
seven	*sette*	30	*trenta*
eight	*otto*	40	*quaranta*
nine	*nove*	50	*cinquanta*
10	*dieci*	60	*sessanta*
11	*undici*	70	*settanta*
12	*dodici*	80	*ottanta*
13	*tredici*	90	*novanta*
14	*quattordici*	100	*cento*
15	*quindici*	200	*due cento*
16	*sedici*	1000	*mille*

Questions

how?   *come?*
how much?   *quanto?*
when?   *quando?*
where?   *dove?*
why?   *perché?*
what?   *che cosa?*

Problems

I don't understand   *non capisco*
I don't know   *non lo so*
I don't speak Italian   *non parlo italiano*
How do you say ... (in Italian)?
    come si dice ... (in italiano)?
Is there anyone who speaks English?
    c'è qualcuno che parla inglese?

Shopping

this one/that one   *questo/quello*
less   *meno*
more   *di più*
how much is it/are they?
  quanto costa/costano?
can I have …?   *posso avere …?*

Travelling

one ticket for...   *un biglietto per...*
single   *solo andata*
return   *andata e ritorno*
does this go to Assisi?
  questo va a Assisi?
airport   *aeroporto*
bus stop   *fermata*
train   *treno*
car   *macchina*
taxi   *tassi*

Hotels

a double/single room
una camera doppia/singola
a double bed   *un letto matrimoniale*
bathroom   *bagno*
Is there a view?   *c'è un bel panorama?*
can I see the room?   *posso vedere la camera?*
when is breakfast?   *a che ora è la colazione?*
can I have the key?   *posso avere la chiave?*

Time

morning   *mattina*
afternoon   *pomeriggio*
evening   *sera*
night   *notte*
soon   *presto/fra poco*
later   *più tardi*
what time is it?   *che ore sono?*
today/tomorrow/yesterday   *oggi/domani/ieri*

Days

Monday   *lunedi*
Tuesday   *martedi*
Wednesday   *mercoledi*
Thursday   *giovedi*
Friday   *venerdi*
Saturday   *sabato*
Sunday   *domenica*

Conversation

alright   *va bene*
right then   *allora*
who knows!   *bo! / chi sa*
good luck!   *in bocca al lupo!* (literally, 'in the
  mouth of the wolf')
one moment   *un attimo*
hello (when answering a phone)
  pronto (literally, 'ready')
let's go!   *andiamo!*
enough/stop   *basta!*
give up!   *dai!*
I like …   *mi piace …*
how's it going?   (well, thanks) *come va?* (bene, grazie)
how are you?   *come sta/stai?* (polite/informal)

Index

Index

Credits

Footprint credits

Text editor: Beverley Jollands
Assistant editor: Alice Jell
Picture editor: Kassia Gawronski
Layout & production: Angus Dawson
Maps: Compass Maps Ltd

Managing Director: Andy Riddle
Commercial Director: Patrick Dawson
Publisher: Alan Murphy
Editorial: Sara Chare, Ria Gane, Jenny Haddington, Felicity Laughton, Nicola Gibbs
Design: Mytton Williams
Cartography: Sarah Sorensen, Rob Lunn, Kevin Feeney, Emma Bryers
Sales & marketing: Liz Harper, Hannah Bonnell
Advertising: Renu Sibal
Business Development: Zoë Jackson
Finance & Administration: Elizabeth Taylor

Print

Manufactured in Italy by EuroGrafica
Pulp from sustainable forests

Footprint Feedback

We try as hard as we can to make each Footprint guide as up to date as possible but, of course, things always change. If you want to let us know about your experiences – good, bad or ugly – then don't delay, go to footprintbooks.com and send in your comments.

Every effort has been made to ensure that the facts in this guidebook are accurate. However, travellers should still obtain advice from consulates, airlines etc about travel and visa requirements before travelling. The authors and publishers cannot accept responsibility for any loss, injury or inconvenience however caused.

Publishing information

FootprintItalia Umbria & Marche
1st edition
© Footprint Handbooks Ltd
May 2009

ISBN 978-1-906098-54-4
CIP DATA: A catalogue record for this book is available from the British Library

® Footprint Handbooks and the Footprint mark are a registered trademark of Footprint Handbooks Ltd

Published by Footprint

6 Riverside Court
Lower Bristol Road
Bath BA2 3DZ, UK
T +44 (0)1225 469141
F +44 (0)1225 469461
www.footprintbooks.com

Distributed in North America by

Globe Pequot Press

The colour maps are not intended to have any political significance.